W9-CFK-662

LEADERSHIP FOR THE PUBLIC SERVICE

Power and Policy in Action

RICHARD A. LOVERD

Northeastern University

To Woody,

Fellow traveler on the
road of public administration!

With best wishes,

Dick

PRENTICE HALL, Upper Saddle River, New Jersey 07458

Library of Congress Cataloging-in-Publication Data

LOVERD, RICHARD A.
  Leadership for the public service: power and policy in action/
Richard A. Loverd.
   p. cm.
  Includes bibliographical references.
  ISBN 0-13-221921-2
  1. Political leadership. 2. Political leadership—United States.
3. Policy sciences. I. Title.
JC330.3.L68 1996
303.3'4'0973—dc20   96-5510
                                                          CIP

Editorial director: Charlyce Jones Owen
Editor-in-chief: Nancy Roberts
Acquisitions editor: Michael Bickerstaff
Editorial/production supervision
  and interior design: Rob DeGeorge
Copyeditor: Ilene McGrath
Prepress and manufacturing buyer: Bob Anderson
Editorial assistant: Anita Castro

This book was set in 10/12 Times Roman by NK Graphics
and was printed and bound by Courier Companies, Inc.
The cover was printed by Phoenix Color Corp.

 © 1997 by Prentice-Hall, Inc.
Simon & Schuster/A Viacom Company
Upper Saddle River, New Jersey 07458

All rights reserved. No part of this book may be
reproduced, in any form or by any means,
without permission in writing from the publisher.

Printed in the United States of America

10 9 8 7 6 5 4 3 2 1

ISBN 0-13-221921-2

PRENTICE-HALL INTERNATIONAL (UK) LIMITED, *London*
PRENTICE-HALL OF AUSTRALIA PTY. LIMITED, *Sydney*
PRENTICE-HALL CANADA INC., *Toronto*
PRENTICE-HALL HISPANOAMERICANA, S.A., *Mexico*
PRENTICE-HALL OF INDIA PRIVATE LIMITED, *New Delhi*
PRENTICE-HALL OF JAPAN, INC., *Tokyo*
SIMON & SCHUSTER ASIA PTE. LTD., *Singapore*
EDITORA PRENTICE-HALL DO BRASIL, LTDA., *Rio de Janeiro*

**for my parents,
two leadership inspirations**

Contents

B. LEGISLATIVE LEADERSHIP

C. BUREAUCRATIC LEADERSHIP

Foreword

As we march toward the end of the twentieth century and into the twenty-first, "politics" is often used as a term of abuse, and its cousin, "government," seems at times to be treated as a synonym for "incompetence." This volume has a very different cast: here "politics" is the craft of identifying important social challenges and building coalitions to meet those challenges; "government" is the social mechanism through which the citizenry can achieve purposes which we cannot accomplish alone or through profit-seeking businesses and voluntary cooperation.

Richard Loverd's approach to the world of politics and government places a primary emphasis on the role of individual leaders in defining possible courses of action and marshaling support for new policies and programs, and on the larger lessons that can be drawn through a careful and systematic look at the experiences of a dozen and more elected and appointed political leaders in the second half of the twentieth century. Here we see the very different perspectives on political strategy and ethical tensions held by President Jimmy Carter and by congressional leaders Tip O'Neill and Howard Baker, the evolution of political understanding (and of the ability to act effectively) between Michael Dukakis's first and second terms as governor, the quite different strategies of leadership used by Mario Cuomo and New Jersey's Christie Whitman, and a variety of other comparisons that stretch our sense of the possible in political life and in governmental action.

As these examples suggest, Loverd adopts a biographical approach to understanding the role of government and its interactions with political life, and his cases are drawn from the American experience. He builds on earlier studies that are substantially biographical, such as Richard E. Neustadt's *Presidential Power,* the volume of essays, *Leadership and Innovation,* and the Cooper–Wright book *Exemplary Public Administrators.*[1] And he expands our understanding in useful ways.

First, the scope of individuals placed under the microscope is wide-ranging, including several presidents, Congressional leaders, governors of states, creative appointed executives, and others. Moreover, while many of these figures have completed their appointed rounds, others—Al Gore and Newt Gingrich, for example, Colin Powell, Christie Whitman, and others—are caught while still in action, allowing the reader to follow their future activities far better informed.

In addition, Loverd provides two opening chapters that offer a valuable framework to guide the reader's examination of the case studies. Here we are reminded, in a systematic way, of the complex intertwining of political feasibility, ethical concerns, bureaucratic hurdles, and the wider historical context which provide opportunities, not unmixed with pitfalls, for those who would devote their energies to public service. The man or woman who would engage in "public service" must inevitably engage in politics and employ the resources of government. Loverd's book helps us to see the possibilities for constructive action, and therefore to retain necessary optimism, as we confront those who would wave the banner of narrow self-interest and urge us to turn away from public service. And beyond optimism, his framework and these case studies can help us identify the strategies that might work, and the ethical and political dilemmas that must be faced, if we want to take an active part in shaping a society whose future can be improved when skillful leadership is combined with energy and disciplined passion.

Jameson W. Doig
Woodrow Wilson School and Department of Politics
Princeton University

1. Richard E. Neustadt, *Presidential Power: The Politics of Leadership from FDR to Reagan* (New York: John Wiley, 1986); Jameson W. Doig and Erwin C. Hargrove, eds., *Leadership and Innovation: A Biographical Perspective on Entrepreneurs in Government* (Baltimore: Johns Hopkins University Press, 1987); Terry L. Cooper and N. Dale Wright, eds., *Exemplary Public Administrators: Character and Leadership in Government* (San Francisco: Jossey-Bass, 1992).

Preface

... all people of great achievement are ambitious. But the key question is whether they are ambitious to be or ambitious to do.[1]
—Jean Monnet

This book is designed to encourage the reader to think about public policy from a leadership perspective, one which stresses that the nature of public policy is very much a reflection of the actions of the leaders who shape it. With the help of leadership cases, it focuses on (1) how leaders gain power, and (2) how that power can be used for constructive policy purposes. In so doing, it aims to provide preparation for those seeking policy leadership roles or wishing to examine the quality of such roles in others.

The book begins with two conceptual chapters, one dealing with gaining power and the other with choosing policy, as a way of preparing the reader for analyzing the cases to follow. The sources and strategies for power are discussed, followed by consideration of the policy process, the five different decision bases that leaders can use in that process, and the resulting five leadership styles.

In putting the concepts to work, the cases themselves, written by a combination of academics and journalists, cover a purposefully wide range of prominent public leaders, from presidents (John F. Kennedy, Gerald Ford, and Bill Clinton), to a president-in-waiting (Vice President Al Gore), to legislators (U.S. House of Representatives Speakers Tip O'Neill and Newt Gingrich, and U.S. Senate Majority Leader Howard Baker), to bureaucrats (National Endowment for the Arts Chairs Nancy Hanks and Jane Alexander, U.S. Department of Housing and Urban Development Secretary Jack Kemp, and General Colin Powell), to governors (Massachusetts Governor Michael Dukakis, New York Governor Mario Cuomo, and New Jersey Governor Christine Todd Whitman), demonstrating a host of different policy leadership approaches. Most are contemporary leaders, and most have been presidents, presidential contenders, or presidential prospects at one time or another in their careers. And while each individual leadership case does not cover every concept presented in the first two chapters, the studies collectively do, thereby providing a book which is both comprehensive and informative.

ACKNOWLEDGMENTS

In many ways, my research for this book began during my graduate studies at the Syracuse University Maxwell School and the Columbia University Business School. At Syracuse the ideas presented by such major figures as Dwight Waldo, Alan Campbell, Spencer Parratt, Roscoe Martin, Frank Marini, H. George Frederickson, James Carroll, Michael Sawyer, W. Henry Lambright, and Michael White left a lasting impression on me, and at Columbia the encouragement and counsel of Leonard Sayles played a major role in moving my studies forward.

In more recent times Princeton University Professor Jameson Doig kept urging me to move this project forward when my spirits would flag. And in the political science department at Northeastern University the enthusiasm and support demonstrated by Robert Gilbert, Christopher Bosso, Suzanne Ogden, Minton Goldman, David Schmitt, and Robert Cord kept me on track.

A special word of thanks is also extended to Michael Dukakis and Howard Baker for taking the time to meet with me in Boston and Washington, respectively, to discuss their leadership approaches, as well as to the funding agencies that provided support for those studies, including the Northeastern University Research and Scholarship Development Fund, the Everett McKinley Dirksen Congressional Leadership Research Center, and the Gordon Fund. In addition, thanks are also extended to the Gerald R. Ford Presidential Library for providing a grant for my study of President Ford's actions during the New York City financial crisis.

And finally, a word of special praise to my own family, my steadfast wife Deborah and children Kate and Rick, for their patience, and impatience, in bringing this project to closure.

Richard A. Loverd
Boston, Massachusetts

1. Noted in Henry A. Kissinger, "With Faint Praise," *New York Times Book Review,* July 16, 1995, p. 7.

CHAPTER 1

Gaining the Power to Lead

RICHARD A. LOVERD

The lifeblood of administration is power . . . of all, it is the most overlooked in theory and the most dangerous to overlook in practice.[1]

—Norton E. Long

If we are strong, our strength will speak for itself. If we are weak, words will be of no help.[2]

—John F. Kennedy

What counts is not necessarily the size of the dog in the fight—it's the size of the fight in the dog.[3]

—Dwight D. Eisenhower

When a leader takes up a new office, how does he or she secure the power necessary to command and gain responsiveness from others? As Richard Neustadt has observed, this is no easy task: "'powers' are no guarantee of power; clerkship is no guarantee of leadership. [Indeed,] the President of the United States has an extraordinary range of formal powers [yet] despite his 'powers' he does not obtain results . . . merely by giving orders."[4] And Leonard Sayles makes much the same point when he writes that "in the modern organization . . . the [leader] must *earn* authority and deference; it's not just given by title or fiat."[5]

Moreover, Sayles goes on to note that, while hierarchy in an organization provides a starting point in trying to specify who outranks whom in terms of formal power, any experienced public official knows that this is only a start. Many individuals and groups have *real power*—meaning the ability to get others to comply with their wishes—that is far greater than their apparent formal status. While an organization chart may show that a number of departments or functions are at the same level, this positioning rarely means that they have the same power. For example, in the federal government, cabinet officers have the same rank, but everyone knows that the secretaries of treasury and state have enormously more clout than those of labor or transportation.[6] Consequently, something more than mere formal power must be at work in shaping how real power is earned.

This chapter will examine how such power can be earned by (1) looking at what the sources of power might be, (2) considering how they might be developed to maximum advantage, and (3) analyzing the use of the elemental behavioral skills of leadership.

THE SOURCES OF POWER

As was noted at the start of this chapter, though limited, the hierarchy, and more particularly the *formal positions* arrayed within it, are not bad places to begin when one is considering the sources of power.[7] The office one holds, and the legitimate, rule-based powers prescribing that position, suggest at least a tentative means for gauging the powers one can expect to wield. Still, as was also noted, the leader who expects to "go by the book" and depends upon authority only as it is defined by position is probably wasting, indeed eroding, influence over time since so many other power sources are available.

For example, beyond the position power of the organization lies the *expert power* of the individual; for the specialized knowledge that a person brings to the job can prove just as important as, if not more than, the job itself. Consequently, when legal questions arise, lawyers can wield power far greater than their positions in an agency might suggest; and much the same can occur when the talents of other experts, such as doctors, economists, computer scientists, and engineers, are in need. Their expertise, more than their positions, lead to heightened influence.

A good example of the significance of expertise over position can be gleaned from a governmental incident involving CBS Board Chairman Thomas Wyman, who in 1983 went to the White House to try to persuade Presidential Counselor Edwin Meese that the syndication rights for movies made for television should be in the hands of the television networks instead of the Hollywood studios. Upon his arrival, he found that, because of a sudden foreign policy crisis, his meeting with Mr. Meese was delayed. So as a courtesy, Mr. Wyman was sent to the office of Craig Fuller, secretary of the Reagan cabinet and a top White House advisor to Meese. While in his office, Mr. Fuller offered his assistance, indicating to Mr. Wyman that he had some familiarity with the syndication controversy. But the CBS head dismissed his offer, preferring to thumb through magazines and wait for Mr. Meese:

Finally, Meese burst into Fuller's office, full of apologies that he simply would not have the time for a substantive talk.

"Did you talk to Fuller?" he asked.

Wyman shook his head.

"You should have talked to Fuller," Meese said. "He's very important on this issue. He knows it better than the rest of us. He's writing a memo for the president on the pros and cons. You could have given him your side of the argument."[8]

Thus, to coin the famous phrase, "what you see may not be what you get." For while Mr. Meese had the position, Mr. Fuller knew the subject, and that expertise made a significant difference in determining who had the real power.

In a somewhat related vein, *informational power*[9] can be equally subtle while adding to the power pool of leaders. The access one has to important information about activities and developments in the organization and the environment, "being in the know," can provide tremendous clout. Indeed, in his book about the "power game" in Washington, journalist Hedrick Smith makes a point of stressing access to information as a major part of being in or out of the "power loop":

> . . . access in the power game is not merely physical; it is mental, too. It is not only entry to the inner sanctum; it is being in the power loop—being chosen to receive the most sensitive information, as fresh grist for the policy struggle. Being "cut out" on information, or being "blindsided" as the power lingo has it, can be crippling.

> Timely inside information is a special form of access that gives a power player the chance to make his move before competitors can react. Like inside tips on the stock market, it is the lifeblood of the government policymaker. Without fresh information a policymaker is forever "behind the power curve," scrambling to catch up. The question in this part of the power game is not "Who can you see?" but "What are you allowed to know?"[10]

And those allowed to be in the know grow smaller and smaller as the information grows more timely and sensitive. For example, within the national security power community, those with access to reports of the *National Intelligence Daily* (put out by the Central Intelligence Agency) are provided with more high-powered and select information than those who might have access only to the *Defense Intelligence Summary* (from the Defense Intelligence Agency), the *Chairman's Brief* (from the military staff of the chairman of the Joint Chiefs of Staff), or the *Secretary's Morning Summary* (from the State Department Bureau of Intelligence and Research for the Secretary of State). And those inner circle chieftains who are allowed to see the singularly secret *FTPO* (*For the President Only*) are likely to be even more knowledgeable, and thus more powerful still, with "only about twenty people qualified to see it: the President, Vice President, their chiefs of staff, and the innermost of the national security circle."[11] Of course, as Benjamin Franklin once observed, "three people can keep a secret, if two of them are dead," and a constant power struggle ensues between those most in the know and those wanting to know more.

Finally, *referent power* too has its place. As the name suggests, this measure uses individuals or groups as points of reference when gauging power. In this regard, the leader's own particular leadership style and personal appeal (or charisma) can serve as a point of reference. His or her manner of speaking, likability, imposing nature, or any number of other traits might come into play.

Much in the same vein, the work group in which the leader labors can carry a similar kind of charismatic cachet. In recent history perhaps no agency more clearly demonstrated this sort of personal appeal than the Peace Corps. Formed in 1961 to meet the needs of underdeveloped nations for trained manpower, this Corps soon became one of the inspirational jewels of the Kennedy administration, drawing talented young men and women in record numbers to serve their country through its capacity to "evoke a faith and enthusiasm that transcend rational calculation."[12]

Beyond immediate individual or group referents, the leader's connections to other individuals or groups in power can also add to influence. What sorts of persons or interests back or oppose this individual? How much influence do they have, and what damage can they do if this leader's initiatives are challenged? In short, who is "wired" to whom in this power network and how well does that referent wiring hold up?

As the newly appointed General Services Administration head under President Jimmy Carter, Georgia businessman Jay Solomon learned some of the perils of network referent power the hard way when he decided to dismiss deputy administrator Robert Griffin. In so doing, he soon discovered that he had fired a close friend of House Speaker Thomas P. "Tip" O'Neill, Jr., and the late President John F. Kennedy, thereby chilling relations between the House and the White House. Subsequently, with the aid of Vice President Walter Mondale, an effort was launched to appease Speaker O'Neill and warm the air by finding Mr. Griffin a newly invented job as a $50,000-a-year White House "senior assistant" to Robert S. Strauss, the president's special trade representative and counselor on inflation; and Mr. Solomon retreated back into the bureaucratic woodwork.[13]

By reviewing the sources of power in this section, we can see that position does indeed reveal only a portion of the power picture. Expertise, information bases and reference points must also be considered. Only then can we begin to get some sense of the power landscape and the disposition of political troops and talent that provides the means for policy leadership. Without knowledge of that territory, power seems a cryptic blur; with it, the focus begins to sharpen.

However, while an understanding of the sources of power begins to sharpen our gaze, seeking out the most effective ways to nurture them remains unclear. More information on how those sources might be developed to maximum advantage is needed. Consequently, in the next section we will address that need by considering the different strategies that might be used to gain power.

DEVELOPING POWER SOURCES TO THE BEST ADVANTAGE

Ways in which policy leaders can develop the preceding power sources to gain power, and thereby obtain responsiveness from others in organizations, can be highlighted by demonstrating (1) ability, (2) credibility, (3) goal-setting, (4) buffering,[14] and (5) coalition-building strategies.

Ability is, of course, generally key to one's being perceived as a legitimate source of authority, and the leader must evidence it from the start. Besides holding considerable credentials and expertise, his or her technical and organizational skills and knowledge in the workplace should be perceived as superior to those of others, beyond reproach, and proven through action again and again.

But ability is only the beginning. An equally important yet much more subtle power challenge lies in establishing *credibility*. To do so, the newcomer must show that he or she is trustworthy and knows the rules of the game, so that the norms, hopes, and values of the people to be supervised will not be violated and the "crust of custom" will not be threatened. In this regard, Hedrick Smith's portrayals of the differing credibility levels of CIA Director William Casey and Federal Reserve Board Chair Paul Volcker during the Reagan years are instructive. While acknowledged as a very able individual, Smith notes that Casey was inclined toward "showing arrogant disdain for Congress and . . . giving evasive, deceptive and dishonest testimony to intelligence committees."[15] This behavior, in turn, led members of Congress to perceive Casey as untrustworthy and unwilling to work within the executive-legislative rules of the game. Paul Volcker, on the other hand, was viewed as "one of the best bureaucratic players in Washington . . . [not merely because he] was a very smart banker and very smart financial analyst [but] because he's a master politician and people believe in him."[16] As one capable of "managing both to flatter the members of Congress by listening to them and getting them to accept him as an oracle,"[17] he learned the crust of custom well, and his credibility reflected that fact.

In addition to individual efforts at credibility, the leader can draw on the credibility of others. He can, for example, be "anointed"[18] by having a senior member already holding status sanction his presence through the formal endorsement of the appointment. This endorsement, usually expressed through some sort of ceremony to indicate a changing of the guard and a transfer of status, should be made known to all relevant parties because, in the absence of that sanctioned ceremony, passing leadership from the old guard to the new can prove difficult, with relations in the direction of the newcomer uncertain and legitimacy unclear. Imagine, for example, how much more difficult it might be for a newly elected president (or, for that matter, those appointed by the president) to take the reins of power without the use of formal announcement and inaugural ceremony.

The credibility of others can be used in other ways as well. Particularly during the early stages, when much has to be learned and earned, the new leader can draw on the talents of superiors, seasoned lieutenants, and colleagues with built-in credibility and knowledge of the system.[19] They can share their knowledge of "the ropes," transmit selected orders from the leader to others in ways which are within acceptable norms, and, in turn, implicitly exhibit support for the new chief through their actions.

Goal setting also adds to leader power when the leader demonstrates a certain measure of innovation, momentum, persistence, and practice. For example, while no one may particularly enjoy being ordered to change routines, perform new work, and head off in new directions, at the same time the absence of such innovative commands tends to generate uneasiness. One may get the sense that, without new edicts from leaders, a business-as-usual climate exists in which there is no forward movement and nothing significant is happening. Consequently, nonroutine, purposeful action which suggests a sense of dynamism or momentum through the promotion of original goals is expected of managers if they are to substantiate their leadership roles and advance the organization.

For example, upon moving from minority leader to majority leader during the early Reagan years, Republican Senator Howard Baker noted the particular need for innovation and momentum when he observed that "There is a difference between being in the minority and being a jungle fighter and shooting from behind trees . . . versus the majority, where you have a program, and where you've got to govern—you've got to do something. You can't just not do something."[20] So too, in the early months of the Bush administration, were similar sentiments raised regarding the need to "do something" when that president's "politics of minimalism" seemed to be leading nowhere. As Princeton Political Science Professor Fred Greenstein observed at the time:

> Being inoffensive builds no credit. A sense begins to develop that there is less there than meets the eye. If Bush makes things too small, when he really wants something, people won't have any reason to pay attention.
>   At some point he might start getting Coolidge jokes. As Dorothy Parker said when she was told Coolidge had passed away, she replied, "How did they know?"[21]

Furthermore, during that process of "doing something" to set new goals in motion, a demonstration of persistence can also add strength. Leaders need to be doggedly and self-confidently persistent[22] in making their claims to have their goals met. Though such behavior may seem obvious, all one need do to acknowledge its importance is recall instances where objectives were advanced by leaders in a half-hearted, subservient, and sporadic style. In those instances, the likelihood of attainment of those goals, and respect for the leader promulgating them, are bound to drop. Conversely, those leaders willing to weather the storm and stick to their objectives in the face of adversity can gain in respect and power.

A good example of such leadership persistence can be seen in the actions of President Clinton during the summer and fall of 1993. That summer few legislative and executive leaders held out much hope for the passage of President Clinton's proposed North American Free Trade Agreement (NAFTA). In July, Speaker of the House Thomas S. Foley thought the proposal was dead, with nothing he, the president, " 'or anyone on the planet' could do to revive it" [and by August,] "the private judgment of most senior members of the White House staff was that the president should abandon the trade accord, doing the best he could "to cover his tracks."[23]

> But Bill Clinton pressed on, growing more rather than less committed as the days passed. Abandoned by two of the three top Democratic leaders in the House, opposed

by usually reliable Democrats in the trade unions and by some important leaders of minority groups and environmental organizations, he kept shoving more and more chips into the pot. . . . [24]

By pressing on and being persistent, the president won his goal of NAFTA legislation that November, a feat which, according to the *New York Times,* "in political terms [represented] the most important achievement of his Presidency. On NAFTA, he looked not like Jimmy Carter, tripping and slipping in his relations with Congress, but like the Lyndon B. Johnson of 1964 and 1965: relentless and resourceful, a fighter and not a fumbler."[25]

One final aspect of the goal-setting process, practice, should also be used by leaders. Directives, as the crux of the leadership role, should be practiced on others in ways which can more reasonably ensure their responsiveness. In particular, Sayles suggests that this is best accomplished "by gradations: moving from very few to the proper level (or frequency) and moving from the most obvious, easily accepted areas to the more ambiguous and potentially controversial." In so doing, "new leaders are cautious, not wanting to be confronted by refusal or to be challenged before their position is established firmly."[26] Thus practice builds responsiveness between leaders and followers and, with time and tact, makes the more difficult orders and goals more acceptable when leaders need to initiate them and followers need to carry them out.

Buffering[27] too has its place in winning follower support. By striving to protect one's own work group from external demands, by shielding them from untoward intrusions that might upset their activities or lessen their influence, the leader builds more group cohesion and more loyalty for him or herself. As Sayles observes, "Nothing proves more about the right to command than the ability to defend."[28]

> Leaders who can buffer their employees and who can go against the organization's grain, against the chain of command, to win benefits and get oppressive rules changed or ignored earn loyal followership—even when other leadership characteristics are inadequate. We have seen many short-tempered, oppressive bosses who would "fight to the death" for their people and who were beloved by appreciative subordinates.[29]

Beyond buffering for one's own group lies the larger leadership challenge of *coalition building,* reaching out and building alliances with other groups in the larger work environment in order to expand one's referent power base and garner benefits for one's self and one's group. In the government work environment this sort of activity is particularly crucial because, as Graham Allison notes, there is a "fundamental constitutional difference" between the fragmented managerial climate of government and the more concentrated one of business:

> In business, the functions of general management are centralized in a single individual: the Chief Executive Officer. The goal is authority commensurate with responsibility. In contrast, in the U.S. government, the functions of general management are constitutionally spread among competing institutions: the executive, two houses of Congress, and the courts. The constitutional goal was "not to promote efficiency but to preclude the exercise of arbitrary power," as Justice Brandeis observed. Indeed, as *The Federal-*

ist Papers make starkly clear, the aim was to create incentives to compete: "the great se-curity against a gradual concentration of the several powers in the same branch, consists in giving those who administer each branch the constitutional means and personal mo-tives to resist encroachment of the others. Ambition must be made to counteract ambi-tion." Thus, the general management functions concentrated in the CEO of a private business are, by constitutional design, spread in the public sector among a number of competing institutions and thus shared by a number of individuals whose ambitions are set against one another.[30]

And of course within this larger, fragmented political work environment that pits am-bition against ambition, even more opportunities for gaining, and losing, power are in the offing.

As the earlier example of the firing and rehiring of Robert Griffin suggests, even the simplest of personnel actions can generate serious power repercussions from outside forces. So too should it be noted that during President Clinton's re-markable bid in building a winning coalition for the passage of North American Free Trade Agreement, "Against the odds, with unlikely conservative Republican allies, he forged a narrow but solid majority that included more Republicans than Demo-crats."[31] Consequently, leaders need to take care in building and maintaining support from those kinds of larger forces in order to maintain and increase power.

When approaching the challenge of coalition building, particularly with regard to leadership from the executive branch, Francis Rourke notes that the following forces need to be nurtured: (1) the general public, (2) the "attentive" publics, or groups that have a salient interest in the leader's agency activities, (3) legislators, and (4) other executive agencies.[32]

As one might suspect, the *general public* tends to be the least reliable base of support, largely ignoring specific public agencies except during times of crisis, when attention is drawn to them. For example, few Americans would likely think about their relationship with the Nuclear Regulatory Commission except when a nuclear plant disaster, such as the one at Three Mile Island, has occurred; and few would tend to think about the Environmental Protection Agency except when smog, sewage, and medical waste spill in their air or on their beaches. This kind of crisis "management by exception" emanating fitfully from the general public results in a more ephemeral than firm basis of support for public agencies.

Given this sporadic concern by the general public, obviously more dependable reference points with other forces need to be forged by agency leaders in order to en-sure that ongoing support for their activities will be present. In this regard, the *"at-tentive" publics* (otherwise known as clienteles, constituencies, or interest groups) can prove far more reliable because each side can derive more specific ongoing ben-efits from the other: the agency can pursue programs and policies that will be of ben-efit to the interest group, while the interest group can, in turn, support the agency's efforts in pursuing a number of key objectives, "including its requests for financial support, its attempts to secure passage of legislation expanding its powers, or its need to defend itself against legislative proposals that threaten its administrative status."[33] Little wonder, then, that the U.S. Forest Service and the National Forest Products Association,[34] the Department of Veterans Affairs and the Veterans of Foreign Wars,[35] the U.S. Department of Agriculture and agribusiness interests,[36] and the Interstate Commerce Commission and trucking interests[37] might work together for mutual benefit.

In a similar vein, so too might *legislators* help agency leaders in their search for support. While agencies can help to formulate and implement programs and policies of interest to legislators and their constituents, legislators can, in turn, provide the legal authority and the funds necessary for agencies to carry them out. Therefore it only follows that such referent relationships as those between the Department of Veterans Affairs and the House and Senate Veterans Affairs Committees, and between the Agriculture Department and the House and Senate Agriculture Committees, would tend to benefit each other.

Finally, in addition to coalition building with the general public, "attentive" publics, and legislators, the *executive agencies* themselves with similar interests, and thus possible conflicts, can band together and form coalitions to support causes of mutual concern. While some may prefer to crush opponents rather than work with them, there are times, in domestic as in international relations, when one agency is better off joining than fighting the other. For example, when a common mission energizes or a common danger threatens both parties more than each endangers the other, cooperative alliances would tend to be in order. In the latter regard, despite the longstanding struggle between the Army Corps of Engineers and the Bureau of Reclamation over jurisdiction over water projects, an agreement was signed between them for the management of water resource development in the Missouri Valley area. In point of fact, this agreement was not due to some newfound faith but rather came about because each saw the need to blunt the threat that a new valley authority under consideration might be established with the comprehensive jurisdiction to take over both their functions.[38]

All of the preceding forces in the fragmented work environment surrounding agency leaders can be used to build coalitions to gain more power. The general public, "attentive" publics, legislators, and executive agencies can each help in winning more support. However, in addition to the mutual approaches noted above, there are some further coalition-building strategies which could be used to increase power, including the following:

1. *"Repackage" organizational skills* to fit a pressing need and look more critical to outsiders. In this regard, Harold Seidman and Robert Gilmour note how public managers came to change the title, and thereby improve the power, of the National Microbiological Institute:

> Programs are packaged in such a way as to elicit congressional and clientele support. General programs have far less political appeal than specific programs. Support can be mobilized more readily for federal programs to combat heart disease, blindness, cancer and mental illness than for such fields as microbiology or for general health programs. For this reason in 1955 the National Microbiological Institute was renamed the National Institute of Allergy and Infectious Diseases. As was explained at the time, the Institute had been handicapped in making its case because "no one ever died of microbiology."[39]

2. *Take advantage of crises.* In the Chinese language the word *wei ji*[40] has a dual meaning, standing for both "crisis" and "opportunity." So too in the process of coalition building should crises be viewed as opportunities for not only proving your abilities but drawing attention to and building support for your needs. For example, if funding for your agency looks as if it will be inadequate, stress that essential services of key concern to legislators, clienteles, or other key executives will be endangered first. Therefore, if a secretary of defense from Massachusetts seeks to cut back on military bases, the Navy should put the Boston Navy Yard at the top of the list; or if the Social Security Administration is unhappy with its operating budget, it should point out that there will be major delays in the delivery of social security checks. Furthermore, if a city is unhappy with its revenues, it should stress that policemen, teachers, and firemen will need to be laid off first.[41]

And for a particularly masterful example of political creativity during crisis, learn from the lesson of Amtrak, which, when faced with possible budget shortfalls in 1976, announced that it would have to abandon the following routes: San Francisco–Bakersfield, St. Louis–Laredo, Chicago–Seattle, and Norfolk–Chicago. In so doing, the agency had cut routes in the states and districts of the key legislators capable of restoring those shortfalls, including California Representative John McFall (chair of the House Appropriations Transportation Subcommittee), Senator John McClellan (chair of the Senate Appropriations Committee), Senator Mike Mansfield (Senate majority leader), Senator Warren Magnuson (chair of the Senate Commerce Committee), Senator Birch Bayh (chair of the Senate Appropriations Transportation Subcommittee), Representative Harley Staggers (chair of the House Commerce Committee), and Senator Robert Byrd (Senate majority whip and a member of the Senate Appropriations Committee). Soon after the announcement, an article in the *Charleston Gazette,* a West Virginia newspaper, noted that Senator Byrd would "either introduce an amendment providing sufficient funds to continue the West Virginia route or try to get language adopted which would guarantee funding for the route of Amtrak."[42]

3. *Farm out portions of your program to other potential adversaries* in order to win them over. For example:

> . . . when the Navy set up its Special Projects Office to handle the service's ballistic missile program, the new office wisely saw that it would need the cooperation or at least the passive compliance of other Navy units in order to succeed. So the Special Projects Office farmed out parts of the program to other Navy units in order to gain, if not their active support, at least their acceptance of the new program.[43]

And in a classic instance, after suffering numerous earlier defeats, aircraft contractor Rockwell International worked with the Department of Defense to win billions of dollars' worth of B-1 bomber legislation in 1982 through the use of a "national production strategy." This strategy farmed out the B-1's production to thousands of subcontractors throughout the nation in 48 of the 50 United States and, in so doing, won substantial support from the bulk of the legislators from those states. Indeed, in the case of the Senate, those favoring the B-1 had an average of $1 billion in constituent contracts and jobs to entice them. Some gained even more. Ohio Democratic Senator Howard Metzenbaum, an earlier opponent of the plane and about to stand for reelection in 1982, changed his mind in the face of $7.4 billion in defense contracts. And in the case of California, President Reagan's home state, the figure was the highest of all: $12.3 billion in B-1 contracts.[44]

4. *Coopt those who might otherwise oppose you.* The term "cooptation," made famous by sociologist Philip Selznick in his well-known study of the Tennessee Valley Authority and its grass roots constituencies, refers to "the process of absorbing new elements into the leadership or policy-determining structure of an organization as a means of averting threats to its stability or existence."[45] Thus in the case of the TVA, an agency charged with the agricultural and electrical development of the Tennessee River basin, constituencies representing "the dominant agricultural leadership in the Tennessee Valley area were afforded a place within its policy determining structure" in exchange for their support. By so doing, the TVA thereby "enhanced its chances for survival by accommodating itself to existing centers of interest and power within its area of operation."[46]

Of course, the price of this sort of accommodation by the TVA, or any agency, means that at times it might have to alter its policies in order to keep clientele support, and that strategy in turn has its dangers. For example, the agency might give away too much of its policy-making discretion to its clientele and become a captive to the very interests whose priorities it sought to overcome. Consequently, agencies need to exercise care in determining how and how much power they need to relinquish to clienteles in order to garner their support without being coopted by them.

A recent study of the use of advisory councils by the Social Security Administration leadership provides clues as to just how a useful agency–clientele cooptive relationship might proceed. Despite the fact that the councils were ordinarily composed of three outside groups—representatives from business, labor, and "the public" (usually professors with an interest in social insurance)—the SSA leadership managed to steer them all in the preferred policy directions by taking pains to (1) limit council membership to persons from those groups who generally supported their program, (2) limit council staff assistance to persons drawn directly or indirectly from the SSA, and (3) limit the council agenda to topics deemed timely by those leaders. In so doing, "there was not much danger that these groups of outsiders would get out of control and produce unwanted recommendations,"[47] and a higher likelihood that they would serve as positive "instruments of executive–legislative relations and independent legitimators of major policy decisions."[48]

5. *Work with the power of the press.* While the media's role as a reflection of the general public, an attentive public, or a fourth branch of government is debatable, the media's power as a mediator[49] in setting the public agenda and shaping working relations between a leader and the forces in the work environment is not. As federal and state public executive Gordon Chase once observed:

> The media provide the essential battleground for public affairs. Officials debate, constituents complain, special interests advocate, and managers defend in the columns of

dailies and pages of weeklies; on the morning, afternoon, and evening news; and over radio's airwaves. Debates between branches of government, among officials within each branch, and between the government and the public are daily occurrences which are dictated in large part by the choices made by editors and reporters about what is interesting and what is relevant for their subscribers to know.[50]

Consequently, in so shaping that battleground, it is important for public leaders to build a rapport with the press which will get their stories across and generate from those editors and reporters the kinds of choices that will increase rather than decrease opportunities for coalition building. While it may not be true that "in this culture, if something is not on the TV nightly news, it didn't happen, it doesn't exist,"[51] clearly the absence of a positive presence on the news will do little to enhance a leader's power.

TAKING CARE IN THE USE OF THE ELEMENTAL BEHAVIORAL SKILLS OF LEADERSHIP: OF PAIR AND SET EVENTS

Thus far we have discussed a variety of the sources and strategies for gaining power in public organizations. However, before we leave this chapter, a review of the elemental skills that provide the basic behavioral underpinnings of leadership would seem to be in order. For no matter how well or through what means power is gained, it can be quickly lost if these skills are not properly used along with those sources and strategies.

Begun through the work of Harvard social-anthropologists Conrad Arensberg and Eliot Chapple[52] and further developed by such scholars as William F. Whyte,[53] George Homans[54] and Leonard Sayles,[55] the study of "social interactions" between members of organizations has proven key to an examination of the behavioral building blocks of leadership. By investigating the interactions between members at the work level with regard to such dimensions as who initiates to whom, when, in what sequence, at what pace, how long, how often, and at what angle (i.e., vertical or lateral), much can be learned about forging the leadership role and diagnosing the relationship between leaders and the led.

In particular, two types of social interaction are significant when one is considering leadership behavior: pair and set events. A *pair event* involves a one-on-one interaction between two people, whereas a *set event* describes an interaction initiated by one person to two or more people. And as Whyte observes, the distinction between these two types of interactions is particularly significant in an investigation of leadership because "organizations and organizational leadership grow out of set events. If human beings could only interact in pair events, man would not be the organization-building animal that we are studying."[56] Moreover, as Sayles notes, it is clear from the studies of anthropologists "that leaders manifest their distinctive roles by periodically initiating orders to all subordinates and getting them to be *simultaneously* responsive to those orders, thereby accomplishing what have come to be called 'set events.' "[57] In their so doing, "such simultaneity is essential to both reinforcing the position of the leader and accomplishing the goals of the group."[58]

However, as Sayles goes on to stress, the successful accomplishment of such set events is hardly automatic for any leader; the behavioral groundwork must be built in advance. In particular, a series of frequent and intense one-on-one pair events need to be performed with followers which will bring them to a point where they will more likely accept a leader's set initiations—not just any pair events, of course; but rather ones which demonstrate an ongoing responsiveness and concern on the part of the leader for the needs of the followers. A continual willingness to listen to any and all subordinates, to provide information and assistance, and, where possible, to solve their individual problems does much to build loyalty between leader and led. Much as the more revered professors tend to be the ones who take the time to treat students as individuals more than as "classes," so too are the better public policy leaders those who pay attention to followers on a one-on-one basis, a basis which, cumulatively, produces a much higher likelihood that subsequent set initiations will yield the desired collective response.

CONCLUDING THOUGHTS ON POWER: "THE DOG IN THE FIGHT AND THE FIGHT IN THE DOG"

By now, as Long noted at the start of this chapter, it should be clear that power does indeed provide the lifeblood of public organizations. Without it, or for that matter without recognition of its presence in others, the leadership of government becomes a hit-or-miss proposition. With it, leaders can direct their own energies along with the energies of others in moving policies forward. Consequently, the search for, and development of, sources of power is a never-ending one.

In conducting that search, power only begins with the position one holds. Expertise, information, and the relation of the leader to others (and they to him) provide additional avenues for power acquisition. Furthermore, the way in which those avenues are pursued makes a great deal of difference. For example, the acquisition of more routine tasks, information, or relationships is hardly a route to power enhancement; it's the nonroutine goal-setting activities and events that garner considerable influence. In addition, a leader's credibility beyond ability multiplies power. And the prudent marshaling of resources and relationships within the workplace and with forces in the larger work environment helps build support. Moreover, regardless of what source or strategy one chooses, careful attention to building pair and set events helps pull in power.

Still, despite the recitation of these power sources and strategies, one key element remains: the degree of importance, or "salience,"[59] the leader places on the need to perform this sort of power-gathering work. If a leader chooses to rest on the existing power garnered and allow it to stand idle, large as it may be, it may soon dissipate; conversely, those hungry enough to pursue the power reservoirs of others may soon have them as their own. Thus, at any given point in time, if power is measured by the "size of the dog in the fight" rather than the "size of the fight in the dog," the current readings may be misleading.

Many a challenge has been lost by those who depended upon overwhelming resources to carry the day, or those who chose to rest rather than resist encroachments on what is, or should be, their turf. For example, in the State Department the leadership in the foreign service chose to limit its activities to diplomacy and avoid such policy-relevant areas as economic forecasting and scientific research; in the absence of a State Department claim, the leadership of other agencies soon took over those functions and claimed them as their own. By contrast, the Defense Department was "much more willing to recruit professionals in areas other than the military, or to upgrade the skills of military officers in order to protect its hegemony over the resolution of national security issues that increasingly turn on expertise in science and technology."[60]

The lesson is that even with large reservoirs of power at the start, low salience can lead an agency down the road to atrophy. Consequently, the motivation to acquire power should be viewed as a continual one, taking place in a continually shifting zero-sum environment where "power floats,"[61] and if you don't reach for it, someone else will.

NOTES

1. Norton Long, "Power and Administration," *Public Administration Review,* Vol. 9, No. 9 (1949), p. 257.

2. "Remarks Prepared for Delivery at the Trade Mart in Dallas, Texas, November 22, 1963," in *Public Papers of the Presidents: 1963* (Washington, D.C.: Government Printing Office, 1964), p. 91.

3. "Excerpts from Remarks at the Republican National Committee Breakfast, Statler Hotel, Washington, D.C.," January 31, 1958," in *Public Papers of the Presidents: 1958* (Washington, D.C.: Government Printing Office, 1959), p. 135.

4. Richard E. Neustadt, *Presidential Power: The Politics of Leadership from FDR to Reagan* (New York: John Wiley, 1986), p. 10.

5. Leonard R. Sayles, *Leadership* (New York: McGraw-Hill, 1979), p. 31.

6. Ibid., p. 111.

7. The following power typology is, in part, derived from John R. P. French and Bertram Raven, "The Bases of Social Power," in *Studies in Social Power,* ed. Dorwin Cartwright (Ann Arbor: University of Michigan Institute for Social Research, 1959), pp. 150–167.

8. Hedrick Smith, *The Power Game* (New York: Random House, 1988), p. xix.

9. This idea was, in part, brought to my attention by Stephen Robbins, *Essentials of Organizational Behavior* (Englewood Cliffs, N.J.: Prentice Hall, 1984), p. 133.

10. Smith, *The Power Game,* pp. 71–72 and 78.

11. Ibid., p. 79.

12. Francis Rourke, *Bureaucracy, Politics and Public Policy*, 3rd ed. (Boston: Little, Brown, 1984), p. 104.

13. See Terence Smith, "Carter Aide Barred from O'Neill Office," *New York Times,* August 3, 1978, p. A13; Terence Smith, "Ousted Friend of O'Neill Is Named to New $50,000 White House Job," *New York Times,* August 4, 1978, and Charles Mohr, "A Jobholder with Friends: Robert Thomas Griffin," *New York Times,* August 4, 1978, p. A6.

14. Elements of these first four power skills were brought to my attention by Professor Leonard Sayles in conversations and in his book *Leadership,* noted above.

15. Smith, *The Power Game*, p. 47.

16. Ibid., p. 53.

17. Ibid., p. 50.

18. Sayles, *Leadership*, p. 46.

19. Ibid., p. 43.

20. Howard Baker, interview by Phil Burton Productions, March 29, 1988, Internal Transcript, The White House, Office of the Press Secretary, Washington, D.C., p. 6.

21. Maureen Dowd, "Bush and the Politics of Minimalism: Some Risks and Some Advantages," *New York Times,* April 14, 1989, p. A18.

22. Sayles, *Leadership*, pp. 48–49.

23. R. W. Apple, Jr., "A High Stakes Gamble that Paid Off: President Emerges as a Tough Fighter," *New York Times,* November 18, 1993, p. 1.

24. Ibid.

25. Ibid.

26. Sayles, *Leadership*, p. 50.

27. Ibid., p. 44.

28. Ibid.

29. Ibid.

30. Graham T. Allison, "Public and Private Management: Are They Fundamentally Alike in All Unimportant Respects?" in Richard J. Stillman, II, *Public Administration: Concepts and Cases,* 5th ed. (Boston: Houghton Mifflin, 1992), p. 288.

31. Apple, "A High Stakes Gamble," p. 1.

32. Rourke, *Bureaucracy, Politics and Public Policy*, pp. 48–87.

33. Ibid., p. 52.

34. James Risser, "The U.S. Forest Service: Smokey's Strip Miners," in *The Culture of Bureaucracy,* ed. Charles Peters and Michael Nelson (New York: Holt, Rinehart and Winston, 1979), p. 146.

35. Milton C. Cummings and David Wise, *Democracy Under Pressure: An Introduction to the American Political System,* 7th ed. (Fort Worth, Tex.: Harcourt Brace Jovanovich, 1993), p. 414.

36. Michael Nelson, "How to Break the Ties that Bind Congress to the Lobbies and Agencies," in Peters and Nelson, *The Culture of Bureaucracy,* p. 276.

37. Stephen Chapman, "The ICC and the Truckers," in Peters and Nelson, *The Culture of Bureaucracy,* p. 156.

38. Rourke, *Bureaucracy, Politics and Public Policy*, p. 78.

39. Harold Seidman and Robert Gilmour, *Politics, Position and Power,* 4th ed. (New York: Oxford University Press, 1986), p. 33.

40. I am indebted to China scholar and colleague Suzanne Ogden for providing me with the translation of this word.

41. Charles Peters, "Firemen First or How to Beat a Budget Cut," in Peters and Nelson, *The Culture of Bureaucracy,* pp. 12–13.

42. Ibid., pp. 11–12.

43. George Berkley, *The Craft of Public Administration,* 4th ed. (Boston: Allyn and Bacon, 1984), p. 396.

44. Frank Greve, "Is the B-1 a Plane Whose Time Has Come," *Philadelphia Inquirer Magazine,"* March 18, 1984, p. 30.

45. Philip Selznick, *TVA and Grass Roots* (Berkeley: University of California Press, 1949), p. 13.

46. Ibid.

47. Martha Derthick, "The Art of Cooptation: Advisory Councils in Social Security," in *Bureaucratic Power in National Policy Making,* 4th ed., ed. Francis Rourke (Boston: Little, Brown, 1986), p. 371.

48. Ibid.

49. See, for example, Richard Davis, *The Press and American Politics: the New Mediator* (New York: Longman, 1992); and Martin Linsky, *Impact: How the Press Affects Federal Policymaking* (New York: W.W. Norton, 1986).

50. Gordon Chase, *How to Manage in the Public Sector* (New York: McGraw-Hill, 1983), p. 149.

51. Keith Blume, *The Presidential Election Show* (South Hadley, Mass.: Bergin and Garvey, 1985), p. 2.

52. Eliot Chapple and Conrad Arensberg, *Measuring Human Relations: An Introduction to the Study of the Interaction of Individuals,* Genetic Psychology Monograph No. 22 (Princetown, Mass.: The Journal Press, 1940).

53. William F. Whyte, *Street Corner Society* (Chicago: University of Chicago Press, 1943).

54. George C. Homans, *The Human Group* (New York: Harcourt, Brace, 1950); see also George C. Homans, *Social Behavior: Its Elementary Forms* (New York: Harcourt Brace, 1961).

55. Leonard R. Sayles, *Behavior of Industrial Work Groups* (New York: John Wiley, 1958).

56. William F. Whyte, *Organizational Behavior: Theory and Application* (Homewood, Ill.: R. D. Irwin, 1969), p. 91.

57. Leonard R. Sayles, *Leadership: Managing in Real Organizations,* 2nd ed. (New York: McGraw-Hill, 1989), p. 38.

58. Ibid.

59. The notion of salience in the power context is particularly well framed in William D. Coplin and Michael K. O'Leary, *Everyman's Prince: A Guide to Understanding Your Political Problems* (North Scituate, Mass.: Duxbury Press, 1976), pp. 1–18.

60. Rourke, *Bureaucracy, Politics and Public Policy,* p. 119.

61. Smith, *The Power Game,* p. 14.

CHAPTER 2

Deciding On the Proper Policy Course

RICHARD A. LOVERD

Perhaps the most essential courage in the public service is the courage to decide.[1]

—Stephen K. Bailey

One can say that three pre-eminent qualities are decisive for the politician: passion, a feeling of responsibility, and a sense of proportion.[2]

—Max Weber

Where one stands depends upon where one sits.[3]

—Rufus Miles

For many scholars,[4] the starting point for any discussion of *policy*—that "general plan of action adopted by a government to solve a problem, counter a threat or pursue an objective"[5]—involves an appreciation of the various stages by which it is made. In particular, the stages of (1) agenda setting, (2) policy formulation, (3) adoption, (4) implementation and (5) evaluation commonly come to mind.

During the *agenda-setting* stage attention is drawn to the ways in which issues of concern to the public become objects of governmental concern and actually get on the government agenda. At the *policy formulation* stage different plans of action are considered for dealing with those issues. In the *adoption* phase a policy is chosen and enacted by the government, and during *implementation* that policy is carried out and enforced. Finally, during the *evaluation* stage the policy is assessed to determine if it has met its goals and accomplished its work.

Obviously policy leaders play a role in this process. They can use the power noted in the preceding chapter and make choices which shape policy outcomes. However, in too many instances those decisions have not been all we would like them to be. History is littered with leaders who overestimated or misused their power by accident or design and made the wrong choices.

As statesman Jean Monnet once observed, ". . . all people of great achievement are ambitious. But the key question is whether they are ambitious to be or ambitious to do."[6] In order to heighten the likelihood that such ambitions will be channeled in meaningful ways, a series of considerations should be employed to help leaders put power in its proper policy perspective and make sound policy decisions.

What sorts of considerations should be used by leaders to help gain a sense of policy proportion and increase the prospect that power will be gauged and used constructively? While numerous frameworks are available,[7] this writer's studies[8] point to a multi-pronged approach which suggests that at least five decision bases be weighed when leaders make policy choices:

1. Rational calculation
2. Ethical imperatives
3. Political desirability
4. Administrative feasibility
5. Systems shifts

As we shall see, each decision base has a distinct emphasis which implies that "where one stands depends upon where one sits" and conveys the need for all such components to be considered when policy decisions are being made.

INDIVIDUALLY DETERMINED DECISION BASES: RATIONAL CALCULATION AND ETHICAL IMPERATIVES

In regard to the decision base of *rational calculation,* a number of scholarly interpretations come to mind. For example, Fred Frohock notes that "rational behavior may be defined as the optimum conjunction of means and ends; or, given any goal, that behavior which secures the posited goal with the least amount of difficulty is the optimum rationality in the circumstances."[9] In a similar vein, Graham Allison refers to "classical 'economic man' and the rational man of modern statistical theory and game theory [as making] optimal choices in narrowly constrained, neatly defined situations," that is, rationality as "consistent, value-maximizing choice within specified constraints."[10] And Schuman and Olufs suggest that "a decision maker is rational if (1) there is a set of existing priorities, (2) when applied to a decision problem, the priorities serve to rank alternatives, and (3) if applied to the same decision twice, the priorities will serve to rank alternatives the same way each time."[11]

More comprehensively, and perhaps more directly, all of these ideas tend to be represented in James Anderson's description of rational decision making, which involves the following progression of logical steps:

1. The decision maker is confronted with a problem that can be separated from other problems or at least considered meaningfully in comparison with them.
2. The goals, values, or objectives that guide the decision maker are known and can be clarified and ranked according to their importance.
3. The various alternatives for dealing with the problem are examined.
4. The consequences (costs and benefits, advantages and disadvantages) that would follow from selecting each alternative are investigated.
5. Each alternative, and its attendant consequences, is then compared with the other alternatives.
6. The decision maker will choose the alternative, and its consequences, which maximizes attainment of his or her goals, values, or objectives.[12]

The result of such a procedure "is a rational decision—that is, one that most effectively achieves a given end. In short, it optimizes; it is the best possible decision."[13]

Clearly, the rational approach has its appeal. After all, would we prefer to have policy makers who are irrational?[14] As Roger Hilsman points out, "We like to think of policy as rationalized, in the economist's sense of the word, with each step leading logically and economically to the next."[15] And James Fesler further counsels that while the theories that form this approach may "seem abstract, their essentials have the appeal of common sense: any sensible person whose goal is to reach another city by car will consider the alternative routes and choose the shortest one."[16]

Therefore, when using rational calculation, the policy leader attempts to make sense of a situation and alternative means to deal with it by considering a problem in very specified terms and, through largely economic perspectives, judging the costs and benefits of proposals according to how well they solve the problem. Along with the facts, the internal logic and consistency of the arguments composed in proposals are examined as they are presented, and the best proposal is selected, regardless of who sponsors or opposes it.[17]

The second decision basis, *ethical imperatives,* is more visceral than logical and keyed to the policy leader's own system of values and personal beliefs concerning the fundamental issues of "what ought to be" in public life. A course of action is chosen not because it is rational so much as because it is "right"; and when it is so chosen, regardless of the array of facts and forces intruding, a path may be taken which is less common and less popular but true to the leader's own values and moral convictions.[18]

By holding to such convictions in decision making, the policy leader can serve as a moral exemplar for others, particularly if those convictions are consistent, that is, "continual to the point of being commonplace," in the behavior of the leader in question. As David Hart notes in distinguishing "moral processes" from "moral episodes," "true morality belongs to our every action and thought, not just to the heightened moments. Morality . . . must never be limited to its exalted moments.

[Consequently,] if one's moral life is defined only by its episodes and confrontations, then most of that life is lived without morality. [As] Montaigne wrote, '. . . to judge a man really properly, we must chiefly examine his ordinary actions and surprise him in his everyday habit.' "[19] And in like manner Terry Cooper observes that "the very legitimacy of moral episodes appears to depend on a prior commitment . . . to moral work. [Indeed] perhaps the crucial difference between whistle blowers and crusaders who contribute to the effectiveness, integrity and openness of public [service] and those who simply draw attention to themselves is the extent to which conscious commitment to virtuous conduct had characterized less visible previous work."[20] Therefore, just as consistency between means and ends is important in rational calculation, so too is consistency in the ongoing level of moral commitment important in assessing the capacity and credibility of the ethical decision maker.

Thus far, the two decision bases presented express perspectives that can be defined on the leader's own consistent terms, with little reference to pressures outside the immediate workplace. They can provide a public official with the illusion of control while, in fact, avoiding other factors in the environment that may be at work, waiting to bash and blunt that individual's choices. In this regard, Schuman and Olufs note that rational approaches "have limited application in accounting for the array of factors at work in public decisions; they are the basis for important techniques, such as benefit-cost analysis, but they do not explain the overall context of decisions . . . ,"[21] a context which can take a leader's decisions to task. And Fesler similarly points out that within the rational decision-making process, only those steps dealing with the identification of alternatives and the calculation and comparison of benefits and costs call for rational analysis. Before those steps, the formulation of the crucial statement of goals, values, or objectives that guides the decision maker is actually "a *prerequisite* of rational analysis," coming from forces *outside the process* (such as Congress, the president, or an agency head) rather than from the process itself.[22]

In the instance of ethical imperatives, similar contextual intrusions can occur when a policy perspective that a leader may deem ethically compelling proves annoying, and perhaps threatening, to those in the larger environment. As Douglas Amy observes, when reacting to the ethical opinions of the policy leader, those individuals and interests "who have a strong commitment to a set of goals or programs . . . would not be pleased by [views] that raised questions about the basic desirability or worth of those programs. And there is a tendency in ethical analysis to raise just those kinds of annoying questions."[23]

Moreover, for the individual leader, raising such "annoying" questions is not always easy and can require considerable courage, for while some leaders may have little difficulty holding true to their convictions, most struggle with them and encounter any number of ethical dilemmas in making policy choices involving such multifaceted, value-laden terms as "liberty," "equality," "the public interest," "public morality," "fairness," "justice," or "the proper role of government." For example, in addressing public morality, Dwight Waldo notes that "much evidence indicates that it is little understood. As presented in the media, including the columns of the pundits, morality in public office is a simple matter of obeying the law, being honest and telling the truth. *Not so!*"[24]

> . . . a decision or action justified as moral because it is judged to be in the interest of the public may be immoral from the standpoint of all, or nearly all, interpretations of moral behavior for individuals. The most common example is killing. When done by an individual it is, commonly, the crime of homicide. When done in warfare or law enforcement on behalf of the public it is an act of duty and honor, perhaps of heroism— presuming the "correct' circumstances. All important governments have committed what would be "sins" if done by individuals, what would be "crimes" if done under their own laws by individuals acting privately.
>
> Those in government who decide and act on behalf of the public will, from time to time, of necessity as I see it, be lying, stealing, cheating, killing. What must be faced is that all decision and action in the public interest is inevitably morally complex, and that the price of any good characteristically entails some bad.[25]

And an awareness of that price is of particular importance to the leaders who make policy decisions because, as Harold Gortner observes, such "an ethical dilemma is a uniquely personal experience. We can turn to others for advice and help in analyzing the problem, but ultimately we must resolve it ourselves and then live with ourselves and the aftereffects."[26]

Perhaps these sorts of competing interpretations and pressures help to explain why, in research conducted by the National Governor's Association, it was discovered that attention to ethical behavior was generally not a central concern. Instead, it was noted that governors "as a group are not philosophers or moral crusaders. They are managers, politicians, problem solvers, and policy setters. Moral questions become important primarily as and when they affect and impinge upon these roles." Indeed, "only in the climactic [Watergate] year of 1974 did there occur extended open discussions of moral issues at the National Governors' Conference, and the ethics resolution adopted then was retained in later years apparently by inertia alone. It was as if once the fever of Watergate had passed, the governors' attention shifted to more immediately pressing matters."[27]

Therefore, when making policy judgments, the leader needs to keep in mind the level of conflict or congruence between the more individually determined decisional approaches of rationality and ethics and those forces present in the larger environment that can alter their meaning and effectiveness.

DECISION BASES FROM THE LARGER CONTEXT: POLITICAL DESIRABILITY, ADMINISTRATIVE FEASIBILITY, AND SYSTEMS SHIFTS

The first decision base involving forces in the larger environment (and most directly corresponding to the discussions of referent power and coalition building presented in Chapter 1) concerns the political pressures or *political desirability* surrounding a policy decision. As one who would normally seek to maintain or expand power in office, the leader needs to ask how much political capital (i.e., power) will be lost or gained from his or her expending energy on a particular decision. In making that determination, it is necessary to keep track of those relevant political actors (i.e., "individuals, groups, and organizations likely to have [an] impact on the decision"[28]) who will respond positively or negatively to different proposals and thereby support or oppose prospective policy choices.

Where collective support is lacking, then bargaining, compromise, and coalition building may be necessary to gain the majority or plurality to win the political battle. In the instance of notably unpopular or controversial decisions, where support may *never* be sufficient, their power ramifications need to be realistically acknowledged and anticipated before, rather than after, the decision is set in motion.[29]

A good example of the rational, ethical, and political bases in action, and the accompanying need to pay attention to environmental as well as individual perspectives when making policy decisions, was related by former House Speaker Thomas P. "Tip" O'Neill in his memoirs recalling his early dealings with President Jimmy Carter on energy policy. For the new president, the energy crisis was serious business and he said so in several of his initial speeches. Perhaps none was more dramatic than his April 18, 1977, address to the nation, when he referred to that crisis as "the moral equivalent of war," and "the greatest challenge our country will face in our lifetime." Immediately after that speech, Speaker O'Neill went up to Mr. Carter, congratulated him, and said:

> "That was a fine address, Mr. President. Now here's a list of members you should call to keep the pressure on, because we'll need their votes."
>
> "No," he replied, "I described the problem to the American people in a rational way. I'm sure they'll realize that I'm right."
>
> I could have slugged him. Did he still think he was dealing with the Georgia legislature?
>
> "Look," I said, trying to control my frustration. "This is politics we're talking about here, not physics. We need you to push this bill through."
>
> "It's *not* politics," he replied. "Not to me. It's simply the right thing, the rational thing. It's what needs to be done."[30]

Obviously, Speaker O'Neill felt differently, noting that "[Mr. Carter] was right in theory but wrong in practice. [While] it was true that his energy plan was a rational response to a real crisis . . . the president just didn't understand how to motivate Congress,"[31] and such motivation would probably require more political horse-trading and coalition building with legislators than any appeal to rationality or ethics.

Much the same demand for environmental sensitivity needs to be recognized when the administrative capabilities of the institutions involved in helping a leader accomplish policy choices are examined. The leader needs to know the *administrative feasibility* that those institutions will work well together in (1) providing useful information to formulate decisions, and (2) bringing decisions to a successful conclusion once they are made. In this administrative category, notions of "coordinated effort," "teamwork," and "workability" come to the fore, reflecting what Simon,

Smithburg, and Thompson characterize as "cooperative group behavior,"[32] perhaps best exemplified in the classic rudimentary case of two persons trying to roll a rock that neither can move alone. Each must coordinate and cooperate with the other, exerting effort at just the right time and place in order to move work forward. If that efficient coordination breaks down, the work of one or many individuals suffers in the process.

In more modern terms, Leonard Sayles makes much the same administrative point when he stresses that "The individual's contribution has no value except insofar as it is made at the right time and place in a sequence. In order to function, the organization must arrange for that contribution to occur at the right time and place."[33] Thus, with a nod to Chuck Yeager, this perspective suggests that arranging for being in the right place at the right time is just as important as having the "right stuff."

Clearly, such administrative capabilities cannot be taken for granted, for as Hilsman notes, "Governments are made up of large organizations [and while] the top leaders do sit formally on top of these organizations, . . . the information they receive is processed by organizations, the policy alternatives from which they choose are analyzed by organizations, and the decisions are carried out by organizations." Furthermore, "Responsibility for different policy areas is divided among different organizations." For example, "The State Department is responsible for political matters and the Defense Department for military matters. The work of these organizations requires that the efforts of a large number of people be coordinated."[34]

And such coordination is not always forthcoming. As President Franklin Roosevelt noted some years ago, the inner workings of any number of organizations can confound direction and hinder task accomplishment:

> The Treasury [Department] is so large and far-flung and ingrained in its practices that I find it is almost impossible to get the action and results I want. . . . But the Treasury is not to be compared with the State Department. You should go through the experience of trying to get any changes in the thinking, policy, and action of the career diplomats and then you'd know what a real problem was. But the Treasury and the State Department put together are nothing as compared with the Na-a-vy. . . . To change anything in the Na-a-vy is like punching a feather bed. You punch it with your right and you punch it with your left until you are finally exhausted, and then you find the damn bed just as it was before you started punching.[35]

Consequently, beyond the rationality, ethics, or politics of a policy, the administrative question as to whether the government has the structural, technical, cultural, and managerial capabilities to accomplish its tasks and move work forward in a way of benefit to its leaders and the public deserves consideration.[36]

The last contextual decision basis involves *systems shifts,* or significant changes in events or conditions beyond the immediate organization that may force a policy decision or alter its approach. This notion is well expressed in an instance that took place during the Kennedy era. McGeorge Bundy, the special assistant for national security affairs, had begun a daily staff meeting by noting to the president that there were four matters up for discussion. The president, in a less than zestful mood that day, responded by asking, "Are these problems I inherited, or are they problems of our own making?"[37]

Both past and current events intrude on a policy leader's decisions.[38] There are pressures from the past that force leaders to inherit problems, and there are also pressures in the present that encourage leaders to address new ones. Indeed, as former White House Chief of Staff Donald Regan has observed, "situations are imposed on the President, not the other way round."[39] Moreover, as one author stresses, "When confronted by fundamental economic, social and demographic movements whose time has come, the President can no more resist history's tides than King Canute could have turned back the sea."[40]

An article in the *New York Times* from the Reagan years, portraying a "new reality" of compromise imposed on the president by economic crisis, demonstrates how shifts in current events can lead to a shift in presidential decision style:

> Mr. Reagan remained staunchly opposed to raising taxes, and even discussing budget matters with the Congress, until the [1987] collapse of the stock market.
> "It made the world different," Mr. Fitzwater [the president's spokesman] said of the crash. It changed the economic outlook, and it changed the political climate."[41]

In a related example from the Bush/Clinton years, the international policy vacuum left by the collapse of the Soviet Union provides an even more dramatic example of how a different world can create a need for new policies, in this instance policies capable of forging a new post-Cold War world order.

In addition to putting pressure on current leaders to change their policy views, systems shifts can also provide opportunities for altogether new leaders to come on the scene with new policies in tow. Gaddis Smith believes that President Jimmy Carter was just such a person. As one who in 1976 "entered office believing that the failure of his predecessors was moral, [Carter had] the good luck to run in the only election since the days of Woodrow Wilson when such an emphasis would lead to victory":[42]

> In 1972, George McGovern tried something very similar and was easily defeated by Richard Nixon. But in 1976 the public . . . was in favor of reform, disillusioned with recent leadership, and more opposed to a military emphasis in foreign policy than at any time since the 1930's.[43]

Interestingly, Smith goes on to point out that "Jimmy Carter did not create that [public] mood. He was like a surfer who is in precisely the right position to catch the one wave of the day that will carry him all the way."[44]

Yet that wave did not last for long. As Smith further observes, soon thereafter new systems shifts were in motion which would eventually contribute to Carter's demise as president:

> By 1977, the public mood was changing. Memories of Vietnam and Watergate were beginning to fade. Public opinion was beginning to shift in favor of more spending on defense and a more assertive foreign policy—in other words, it was returning to a normal

condition. Jimmy Carter as the prophet assailing American wickedness was now out of step. By 1979, Carter had changed his approach, emphasizing American strength more than human values. But this did not bring him immunity from the earlier image of weakness or prevent him from acquiring a new image of inconsistency.[45]

Therefore, just as timing plays an important role in the coordination of people in administrative situations, so too is it important in the coordination of leadership actions with larger systems shifts. Policies, and the leaders who promote them, need to be in tune with their times.

CONCLUDING THOUGHTS ON THE COURSE OF POLICY: DECISION BASES AND LEADERSHIP STYLES

At the start of this chapter, mention was made of the policy process and the role that policy leaders play in shaping that process, particularly with regard to the decisions they make in helping to shape policy outcomes. It was further noted that in too many instances their choices, and the power which propels them, have led to unfortunate results.

As a way of remedying those results and providing policy leaders with a greater sense of proportion, it was then suggested that they view their decisions from a multi-pronged perspective involving at least five vantage points, or decision bases, perhaps best expressed in the following key questions:

1. Rational calculation: Does my decision make sense?
2. Ethical imperatives: Is it right?
3. Political desirability: Will it enhance my power?
4. Administrative feasibility: Is it workable?
5. Systems shifts: Is the timing right, and are there events or conditions in the past or present that might be intruding?

It was expected that these vantage points would help leaders to adjust to a variety of situations and make the most effective policy decisions.

However, it should be noted that, leaders being human, not all of them weigh these decision bases in the same ways. By either talent or inclination, each has personal preferences which emphasize some vantage points more than others and reveal themselves in their leadership styles. And, of course, those styles can in turn limit a leader's ability to adjust to different public situations.

For example, some leaders may exhibit a preference for *political leadership* and focus on the accumulation of power as a means to winning the policy game. Others may look toward the technical or moral sides of policies and ignore politics. In those instances *professional leadership* (stressing the rational use of technical knowledge as a means of winning deference from others) or *ethical leadership* (emphasizing the use of honorable words and deeds as a means for encouraging responsible behavior from the government and its citizens) would tend to be favored. Still other leaders might prefer *administrative leadership* as their means to satisfaction by concentrating on the need to coordinate the group efforts necessary to make past and present policy efforts workable. Finally, rather rarely in fact, still others might go beyond the everyday transactional aspects of their craft and reach for *transformational leadership*[46] by utilizing the systems shifts available to exercise the vision and character to set new, revolutionary directions for the government.

As we evaluate the cases which follow, we should consider not only power and policy perspectives per se, but also the leadership styles that tend to reflect that power and policy in action. As we do so, the following series of questions could serve as helpful guides:

1. Is this leader's power increasing or decreasing? Why?
2. What stages of the policy process do you see at work?
3. What kinds of policy decision bases, and resulting leadership styles, are being emphasized by this leader?
4. Would you have exercised policy leadership differently? Why or why not?

NOTES

1. Stephen K. Bailey, "Ethics and the Public Service," in *Public Administration and Democracy: Essays in Honor of Paul H. Appleby,* ed. Roscoe C. Martin (Syracuse, N.Y.: Syracuse University Press, 1965), p. 296.

2. Max Weber, "Politics as a Vocation," in H. H. Gerth and C. Wright Mills, eds. *From Max Weber: Essays in Sociology* (New York: Oxford University Press, 1946), p. 115.

3. Cited in Harold Seidman and Robert Gilmour, *Politics, Position and Power,* 4th Ed. (New York: Oxford University Press, 1986), p. 21.

4. See, for example, Charles O. Jones, *An Introduction to the Study of Public Policy,* 2nd. ed. (Boston: Duxbury, 1978); John W. Kingdon, *Agendas, Alternatives and Public Policies* (New York: Harper-Collins, 1995); James E. Anderson, *Public Policymaking: An Introduction,* 2nd ed. (Boston: Houghton Mifflin, 1994); Dennis J. Palumbo, *Public Policy in America: Government in Action* (Fort Worth, Tex.: Harcourt Brace, 1994); and Stella Z. Theodoulou, "How Public Policy is Made," in *Public Policy: The Essential Readings,* ed. Stella Z. Theodoulou and Matthew A. Cahn (Englewood Cliffs, N.J.: Prentice Hall, 1995).

5. Kenneth Janda, Jeffrey M. Berry, and Jerry Goldman, "Policymaking," A Supplement to Accompany Kenneth Janda, Jeffrey M. Berry, and Jerry Goldman, *The Challenge of Democracy: Government in America,* 2nd ed. (Boston: Houghton Mifflin, 1994), p. 3. Similar definitions are provided by Anderson and Palumbo.

6. Noted in Henry A. Kissinger, "With Faint Praise," *New York Times Book Review,* July 16, 1995, p. 7.

7. See, for example, Madeline Wing Adler and Frederick S. Lane, "Governors and Public Policy Leadership," in *Governors and Higher Education,* ed. Samuel Gove and Thad Beyle (Denver: Education Commission of the States, 1988); Graham Allison, *Essence of Decision* (New York: HarperCollins, 1971); Thomas R. Dye, *Understanding Public Policy,* 8th ed. (Englewood Cliffs, N.J.: Prentice Hall, 1995); Daniel C. McCool, *Public Policy Theories, Models, and Concepts: An Anthology* (Englewood Cliffs, N.J.: Prentice Hall, 1995); Stuart Nagel, ed., *Encyclopedia of Policy Studies,* 2nd ed. (New York: Marcel Dekker, 1994); and Jameson W. Doig and Erwin Hargrove, *Leadership and Innovation: A Biographical Perspective on Entrepreneurs in Government* (Baltimore: Johns Hopkins University Press, 1987).

8. See, for example, Richard A. Loverd, "Adding More of a Management Thrust to Public Personnel Perspectives," *Policy Studies Journal,* Fall 1982; Richard A. Loverd, "Approaching the Management of Public Personnel: A United States Perspective," *International Studies of Management and Organiza-*

tion, Fall 1982; Richard A. Loverd, "The Challenge of a More Responsible, Productive Public Work-place," Featured Topic, *Public Productivity and Management Review,* Fall 1989; and Richard A. Loverd, "Presidential Decision Making During the 1975 New York City Financial Crisis," *Presidential Studies Quarterly,* Spring 1991.

9. Fred M. Frohock, *The Nature of Political Inquiry* (Homewood, Ill.: Dorsey Press, 1967), p. 132.

10. Allison, *Essence of Decision,* pp. 29–30.

11. David Schuman and Dick W. Olufs, III, *Public Administration in the United States,* 2nd ed. (Lexington, Mass.: D.C. Heath, 1993), p. 452.

12. Anderson, *Public Policymaking,* p. 122.

13. Ibid.

14. In this regard, one might consult Mary Zey, ed., *Decision Making: Alternatives to Rational Choice Models* (Thousand Oaks, Calif.: Sage Publications, 1992).

15. Roger Hilsman, *The Politics of Policy Making in Defense and Foreign Affairs: Conceptual Models and Bureaucratic Politics* (New York: Prentice Hall, 1987), pp. 60–61.

16. James W. Fesler, *Public Administration: Theory and Practice* (Englewood Cliffs, N.J.: Prentice Hall, 1980), p. 212.

17. See, for example, "Rational Decision Making," in Fesler, *Public Administration;* Ralph Hambrick and William Snyder, *The Analysis of Policy Arguments* (Croton-on-Hudson, N.Y.: Policy Studies Associates, 1976); and "Economic Rationality," in Paul Diesing, *Reason in Society* (Urbana: University of Illinois Press, 1962).

18. See, for example, Wayne A. R. Leys, *Ethics for Policy Decisions* (Englewood Cliffs, N.J.: Prentice Hall, 1952); Jeremy Paul, Amy Gutmann, and Dennis Thompson, *Ethics and Politics* (Chicago: Nelson-Hall, 1984); Joel Fleishman, Lance Liebman, and Mark Moore, *Public Duties: The Moral Obligations of Government Officials* (Cambridge, Mass.: Harvard University Press, 1981); William L. Richter, Frances Burke, Jameson W. Doig, eds., *Combating Corruption/Encouraging Ethics: A Sourcebook for Public Service Ethics* (Washington, D.C.: American Society for Public Administration, 1990); Harold F. Gortner, *Ethics for Public Managers* (New York: Praeger, 1991); and Peter Madsen and Jay M. Shafritz, eds., *Essentials of Government Ethics* (New York: Meridian, 1992).

19. David K. Hart, "The Moral Exemplar in an Organizational Society," in *Exemplary Public Administrators: Character and Leadership in Government,* ed. Terry L. Cooper and N. Dale Wright (San Francisco: Jossey-Bass, 1992), pp. 23–24.

20. Terry L. Cooper, "Reflecting on Exemplars of Virtue," in Cooper and Wright, *Exemplary Public Administrators,* p. 336.

21. Schuman and Olufs, *Public Administration,* pp. 453–454.

22. Fesler, *Public Administration,* p. 214. For more related to this point, see Christopher J. Bosso, "The Practice and Study of Policy Formation," in Nagel, *Encyclopedia,* pp. 95–113.

23. Douglas J. Amy, "Why Policy Analysis and Ethics Are Incompatible," *Journal of Policy Analysis and Management,* 3, no. 4 (1984), p. 582.

24. Dwight Waldo, *The Enterprise of Public Administration* (Novato, Calif.: Chandler and Sharp, 1980), p. 100.

25. Ibid., pp. 100–101.

26. Gortner, *Ethics for Public Managers,* p. 14.

27. Robert Dalton, "Governors and Ethics," in *Being Governor: The View from the Office,* ed. Thad L. Beyle and Lynn R. Muchmore (Durham, N.C.: Duke University Press, 1983), p. 76.

28. William D. Coplin and Michael K. O'Leary, *Political Analysis Through the Prince System,* PS 23 (Croton-on-Hudson, N.Y.: Policy Studies Associates, 1983), p. 15.

29. See, for example, Seidman and Gilmour, *Politics, Position and Power;* Eugene Bardach, *The Skill Factor in Politics* (Berkeley: University of California Press, 1972); and Barbara Hinckley, *Coalitions and Politics* (New York: Harcourt Brace Jovanovich, 1981).

30. Thomas P. O'Neill, Jr., *Man of the House: The Life and Political Memoirs of Speaker Tip O'Neill* (New York: Random House, 1987), p. 320.

31. Ibid.

32. Herbert Simon, Donald Smithburg, and Victor Thompson, *Public Administration* (New York: Alfred Knopf, 1950), p. 4.

33. Leonard Sayles, *Managerial Behavior* (New York: McGraw-Hill, 1964), p. 22.

34. Hilsman, *The Politics of Policy Making,* p. 55. In a related vein, see also Allison, *Essence of Decision,* pp. 67–100.

35. Quotation from M. S. Eccles, in Allison, *Essence of Decision,* p. 86.

36. See, for example, Simon, Smithburg and Thompson, *Public Administration;* and Sayles, *Managerial Behavior.*

37. Charles J. V. Murphy, "Cuba: The Record Set Straight," *Fortune,* September 1961, p. 92.

38. See, for example, Richard Neustadt and Ernest May, *Thinking in Time* (New York: Free Press, 1986); and Leonard Sayles and Margaret Chandler, *Managing Large Systems* (New York: Harper and Row, 1971).

39. Ibid.

40. Mel Elfin, "Shrinking the Oval Office," *U.S. News and World Report,* December 7, 1987, p. 28.

41. Steven V. Roberts, "Reagan's New Reality: Compromise," *New York Times,* November 13, 1987, p. A16.

42. Gaddis Smith, *Morality, Reason and Power: American Diplomacy in the Carter Years* (New York: Hill and Wang, 1986), p. 241.

43. Ibid., p. 242.

44. Ibid.

45. Ibid.

46. A related, albeit somewhat different version of this concept, "transforming leadership," was first brought to my attention by James MacGregor Burns through a discussion with him at Villanova University and the subsequent study of his book on *Leadership* (New York: Harper and Row, 1978).

CHAPTER 3

John F. Kennedy:
Moral Leadership in Civil Rights

*ROBERT E. GILBERT**

PRE-PRESIDENTIAL CIVIL RIGHTS RECORD

At the time John F. Kennedy launched his formal campaign for the presidency in 1959, major civil rights leaders in the United States regarded him as something of an enigma. They were quite aware that at the 1956 Democratic convention, when Adlai Stevenson had departed from precedent by throwing the choice of his vice presidential running mate to the delegates, Kennedy had emerged as the clear choice of the South. Of the 334 southern convention delegates, Kennedy had won 249½ of their votes on the second and final ballot, capturing unanimous support among the Arkansas, Georgia, Louisiana, Mississippi, South Carolina, Texas, and Virginia delegations.[1] Kennedy's southern support is somewhat deceptive, however, and can be attributed primarily to two factors.

First, his principal opponent, who went on to win the vice presidential nomination, was Tennessee's Senator Estes Kefauver, a liberal. Kefauver was perceived as something of a renegade throughout much of the South. As a young congressman, he had taken a clear stand against the poll tax, long used as a means of preventing poor blacks and whites from voting. Also, in 1949, as a senator, he had infuriated much of the South by announcing his support for a rule change in the Senate which would

---

*From Robert E. Gilbert, *Political Communication and Persuasion,* vol. 6, pp.1–19. Washington, D.C.: Taylor and Francis, Inc. Reproduced with permission. All rights reserved.

have limited debate, thereby eroding the power of the filibuster as a southern means for stopping or at least delaying action on civil rights and other legislation. At the 1956 Democratic convention, the South retaliated by casting the lion's share of its votes against the Tennessee senator rather than for his Massachusetts colleague.[2]

The second reason for Kennedy's 1956 strength in the South was very simply the fact that the South did not know where Kennedy stood on the civil rights question. In 1957, however, southerners were to learn something of the Kennedy view as a result of the congressional struggle over the civil rights bill of that year. While Kennedy basically favored that legislation, his cautious role in the fight over its adoption should be noted. For the sake of clarity, Kennedy's behavior can be divided into two phases: first, his participation in the parliamentary maneuvering preceding the bill's passage and, second, his attitude toward the substance of the legislation itself.

The Civil Rights Bill of 1957 was the first piece of legislation since the Civil War designed specifically to benefit blacks.[3] Liberals in the Senate were strongly committed to its passage and feared that southern congressional power might lead to its defeat. Of particular concern to the backers of the bill was Senator James Eastland (D–Miss.), chairman of the Judiciary Committee, who was expected to try to emasculate the legislation. As a result of this fear, Democratic liberals, joined by some Republican senators, launched an attempt to have the bill bypass Eastland's committee and go directly to the Senate floor.[4] However, since John Kennedy felt that such a move would set a dangerous precedent, he refused to support it, arguing that supporters of the bill should rely instead on the threat of a discharge petition.[5] His insistence on following the normal procedures of Senate business irritated Senate liberals and disappointed civil rights advocates. Kennedy's position in this instance was symbolic of his somewhat conservative attitude toward the political process. He tended to be a cautious liberal rather than a radical reformer. He believed in operating slowly through established structures and was rather reluctant, in most instances, to reach beyond those structures.

Apart from his negative attitude toward the Judiciary Committee bypass, Kennedy strongly supported the legislation itself. He even took to the floor of the Senate to endorse a controversial provision which permitted the attorney general of the United States to use injunctive power to enforce school desegregation, "hence allowing greater use of civil sanctions instead of cumbersome criminal prosecution."[6] This proposal, however, was later deleted from the legislation.

Some civil rights proponents were somewhat concerned by Kennedy's stand on an amendment sponsored by Senator Joseph O'Mahoney (D–Wyo.) which called for jury trials in criminal contempt cases in the area of voting rights. If southern white election officials charged with wrongdoing under the act should then be brought before southern white juries, the voting rights section of the bill might well be rendered meaningless. Kennedy, again deserting and antagonizing most Senate liberals, supported the amendment. He did so partially for political reasons—he wanted to minimize southern opposition to passage of the bill and also to his own political advancement. Yet it should be noted that he had received advice from Professors Paul Freund and Mark de Wolff Howe of the Harvard University Law School that the

O'Mahoney amendment would "probably not hurt the effectiveness of the bill in a major way"[7] and read into the *Congressional Record* excerpts of their advice to him.[8] James MacGregor Burns concludes that "these arguments helped Kennedy take the position toward which he had already leaned for political reasons."[9]

In sum, the pattern of Kennedy's behavior in the 1957 struggle for civil rights legislation was one of caution and moderation. Although a supporter of the 1957 bill, Kennedy was unwilling to antagonize completely the southern power structure on either the Judiciary Committee bypass or the O'Mahoney jury trial amendment. Thus, the strength of his commitment to the cause of civil rights was still unclear at the time he launched his bid for the 1960 presidential nomination of the Democratic Party. As Schlesinger recounts:

> In the late fifties civil rights advocates regarded him as sympathetic . . . but detached. [Martin Luther] King, who breakfasted with him in New York a month before the 1960 Convention, later said he displayed at this time a definite concern, but . . . not what I would call a "depthed" understanding. Most civil rights leaders preferred Humphrey or Stevenson for the Democratic nomination.[10]

THE 1960 PRESIDENTIAL CAMPAIGN

The Democratic National Convention of 1960 adopted a strong civil rights plank in its platform. In that document, Democrats committed themselves to the elimination of literacy tests and poll taxes as requirements for voting, urged that the attorney general be empowered to file civil injunctive suits in federal courts to prevent the denial of any civil right because of race, called for the establishment of a Fair Employment Practices Commission, recommended the strengthening of the powers of the Civil Rights Commission, and advocated the end of racial discrimination in public education. The Democratic platform also pledged that a new Democratic administration would "take action to end discrimination in Federal Housing programs, including Federally assisted housing," would use "its full executive powers to assure equal employment opportunities and to terminate racial segregation throughout Federal services and institutions, and on all government contracts," and would provide "moral and political leadership . . . to make equal opportunity a living reality for all Americans."[11]

Throughout his campaign for president in 1960, John F. Kennedy was true to the Democratic platform, speaking frequently and eloquently about the need for civil rights progress in the United States. He did so not only in such northern cities as New York, Philadelphia, Detroit, and San Francisco[12] but also in cities of the South. As examples, in Greensboro, North Carolina, on September 17 and in Memphis, Tennessee, on September 21, he advocated an America where all persons are truly free and where all enjoy their full constitutional rights. In Warm Springs, Georgia, on October 10, he urged that "we must assure every citizen of the full protection of his constitutional rights and equal opportunity to participate with every other American in every phase of our national life." In Columbia, South Carolina, also on October 10, he asserted:

> I think it is clear . . . that if we are to have progress in this area [civil rights], and we must have progress to be true to our ideals and responsibilities, then Presidential leadership is necessary so that every American can enjoy his full constitutional rights. Some of you may disagree with that view but at least I have not changed that view in an election year, or according to where I am standing.[13]

While the Democratic nominee voiced support for the general goal of equal rights and equal opportunity in all sections of the country, closer scrutiny discloses that his campaign pronouncements on the subject can be divided into several different categories. First, he often linked fair treatment for those of minority races to fair treatment for those of minority religions. This was not a surprising strategy in light of the fact that his own Catholic religion had emerged as a major issue in the 1960 campaign and was being used against him by some of his opponents.[14] The Democratic nominee joined the issue of racial and religious liberty in Oakland, California, where on September 8, 1960, he asserted that "the Democratic Party intends to use the full legal and moral authority of the Federal Government, including, in particular, the Presidency itself, to put an end to racial and religious discrimination in this country of ours." In Harrisburg, Pennsylvania, on September 15, Kennedy stated, "we must make sure that every American—of every race, religion, and age—has equal opportunity to find a job." On September 25, he took the same approach in Cleveland, Ohio, when he said, "We want fair treatment for all Americans, regardless of where they live or what their occupation, regardless of their race, their creed or their color." Three days later in Buffalo, New York, Kennedy announced that he wanted "to provide equal opportunity for all Americans, regardless of their race or regardless of their religion, for any job they are competent to hold in any part of the United States, for any office." The future president took a similar position in campaign remarks delivered in such places as Newark, New Jersey (September 15); Minneapolis, Minnesota (October 1); and Venice, Illinois (October 3).[15]

Second, Kennedy used the foreign policy interests of the United States as an argument for civil rights progress for black Americans at home. In remarks delivered in Los Angeles, California, on September 9, 1960, Kennedy asked:

> Can we honestly say that it doesn't affect our security and the fight for peace when Negroes and others are denied their full constitutional rights, when we in this country who are a white minority around the world are asking for the friendship of Negroes and colored people stretching all around the globe and whose good will, whose support, whose common interest we seek to develop in the coming years?

In New York City, on October 12, 1960, Kennedy asserted that "We must wipe out all traces of discrimination and prejudice against Negroes at home if we are to win the respect and friendship of the Negro peoples of Africa." He reiterated this theme in his final campaign appearance, in Boston, Massachusetts, on November 7, 1960, when he remarked, "by assuring every American, of every race and creed, equal opportunity in all the activities of our national life . . . we can convince the people of the developing nations that the road to progress is freedom's road—that democracy, not communism, offers the brightest hope for their future."[16]

Third, Kennedy indicated that he would use his executive power and influence, if elected president, to bring about change in the United States, and he attacked President Eisenhower for not having done so. In Portland, Oregon (September 7, 1960), Kennedy decried an "executive branch which has shown no real concern for civil rights." Two days later he spoke in Burbank, California, and remarked that "I don't think that the president has used his executive power fully in the fight for equal rights and I do not think that this Administration has been particularly vigorous in setting a moral atmosphere for the implementation of the Supreme Court decisions." In East Saint Louis, on October 3, 1960, Kennedy asserted, "It is the president of the United States who can set the goals for the country in . . . equality of rights for all Americans, regardless of their race or color." And in New York City, on October 12, he pledged "moral and persuasive leadership by the President to create the conditions in which compliance with the constitutional requirements of school desegregation takes place; this is the kind of leadership I intend to give."[17]

Fourth, Kennedy repeatedly linked civil rights progress with the Democratic Party. In Newark, New Jersey, on September 15, 1960, he proclaimed, "So long as there are millions of our fellow Americans in parts of the country who are denied their equal opportunity . . . so long is there a need for the Democratic Party." On September 9, 1960, Kennedy asserted in Los Angeles, California, that "we are even prouder of the fact that the Democratic Party—in its platform—has a program of future action which will insure equality of opportunity to all Americans." In Paterson, New Jersey, on September 15, he pledged that "if we are elected in November, . . . we will carry on in this country the same policies which have distinguished for so many years other great Democratic Administrations, the equality of opportunity for our people, the protection of their rights." And in Minneapolis, on October 2, 1960, he told his audience that the Democratic Party stands for the principle of equal rights and "a fair chance for all Americans."[18]

Fifth, Kennedy used some of his campaign appearances to indicate support for the sit-in movement that was beginning to appear in several of the southern states. On September 3, in San Francisco, he remarked, "I want every American free to stand up for his rights, even if sometime he has to sit down for them." Five days later, in Oakland, California, he repeated very much the same theme, saying, "we believe in the right of every American to stand up for his rights, even if to do so he has to sit down for them."[19]

Sixth, Kennedy indicated support for specific actions and policies relevant to civil rights progress. In Los Angeles, for example, he remarked, "we must strengthen the President's Civil Rights Commission. We must grant the Attorney General power to enforce all constitutional rights. We must wipe out discriminatory poll taxes and literacy tests, and pass effective anti-bombing and anti-lynching legislation." After calling attention to the fact that there were no black federal district judges in the United States, Kennedy told the National Bar Association on August 31, 1960:

With more than 4,000 Negro lawyers in this country, there are many outstanding Negroes from whom to choose future judges. I assure you that in a new Democratic Administration there will be far better representation, on the basis of merit, of persons of all our racial groups, including particularly those who in the past have been excluded on the basis of prejudice.

Also, Kennedy frequently called attention to the fact that there were only 26 black foreign service officers out of 6,000 and that "we have to do better" (Battle Creek, Michigan, October 14, 1960; Fairborn, Ohio, October 17, 1960; Brooklyn, New York, October 20, 1960; Madison, Wisconsin, October 23, 1960; Los Angeles and San Francisco, California, November 1 and 2, 1960).[20]

Interestingly, the civil rights campaign promise most commonly associated with Kennedy's quest for the presidency was his "stroke-of-the-pen" comment relative to housing discrimination.[21] In late summer 1960, Kennedy joined 23 other Democratic senators in signing a statement condemning the Eisenhower administration for its failure to issue an executive order calling for an end to racial discrimination in federal housing programs.

As he began traveling across the country, he promised, from time to time, to issue such an order and end discrimination in federal housing "by a stroke of the pen." This was a pledge that would haunt Kennedy throughout most of the first two years of his administration, because that order, despite the urging of civil rights groups, was not forthcoming. Burke Marshall reported that Kennedy later joked ruefully about his "stroke-of-the-pen" remark, blaming Ted Sorensen for having written the speech that contained that pledge. Sorensen responded that he had nothing to do with it, "and the president remarked that nobody wrote it or something like that. But 'the stroke of the pen,' the president kept muttering that phrase: Who put those words in my mouth?"[22]

Kennedy's supportive attitude toward the sit-in movement has already been cited. That support and the dramatic campaign event which it spawned proved to be extremely important to his election to the presidency. During the 1960 campaign, perhaps no single event was more important in rallying black voters to the Democratic ticket than one involving Dr. Martin Luther King. On October 19, 1960, King and more than 50 of his associates were arrested in an Atlanta department store for refusing to leave a table in its restaurant. Although all of King's sit-in companions were soon released, King himself was kept in prison and then sentenced to four months at hard labor at the Georgia State Penitentiary.

Theodore White reported that prior to King's arrest, Kennedy had been warned by at least three southern governors that if he intruded himself into southern affairs by endorsing King, "the south could be given up as lost to the Democratic ticket."[23] Nevertheless, despite this threat and the admonition he received from some of his advisors, Kennedy did intervene by personally telephoning King's wife and by having his brother Robert telephone the Georgia judge who had sentenced the civil rights leader to urge his release. King was soon free on bail, pending an appeal, thereby ending widespread fears that he would be murdered while in prison.

Word of the Kennedy brothers' intervention spread rapidly throughout the black community. A number of black leaders, among them King's minister father, endorsed Kennedy for the presidency. The president of the Protestant Council of New York, Dr. Gardner Taylor, who was also pastor of one of the nation's major black churches, announced, "This is the kind of moral leadership and direct personal concern which this problem [social justice] has lacked in these critical years."[24] In an effort to capitalize on these developments, the Democratic campaign organization distributed a million pamphlets describing the episode at black churches across the country two days before the election.[25]

Kennedy's intervention, as well as the overall efforts of his civil rights campaign team, seemingly had an impact on black voters. In one of the closest presidential elections in history, Kennedy captured 49.7% of the total popular vote to 49.6% for his Republican opponent, Richard M. Nixon. Among white voters, Nixon prevailed 52 to 48%. But among the black electorate, Kennedy amassed 75% of the vote. Four years before, the Democratic candidate had received only 60% of the black vote.[26] Kennedy's support among black voters was extremely important in enabling him to capture the electoral votes of three large industrial states (Illinois, Michigan, New Jersey), where his popular vote margin over Nixon was paper-thin. So narrow was Kennedy's victory that some observers have credited it to the strong support he received from black voters.[27]

THE PRESIDENTIAL YEARS

In his book *Pragmatic Illusions,* Bruce Miroff attacked John F. Kennedy, as president, for failing to serve as the nation's educator on the matter of civil rights. He charged that "Kennedy had nothing new to teach to the American public" and that Kennedy's "approach failed to confront the moral questions [the civil rights struggle] posed and the profound consequences it held for American society." He wrote further, "If he accepted (sometimes) his presidential responsibility to act, he never fully appreciated the equally important responsibility to educate. On no other subject was political education so vital in the early 1960s; on no other subject did Kennedy prove so deficient as an educator."[28] After reviewing the record, Miroff's judgment seems overly harsh.

John Kennedy was an extremely mediagenic chief executive. Articulate, urbane, and witty, he was the most proficient handler of the media since Franklin Roosevelt had sat in the White House.[29] In Kennedy's day, television had become a vital component of the media, and his telegeneity became a powerful asset to his presidency. Kennedy was the first president to conduct live, televised press conferences, at which he invariably excelled, and he held 63 during his 34 months in office. The primary purpose of these conferences, according to one of Kennedy's closest aides, "was to inform and impress the public more than the press."[30] Another aide described them as "the central forum of presidential contact."[31]

The American Research Bureau found that there was a 10% increase in the number of television sets in use every time the president took to the airwaves.[32] Typically conducted during daytime hours, these conferences drew average television audiences of some 18 million.[33] In short, Kennedy's meetings with the press were media events which captivated much of the nation and provided him with a powerful national pulpit.[34]

At any number of his press conferences, Kennedy was asked questions which pertained to civil rights. Unlike some other contemporary presidents, Kennedy never used those questions as a vehicle for attacking the courts or indicating his disapproval for court actions. Instead, he responded in a way which left little doubt as to his own personal convictions, even when somewhat controversial tactics were employed by civil rights groups. For example, at a press conference held on July 19, 1961, Kennedy was asked his view of the freedom rider movement,[35] and he replied:

> I think the Attorney General has made it clear that we believe that everyone who travels, for whatever reason they travel, should enjoy the full constitutional protection given to them by the law and by the Constitution. They should be able to move freely in interstate commerce.[36]

This and many other of Kennedy's press conference remarks form a mosaic of support for progress in the area of human rights. Delivered before large television audiences, they indicated the president's disdain for racism, his insistence on equal rights and opportunities, his belief in the moral dimensions of the issue, and, in his final months in office, his refusal to allow the political consideration of his own projected reelection to interfere with his commitment to the cause. Scrutiny of the president's press conference comments reveals his view on a wide range of issues relevant to civil rights and indicates his intent to serve as the nation's teacher.

With regard to education, Kennedy frequently and unequivocally advocated integration of public schools. On February 8, 1961, just a few weeks after his inauguration, the new president asserted, "it is my position that all students should be given the opportunity to attend public schools regardless of their race, and that is in accordance with the Constitution. "[37] On August 30, 1961, he publicly congratulated the governor of Georgia, the mayor, police chief, and superintendent of schools of Atlanta, and the parents, students, and citizens of that city for the successful integration of four high schools with "courage, tolerance, and above all, respect for the law."[38] With reference to the integration of New Orleans schools, President Kennedy told his national audience, "I believe strongly that every American should have the opportunity to have maximum development of his talents, under the most beneficial circumstances, and that is what the Constitution provides."[39]

Kennedy was even more outspoken in his commitment to voting rights for all Americans. During his first press conference as president, held on January 25, 1961, and watched by some 65 million people,[40] Kennedy said, "I am extremely interested in making sure that every American is given the right to cast his vote without prejudice to his rights as a citizen. And therefore, I can state that this Administration will pursue the problem of providing that protection with all vigor."[41] On November 8,

1961, Kennedy announced, "there have been more suits filed to provide for voting and there will continue to be a concerted effort by this administration to make it possible to vote under the laws and directions provided by Congress."[42] Ten months later, the president commended "those who are making every effort to register every citizen. They deserve the protection of the United States Government, the protection of the state, the protection of local communities, and we shall do everything we possibly can to make sure that that protection is assured."[43]

In the face of the violence which often confronted civil rights workers in the South, Kennedy expressed indignation and outrage. At a press conference held on September 13, 1962, he remarked: "The United States Constitution provides for freedom to vote, and this country must permit every man and woman to exercise their franchise. To shoot, as we saw in the case of Mississippi, two young people who were involved in an effort to register people—to burn churches in reprisal, I consider both cowardly as well as outrageous." He went on to say, "The United States now has a number of FBI agents in there and as soon as we are able to find out who did it, we'll arrest them."[44] On April 24, 1963, President Kennedy asserted:

> We had outrageous crimes, from all accounts, in the state of Alabama in the shooting of the postman who was attempting in a very traditional way to dramatize the plight of some of our citizens, being assassinated on the road. We have offered to the state of Alabama the services of the FBI in the solution of the crime.[45]

Kennedy also indicated his disapproval with the status quo in the way black citizens were being treated in the South. On February 15, 1961, he was asked his reaction to the decision by the Civil War Centennial Commission that it had no authority to provide hotel rooms for Negroes who attended meetings in the South. His answer was unequivocal:

> The Centennial [Commission] is an official body of the United States government, federal funds are contributed to sustaining it, there have been appointments made by the federal government to the Commission, and it's my strong belief that any program of this kind in which the United States engages should provide facilities and meeting places which may— do not discriminate on the grounds of race and color. We cannot leave the situation as it is today.[46]

On August 1, 1962, he took a similar position with regard to the status of black citizens of Albany, Georgia. Kennedy asserted that "We are going to attempt, as we have done in the past, to try to provide a satisfactory solution and protection of the constitutional rights of the people of Albany and I will continue to do so. And the situation today is completely unsatisfactory from that point of view."[47]

In 1963, civil rights leaders and groups focused much of their attention on the August 28 march on Washington. That march brought 250,000 persons of all races to the nation's capital to demonstrate their support for the cause of equal rights and equal opportunity. While some political figures in the country were made uncomfortable by the prospect of such a massive demonstration in Washington, President Kennedy, on July 17, publicly proclaimed, "I think that's in the great tradition. I look forward to being here. I am sure members of Congress will be here. We want citizens to come to Washington if they feel that they are not having their rights expressed."[48] On August 20, he told the press and the nation, "I have been asked for an appointment and I will be glad to see the leaders of the organizations who are participating on that day."[49]

Finally, and importantly, in addition to speaking forthrightly concerning a number of specific civil rights issue areas, President Kennedy directed the attention of the country to the moral dimensions of the civil rights struggle, a struggle which he described on at least one occasion as "a national crisis of great proportions."[50] Many of his press conference remarks reveal that this president was trying to serve as a national educator, pointing out the role that must be played by individuals and by governmental and nongovernmental groups in changing thought and behavior patterns in the area of civil rights. On May 6, 1961, he remarked:

> Now the Federal Government cannot compel that. All we can do is indicate the need. . . . We are asking the people of this country to try, regardless of their own personal views, to reach— to come closer to the constitutional concept of equality of opportunity for all Americans, regardless of their race or creeds.[51]

During a meeting with the press on August 1, 1962, Kennedy commented on demonstrations in the state of Georgia by saying:

> I find it wholly inexplicable why the city council of Albany [Georgia] will not sit down with the citizens of Albany, who may be Negroes, and attempt to secure them, in a peaceful way, their rights. The United States Government is involved in sitting down at Geneva with the Soviet Union. I can't understand why the government of Albany . . . cannot do the same for American citizens.[52]

On May 8, 1963, the president spoke clearly of civil rights in the context of national morality, by saying that "I've attempted to make clear my strong view that there is an important moral issue involved in the equality for our citizens and that until you give it to them, you are going to have difficulties."[53]

Two months later, on July 17, 1963, Kennedy lectured the country as its most visible teacher. He pointed out in frank terms:

> Some of the people . . . who keep talking about demonstrations never talk about the problem of redressing grievances. . . . You just can't tell people, "Don't protest," but on the other hand, "We are not going to let you come into a store or restaurant." It seems to me it is a two-way street. . . . I would suggest that . . . those people who have responsible positions in Government and in business and labor do something about the problem which leads to the demonstrations.[54]

At a press conference on August 1, 1963, Kennedy again pressed the country on the need for change. He remarked that

> Merely because the demonstrations have subsided does not seem to me, those who are in a position of responsibility, does not mean that we should go to sleep and forget the

problem, because that is no solution. . . . I would hope that if there is a period of quiet, we should use it and not merely regard it as an end of the effort.[55]

On October 23, 1963, in one of his last press conferences before his assassination, Kennedy urged the U.S. Steel Corporation, a major force in Birmingham, Alabama, to "use its influence on the side of comity between the races," saying that since the federal government alone cannot solve the problem, business, labor, and every citizen has a responsibility in trying to do so.[56]

The number of questions pertaining to civil rights which were put to Kennedy at press conferences escalated sharply during his years in the White House, from a total of 10 in 1961 and 9 in 1962 to some 25 in the ten months of 1963 during which he served as president.[57] Most of those questions were answered by the president in a way which made the administration's commitment to the cause absolutely clear. No lack of conviction could tempt any opponent of civil rights to take easy comfort in an ambivalent or equivocating national executive. When, for example, the governor of Alabama, George Wallace, announced that his state would never yield to integration in education and seemed on the verge of testing the president's resolve on the issue, Kennedy told the nation (and Wallace) at his May 22, 1963, press conference:

> I know there is great opposition in Alabama, and indeed in any state, to federal marshals and federal troops. And I would be very reluctant to see us reach that point. But I am obligated to carry out the court order. That is part of our constitutional system. There is no choice in the matter. We are a people of laws and we have to obey them.[58]

It is interesting to remember President Eisenhower's words in a similar situation six years earlier. Eisenhower had faced the intransigence of the governor of Arkansas, Orville Faubus, over the issue of school integration. When questioned in July 1957 about his plans to deal with the pending crisis, that president replied:

> I can't imagine any set of circumstances that would ever induce me to send Federal troops . . . into any area to enforce the orders of a federal court, because I believe that common sense of America will never require it. Now there may be that kind of authority resting somewhere but certainly I am not seeking any additional authority of that kind, and I would never believe that it would be a wise thing to do in this country.[59]

Faubus, understandably, interpreted Eisenhower's words as a sign of weakness and irresolution and openly violated federal court orders two months later. Eisenhower responded by sending troops into Little Rock. Perhaps the president could have avoided the need to make a military response in September if his words and intentions had been stronger and clearer in July.[60]

In 1963, however, no such ambiguity could be found in President Kennedy's words on the subject of integration in Alabama. Not even the most intransigent governor could doubt that Kennedy meant to carry out the dictates of the law.

Kennedy's critical remarks aimed at some southern states and local communities and his insistence that federal power could intervene to protect individual civil rights were supported strongly by Democrats and overwhelmingly by Kennedy partisans. The nation as a whole supported him only marginally, as did those who classified themselves as politically independent. Republicans, however, adhered to the principle of states' rights by a large margin, as, not surprisingly, did the South. Table 3-1[61] presents data collected in October 1963 for each of these groups as well as a more complete geographical breakdown.

It is worth noting that on the states' rights issue, Kennedy supporters clearly seemed to be taking their lead from the president. They adopted a more liberal (pro-federal government) position than any of the other population subgroups whose opinions were measured by the Gallup organization. This conforms to the findings of previous research that those who are most supportive of the president are more enthusiastic about the policies which he espouses.[62]

John F. Kennedy supplemented his press conference remarks on civil rights with several important public addresses, some of which were delivered in the South. Following the Birmingham crisis, for example, he spoke at Vanderbilt University in Nashville, Tennessee, and told his audience that attempts by blacks to secure their rights were "in the highest tradition of American freedom."[63]

Undoubtedly, however, the most memorable civil rights speech by President Kennedy was his nationally televised address of June 11, 1963. Trying to create the environment in which the civil rights bill which he would send to Congress eight days later would be passed,[64] Kennedy moved forcefully to change the thought processes of the American majority toward the rights of one of the nation's largest minorities. In that historic address, the president spoke in dramatic terms:

> We are confronted primarily with a moral issue. It is as old as the scriptures and is as clear as the American Constitution. The heart of the question is whether all Americans are to be afforded equal rights and opportunities, whether we are going to treat our fellow Americans as we want to be treated. If an American, because his skin is dark, cannot eat lunch in a restaurant open to the public, if he cannot vote for public officials who represent him, if, in short, he cannot enjoy the full and free life which all of us want, then who among us would be content to have the color of his skin changed and

TABLE 3-1   EACH STATE SHOULD/SHOULD NOT HAVE THE RIGHT TO DECIDE WHAT TO DO ABOUT INTEGRATION

	SHOULD	SHOULD NOT
National	43	48
Democrats	36	56
Kennedy Supporters	31	61
Independents	42	46
Republicans	53	39
Easterners	36	54
Westerners	36	53
Midwesterners	33	58
Southerners	64	28

stand in his place? Who among us would then be content with the counsels of patience and delay?

In a passage noteworthy for its eloquence as well as for its frankness, Kennedy added:

> We preach freedom around the world, and we mean it, and we cherish our freedom here at home, but are we to say to the world, and much more importantly, to each other, that this is a land of the free except for the Negroes, that we have no second class citizens except the Negroes, that we have no class or caste system, no ghettoes, no master race, except with respect to the Negroes? . . . Next week I shall ask the Congress of the United States to act, to make a commitment it has not fully made in this century to the proposition that race has no place in American life or law.[65]

Here Kennedy was trying to teach the American public that law, even though important, would not be enough, that they themselves would have to change the ways in which they interacted with each other, that the nation would have to undergo fundamental, even radical, alterations in its standards of values and norms. The president was lecturing the public on an important theme—racism was not only a national but also an individual problem, and it would have to be dealt with not only in the halls of Congress, but in the minds and hearts of the American people.

As the administration progressed, the president's growing interest in and commitment to the cause of civil rights was being perceived and recognized by the country. Unfortunately, however, much of the country perceived and recognized it in negative terms. In the summer of 1962, a plurality of Americans, albeit small, believed that the pace of racial integration being set by the Kennedy administration was "just about right." Within two months, however, public opinion showed a marked shift. By October 1962, a sizable plurality of Americans believed that the administration was pushing racial integration too fast and that plurality would not only persist but also grow throughout Kennedy's remaining months in the White House. Table 3-2[66] presents the relevant Gallup poll data for this period.

Even among nonsouthern white Americans, Kennedy's actions and statements

TABLE 3-2   NATIONAL OPINION ON KENNEDY'S PUSHING OF RACIAL INTEGRATION

	TOO FAST	NOT FAST ENOUGH	JUST RIGHT
August 1962	32	11	35
October 1962	42	12	31
May 1963	36	18	32
June 1963	41	14	31
July 1963	48	11	41*
August 1963	50	10	40*
September 1963	50	11	27
October 1963	46	12	31

* Includes those with no opinion.

TABLE 3-3   NONSOUTHERN WHITE OPINION ON KENNEDY'S PUSHING OF RACIAL INTEGRATION

	TOO FAST	NOT FAST ENOUGH	JUST RIGHT
August 1962	27	11	37
May 1963	34	17	33
June 1963	35	13	36
July 1963	48	n/a	n/a
October 1963	45	12	30

relevant to civil rights were increasingly perceived as pushing racial integration "too fast." Table 3-3[67] presents data collected over the final 15 months of the Kennedy administration for whites outside the South.

Interestingly, among Democrats alone, Kennedy's activism was viewed more favorably. Between October 1962 and October 1963, the change in public opinion was only marginal, showing, in fact, a slightly more positive attitude toward the civil rights activism of the president. In the former year, 38% of Democrats viewed the administration's civil rights activities as "just right," while 35% felt they represented moving "too fast." A year later, while national data indicated growing alienation from the Kennedy administration's civil rights stance, 40% of Democrats viewed the intensity of Kennedy's efforts on the racial integration issue as "just right," while 36% felt that the president was moving too quickly.[68] At least among Democrats, therefore, Kennedy's educational efforts seemed to be having their desired effects.

As the civil rights movement intensified throughout 1963, the president's popularity began to erode.[69] The first wave of the white backlash seemed to show itself almost at the very moment when Kennedy's 1964 reelection campaign was being contemplated. The Harris poll disclosed that during 1963, the civil rights issue had alienated approximately 4.5 million white voters against the Kennedy administration.[70] Lubell found that Kennedy's support in the South had collapsed. Moderate Governor Terry Sanford of North Carolina believed that even his state would vote against Kennedy if the election were held in November 1963 instead of November 1964.[71] Nationwide, Kennedy's standing in the Gallup poll dropped from a 60% approval level to 47%. According to Sorensen, the president "confided to one Negro leader that 'this issue could cost me the election, but we're not turning back.' "[72] True to his word, the president did not back away from the cause or modify his support for it.

At his August 1, 1963, press conference, Kennedy was asked by a reporter whether "civil rights are worth an election." He responded:

> Every effort should be made to protect the rights of all our citizens, and advance their right to equality of opportunity. Education, jobs, security, the right to move freely about our country, the right to make personal choices—these are matters which it seems to me are very essential, very desirable, and we just have to wait and see what political effect they have. But I think that the position of the government, the administration is well known, and I expect it will continue to follow the same course it has followed in the past.[73]

A month later, Kennedy assessed more fully the political ramifications of the civil rights movement. During a September 2 interview with Walter Cronkite, he was asked whether the civil rights situation would affect his chances for reelection and whether he thought that he would lose some southern states in 1964. Kennedy's reply was candid:

> Well, obviously it is going to be an important matter. It has caused a good deal of feeling against the Administration in the south—also, I suppose, in other parts of the country. . . . I lost some southern states in 1960 so I suppose I will lose some, maybe more, in 1964. . . . I am not sure that I am the most popular figure in the country today in the south, but that is all right.[74]

Finally, on September 12, 1963, shortly before his assassination, Kennedy was asked by a reporter for his reaction to a Gallup poll which indicated that 50% of the American people felt that he was pushing integration too quickly. The president responded:

> The same poll showed forty percent or so thought it was more or less right. I thought that was rather impressive because it is change; change always disturbs, and therefore I was surprised that there wasn't greater opposition. I think we are going at about the right rate.[75]

Even though some of his closest aides believe that Kennedy was confident that he would have been reelected in 1964,[76] the president's persistence in his support for civil rights in the face of declining levels of public support for his administration is impressive. He was trying to mobilize public sympathy for a major cause and was not deflected from the effort by widespread arguments that he was trying to move too quickly. In short, Kennedy was serving as a national educator on a subject which was unpalatable to much of the nation. Although the lesson he attempted to convey was causing his own popularity to decline, he persisted in trying to teach the nation that the accident of race cannot be the standard by which some of the American people will be judged by their fellow citizens.

CONCLUSIONS

Scholars have long emphasized the important role which presidents play in trying to shape public opinion.[77] While presidents often direct their attention toward improving their own standing in public opinion polls, occasionally they have been even more concerned about mobilizing public support for a specific program or a set of goals which they perceive as important.[78] In the foreign policy realm, presidents often exert significant influence over public opinion, because the public tends to take foreign policy "cues" from the president.[79] The situation, however, is considerably more complex in the area of domestic policy, because the public's predispositions there are likely to be stronger and the role of Congress and even the states more prominent.

With respect to civil rights for black Americans in the early 1960s, not only did much of the country have definite predispositions on the issue, but those predispositions often tended to be both resistant and emotional. In the 1960 presidential election, Kennedy's margin of victory had been extraordinarily narrow, and his support in Congress was tenuous, at least in part, because of that narrow victory. He was understandably reluctant to embrace such a controversial issue as civil rights early in his administration; he saw it as divisive to the country and as damaging to his relationships with Congress and with his own political party.

The 1950s, after all, had been a time of quiet, a time when potentially explosive problems were somewhat smothered under the comforting and warm personality of Dwight D. Eisenhower.[80] In the early 1960s, President Kennedy confronted a nation that was largely asleep. While dramatic events would finally shake the nation out of its slumber, those events would not reach their peak until late into the Kennedy years and even thereafter.

The freedom rides, sit-ins, and the march on Washington, as well as media coverage of the occasionally violent resistance to civil rights that manifested itself in the South, all focused sustained attention on the problem of racism in the early 1960s and made necessary some response by the president and the executive branch he headed. Instead of refusing, as his immediate predecessor in the White House had done, to take any positive action on civil rights because it might "inflame racial feelings,"[81] Kennedy used his position as president, slowly at first but with growing resolve, to teach the nation the moral, as well as the legal, imperatives of equal treatment under the law. He tried hard, through statements and speeches on the subject as well as through private meetings with business, labor, and community leaders, to create the environment in which substantial change could come.

It is not possible to determine what the state of public opinion toward civil rights would have been in the United States at that time if Kennedy had not spoken out so forcefully on the issue. It is clear, however, that public resistance was strong throughout much of the country and that it grew stronger in the months before Kennedy's assassination. As might be expected, southern whites were particularly unhappy with the president's civil rights activism. Between August 1962 and October 1963, the percentage of southern whites believing that Kennedy was moving too quickly on the racial front increased from 59 to 73 percent.[82] Nonsouthern whites, as previously noted, also showed increasing concern that Kennedy was pushing racial integration too quickly.

Yet among the members of Kennedy's own party, support for his civil rights activities ran contrary to the national norm. A plurality of Democrats felt that the intensity of Kennedy's efforts in civil rights was "just about right," and that plurality of support persisted, and even grew somewhat, during Kennedy's last year in office, when the civil rights movement took on crisis dimensions. Also, the president's deepening commitment to the cause was viewed favorably by black Americans, who saw him as a friend and ally.[83]

Despite these pockets of support, the decline in Kennedy's overall popularity accelerated during his final months in office. Between late June and mid-October

1963, his lead over Senator Barry Goldwater, a likely opponent in 1964, decreased from 26 to 16 points in the Gallup poll. In the South, Goldwater actually led Kennedy in mid-October by a margin of 55 to 45%.[84] Moral leadership obviously can carry a heavy price.

It is important to note that President Kennedy's efforts to persuade the nation that progress was needed in the area of civil rights often were accompanied by more practical steps to bring about that progress. Previous studies have focused on the civil rights policies and accomplishments of the Kennedy administration in such areas as employment, housing, litigation, legislation, and judicial appointments.[85] It is not the intention here to replicate or contradict those earlier works. Rather, John F. Kennedy's contributions to the cause of civil rights as a teacher and moral leader have been the sole focus of this analysis, because they served as a necessary backdrop for the more concrete actions that were taken in this sensitive area.

While Kennedy's executive actions and achievements clearly are essential to any comprehensive evaluation of his civil rights record, the dramatic evolution of his willingness to serve as moral leader and national educator on the issue should neither be overlooked nor underestimated. Although the president's commitment to civil rights was damaging his popularity as he approached the date of his own anticipated reelection campaign in 1964, he persevered, apparently sharing the view of Franklin D. Roosevelt, who once said that "all great Presidents were leaders of thought at times when certain historic ideas in the life of the nation had to be clarified."[86]

Overcoming his initial caution and reticence, President Kennedy emerged as a significant leader of the civil rights movement in the latter months of his administration. As one of his critics has written, "a people can be nourished to believe that there are necessary things to be done, which they have overlooked, and that they have the necessary capacity to do them."[87] Kennedy as president tried to provide his people with that nourishment.

NOTES

1. *New York Times,* August 18, 1956, p. 1.

2. Jack Anderson and Fred Blumenthal, *The Kefauver Story* (New York: Dial Press, 1956), pp. 131–32.

3. The Civil Rights Act of 1957 established the Commission on Civil Rights and gave it the duty to investigate charges that "certain citizens of the United States are being deprived of their right to vote and have their vote counted by reason of their color, race, religion, or national origin, . . . study and collect information concerning legal developments constituting a denial of equal protection of the laws under the Constitution, and appraise the laws and policies of the Federal Government with respect to equal protection of the laws under the Constitution." The legislation also provided for the appointment of an additional Assistant Attorney General and for trial by jury, "to punish criminal contempts of court growing out of civil rights cases." Public Law No. 85-315, 71 Stat. pp. 634–38.

4. According to a seldom invoked senatorial rule, a senator may move that a bill bypass committee consideration and become immediately pending business on the floor of the Senate. Such a move requires majority consent.

5. *John Fitzgerald Kennedy: A Compilation of Statements and Speeches Made During His Service in the United States Senate and House of Representatives,* Legislative Reference Service, Washington, D.C., 1964, p. 537.

6. James MacGregor Burns, *John Kennedy* (New York: Avon Books, 1959), p. 192.

7. Ibid., p. 193.

8. *Kennedy: A Compilation,* p . 538.

9. Burns, *John Kennedy.*

10. Arthur M. Schlesinger, *A Thousand Days* (Boston: HoughtonMifflin, 1965), p. 928.

11. *National Party Platforms 1840–1972,* comp. Donald B. Johnson and Kirk H. Porter (Urbana: University of Illinois Press, 1973), pp. 599, 600.

12. Senate Committee on Commerce, Subcommittee of the Subcommittee, *Report of the Committee on Commerce, The Speeches of Senator John F. Kennedy in the Presidential Campaign of 1960. 87th Congress,* Ist session, Report 994, part 1, pp. 570, 1224, 361, 172.

13. Ibid., pp. 307, 544, 550.

14. William H. Flanigan and Nancy H. Zingale, *Political Behavior of the American Electorate,* 3rd ed. (Boston: Allyn and Bacon, 1975), p. 81.

15. *Report of the Committee on Commerce,* pp. 173, 1021, 361, 398.

16. Ibid., pp. 191, 570, 1266.

17. Ibid., pp. 159, 186, 453, 576.

18. Ibid., pp. 246, 1011, 245, 432.

19. Ibid., pp. 95, 173.

20. Ibid., pp. 1011, 977–78, 1132, 632, 670, 715, 846, 865.

21. Ibid., p. 910.

22. Burke Marshall, *Oral History,* John F. Kennedy Library, Boston, p. 55.

23. Theodore H. White, *The Making of the President 1960* (New York: Atheneum Publishers, 1961), p. 321.

24. Charles V. Hamilton, *The Bench and the Ballot* (New York: Oxford University Press, 1973), p. 79.

25. White, *Making of the President,* p. 323.

26. Mark R. Levy and Michael S. Kramer, *The Ethnic Factor: How America's Minorities Decide Elections* (New York: Simon and Schuster, 1973), p. 43.

27. Theodore White suggested that "it is difficult to see how Illinois, New Jersey, Michigan, South Carolina, or Delaware (with 74 electoral votes) could have been won had the Republican–Democratic split of the Negro wards and precincts remained as it was, unchanged from the Eisenhower charm of 1956." White, *Making of the President,* p. 354. Also, Arthur Schlesinger wrote that without black support in 1960, "Kennedy could not have carried Illinois and Michigan, not to mention Texas, South Carolina and possibly Louisiana." Schlesinger, *A Thousand Days,* p. 930.

28. Bruce Miroff, *Pragmatic Illusions: The Presidential Politics of John F. Kennedy* (New York: David McKay Company, 1976), pp. 7, 224.

29. For an interesting contrast between the Kennedy and Roosevelt media styles, see Samuel Kernell, *Going Public: New Strategies of Presidential Leadership* (Washington, D.C.: Congressional Quarterly Press, 1986), pp. 63–66, 69–76.

30. Theodore C. Sorensen, *Kennedy* (New York: Harper and Row, 1965), p. 322.

31. Schlesinger, *A Thousand Days,* p. 716.

32. Robert MacNeil, *The People Machine* (New York: Harper and Row, 1968), p. 297.

33. Ibid.

34. For a further discussion of Kennedy's television proficiency, see Elmer E. Cornwell, *Presidential Leadership of Public Opinion* (Bloomington: Indiana University Press, 1965), pp. 188–206, 281–83; Robert E. Gilbert, *Television and Presidential Politics* (North Quincy, Mass.: Christopher Publishing House, 1972), pp. 286–88.

35. Kennedy had sent 600 deputy U.S. marshals to Alabama to protect the Freedom Riders (Harold Fleming, "Federal Executive and Civil Rights," *Daedalus* [Fall 1965]: p. 935) and had ordered the FBI to investigate the burning of a Freedom Rider bus in Anniston, Alabama. As a result of this latter action, nine men were subsequently indicted by a federal grand jury (Burke Marshall, *Papers,* "Progress in the Field of Civil Rights, A Summary, January 20 to November 20, 1961," John F. Kennedy Library, Boston, p. 3).

36. *Public Papers of the Presidents of the United States, John F. Kennedy, 1961* (Washington, D.C.: Government Printing Office, 1962), p. 517.
37. Ibid., p. 69.
38. Ibid., p. 572.
39. *Public Papers of the Presidents of the United States, John F. Kennedy, 1962* (Washington, D.C.: Government Printing Office, 1963), p. 69.
40. Harold Mendelsohn and Irving Crespie, *Polls, Television and the New Politics* (Scranton, Pa.: Chandler Publishing Co., 1970), p. 274.
41. *Public Papers, 1961,* p. 10.
42. Ibid., p. 703.
43. *Public Papers, 1962,* p. 677.
44. Ibid., p. 676.
45. *Public Papers of the Presidents of the United States, John F. Kennedy, 1963* (Washington, D.C.: Government Printing Office, 1964), p. 347.
46. *Public Papers, 1961,* p . 217.
47. *Public Papers, 1962,* pp. 592–93.
48. *Public Papers, 1963,* pp. 572–73.
49. Ibid., p. 631.
50. Ibid., p . 615.
51. *Public Papers, 1961,* p. 355.
52. *Public Papers, 1962,* p. 593.
53. *Public Papers, 1963,* p. 378.
54. Ibid., p. 573.
55. Ibid., p. 617.
56. Ibid., p. 831.
57. See *Public Papers, 1961, 1962, 1963.*
58. *Public Papers, 1963,* p. 418.
59. *Public Papers of the Presidents of the United States, Dwight D. Eisenhower, 1957* (Washington, D.C.: The National Archives, 1958), p. 546.
60. For a discussion of the president's power to persuade, see Richard E. Neustadt, *Presidential Power* (New York: John Wiley and Sons, 1980).
61. George H. Gallup, *The Gallup Poll, Public Opinion 1935–1971,* vol. 3 (New York: Random House, 1972), p. 1851.
62. Samuel Kemel, *Going Public* (Washington, D.C.: Congressional Quarterly Press, 1986), p. 150.
63. *Public Papers, 1963,* p. 408.
64. For a discussion of Kennedy's legislative efforts in the area of civil rights, see Robert E. Gilbert, "John F. Kennedy and Civil Rights for Black Americans," *Presidential Studies Quarterly* (Summer 1982): 393–97.
65. *Public Papers, 1963,* p. 469.
66. Gallup, *Poll,* pp. 1769, 1789, 1823, 1828, 1832, 1838, 1844, 1852.
67. Ibid., pp. 1769, 1823, 1828, 1832, 1852.
68. Ibid., pp. 1789, 1852.
69. John E. Mueller, "Presidential Popularity from Truman to Johnson," *American Political Science Review* (March 1970): pp. 20, 30.
70. Schlesinger, *A Thousand Days,* p. 968.
71. Sorensen, *Kennedy,* p. 505.
72. Ibid., p. 506.
73. *Public Papers, 1963,* p. 615.
74. Ibid., p. 650.

75. Ibid., p. 677.

76. Both Schlesinger and Sorensen cite Kennedy's belief that he would win reelection in 1964. (Schlesinger, *A Thousand Days,* p. 1016; Sorensen, *Kennedy,* p. 506.)

77. Neustadt cites the importance of public prestige in the exercise of presidential power. See Neustadt, *Presidential Power,* pp. 64–79. Also see George C. Edwards III, *The Public Presidency* (New York: St. Martin's Press, (1983); Cornwell, *Presidential Leadership of Public Opinion;* Kernel, *Going Public.*

78. The president's effectiveness in shaping public opinion has been examined in various studies. See, for example, Benjamin I. Page and Robert Y. Shapiro, "Presidents as Opinion Leaders: Some New Evidence," *Policy Studies Journal,* Vol. 12 (June 1984): pp. 647–62. See also Lyn Ragsdale, "The Politics of Presidential Speechmaking, 1949–1980," *American Political Science Review* (December 1984): pp. 971–84.

79. Edwards, *The Public Presidency,* p. 43. Also see Bernard C. Cohen, *The Press and Foreign Policy* (Princeton, N.J.: Princeton University Press, 1968), pp. 20–21.

80. See Norman A. Graeber, "Eisenhower's Popular Leadership," in *Eisenhower as President,* ed. Dean Albertson (New York: Hill and Wang, 1963), pp. 147–59; also Harvey G. Zeidenstein, "Presidential Popularity and Presidential Support in Congress," *Presidential Studies Quarterly* (Spring 1980): p. 228.

81. Stuart Gerry Brown, *The American Presidency* (New York: MacMillan, 1966), p. 107.

82. Gallup, *Poll,* pp. 1769, 1852.

83. William C. Spragens, "John F. Kennedy," in *Popular Images of American Presidents,* ed. William C. Spragens (New York: Greenwood Press, 1988), p. 456.

84. Gallup, *Poll,* pp. 1830, 1847.

85. See, for example, Carl M. Brauer, *John F. Kennedy and the Second Reconstruction* (New York: Columbia University Press, (1977); Aida di Pace Donald, ed., *John F. Kennedy and the New Frontier* (New York: Hill and Wang, 1966), pp. 138–64; Harry Golden, *Mr. Kennedy and the Negroes* (New York: World Publishing Co., (1964); Gilbert, "John F. Kennedy," pp. 386–99.

86. Edwards, *The Public Presidency,* p. 38.

87. Henry Fairlie, *The Kennedy Promise* (Garden City, N.Y.: Doubleday, 1973), p. 364.

CHAPTER 4

Gerald Ford:
Changing Course During the New York
City Financial Crisis

RICHARD A. LOVERD*

I can tell you, and I tell you now, that I am prepared to veto any bill that has as its purpose a Federal bailout of New York City to prevent default.[1]

—Gerald R. Ford

. . . I have decided to ask Congress when it returns from recess for authority to provide a temporary line of credit to the State of New York to enable it to supply seasonal financing of essential services for the people of New York City.[2]

—Gerald R. Ford

INTRODUCTION

During the period from May to November 1975 New York City was on the brink of financial death. Heavily in debt, on the verge of bankruptcy, and unable to borrow money in the private credit markets,[3] it turned to the federal government for help,

* This case was originally published as Richard A. Loverd, "Presidential Decision Making During the 1975 New York City Financial Crisis: A Conceptual Analysis," *Presidential Studies Quarterly*, vol. XXI, no. 2 (Spring 1991), and is reprinted with the permission of the Center for the Study of the Presidency, publisher of *Presidential Studies Quarterly*. Research for this study was funded by the Gerald R. Ford Presidential Library, Ann Arbor, Michigan.

only to find a rather unreceptive President Ford in office. Indeed, after meeting with Mayor Abraham Beame and Governor Hugh Carey on May 13, 1975, President Ford made clear in a letter to the mayor the following day that no federal aid would be forthcoming and "that the proper place for any request for backing and guarantee is with the State of New York."[4] Six months later, on November 26, 1975, support from the president materialized when he announced that he would submit a bill to Congress authorizing federal loans to New York City of up to $2.3 billion a year through June 1978.

Why did the president say "no" in May and "yes" in November? For the most part, little has been written regarding Mr. Ford's deliberations in shifting policy positions on the New York City issue. Instead, writers have tended to focus on the heroic or manic maneuvers of state and the city officials during the crisis.[5] In this case, with the help of a conceptual decision framework, firsthand federal accounts, and archival research performed at the Gerald Ford Library, an attempt will be made to redress this literary imbalance by taking the presidential perspective and exploring the reasons behind the president's policy decisions.

JUST SAY, AND KEEP ON SAYING, NO

At the outset, why, in the words of the *Daily News,* did President Ford tell New York City to "drop dead?"[6] Before examining this question at length, we should note that, in point of fact, Gerald Ford was not the first federal official to say no to aid; Treasury Secretary William Simon held that distinction. On May 6, 1975, one week before seeing the president, Governor Carey and Mayor Beame met with Secretary Simon and other senior officials, seeking support for legislation to provide approximately $1 billion in federal credit to the city for a 90-day term. Soon thereafter, on May 8, a decision followed from the secretary denying their request for aid. That this denial was done with the president's knowledge and consent is made clear in a May 8 memorandum from L. William Seidman, assistant to the president for economic affairs, to Mr. Ford, informing him that "Secretary Simon intends to announce today that the U.S. Government is unable to do anything further to help the City's financial condition. He will announce this is being done with your approval."[7]

Therefore, when the mayor and the governor finally did meet with the president on May 13, they were seeking a "second opinion" for infusions of funds to New York City. This renewed attempt was duly noted on the day of the meeting when Jim Cannon, assistant to the president for domestic affairs, wrote in a memo to the president prior to the session that its purpose was "to apprise you of the fiscal crisis New York City faces in the next two weeks and to appeal Secretary Simon's decision not to support legislation giving Treasury authority to loan New York City federal funds."[8] Twenty-four hours later the president responded to their appeal in a May 14 letter to Mayor Beame which seconded the secretary's negative sentiments.

Still, the question remains: why did President Ford say no to aid? In the first place, from a *rational* standpoint, the president thought aid to New York City did not make sense. For example, in his analysis of the crisis in a draft statement written May 12, he observed that "Although New York City's fiscal problems are enormous, they come down to this":

> The city has been living beyond its means for many years. The cost of the services the city provides has been rising almost twice as fast as the city's capacity to pay for them. The difference between annual income and outgo has been made up in large part by borrowing—and now the size of New York City's debts are so great that banks are finding it difficult to extend credit to New York City.
>
> But the problem is not new. The New York City fiscal situation was analyzed by a non-partisan State Study Commission for New York City and also by the State Charter Revision Committee for New York City. Both concluded, in effect, that the city's revenue base, big as it is, is simply not large enough to finance all the services that New York City provides.[9]

And in his memoirs, Ford further noted that since 1965, the city's budget had tripled, expenses had increased by an average of 12 percent while revenues had risen by less than 5 percent, and the federal government had contributed an annual sum of $3.5 billion, or 25 percent of the city's budget.[10] Therefore, as he wrote in his May 14 letter to Mayor Beame, he felt that since "the City's basic financial condition is not new but has been a long time in the making without being squarely faced . . . , a ninety day Federal guarantee by itself would provide no real solution but would merely postpone, for that period, coming to grips with the problem."[11]

So how should New York come to grips with the problem? Instead of its continuing past flawed financial practices, the president stressed that "For a sound judgment to be made on this problem by all concerned, there must be presented a plan on how the City would balance its budget," a balance which required "an evaluation of what the City can do through curtailment of less essential services and subsidies and what activities the City can transfer under existing laws to New York State."[12]

And what about the federal role in funding the city? In essence, Ford saw no such role. He believed that the "proper place" for any request for backing and guarantee was the State of New York: "it seems both logical and desirable for the State of New York to arrange under its laws a 'bridge loan' to the City in the amount that you estimate will be needed during the City's fiscal year."[13] Indeed, about the only actions the president indicated the federal government would take is monitor the city credit situation "very closely" through Secretary Simon and the Federal Reserve Board, and "keep me informed."[14]

And finally, in the absence of a rescue, what about the dangers of having the city default on its obligations? While New York city and state officials warned of catastrophic consequences for the American banking community, Ford's advisors told him otherwise. In preparation for the May 13 meeting, the president reviewed "Proposed Comments on the Consequences of a Default by New York" from Robert A. Gerard, director of the Office of Capital Markets Policy for the Treasury Department; Alan Holmes, vice president of the Federal Reserve Bank, New York City; and J. C. Partee, managing director for research and economic policy for the Federal Reserve Board, which indicated that "the cataclysm threatened by some city officials and some bankers is unlikely" (Gerard), "It is not anticipated that there would be widespread collapse of the markets in state and local issues" (Holmes), and "A default on its note issues would probably not have significantly adverse effects on the national economy . . . (Partee). Indeed, Mr. Gerard went on to suggest that "A default could trigger the kind of radical fiscal action by the city which is required [to] induce the banking community—probably with the blessing of the Fed—to provide the city with the cash to cure the default."[15] Moreover, as the president noted in his memoirs, Federal Reserve Board Chairman Arthur Burns never agreed with the dire consequences of default and "kept cautioning me . . . [not to] let them sell you a bill of goods."[16]

Thus, from a rational standpoint, federal aid for New York City's fiscal problems made little sense because (1) the city had been living beyond its means for many years; (2) a 90-day guarantee would not solve the city's financial problems but only delay the day of reckoning; (3) no plan was in evidence to indicate how the city would balance its budget; (4) the logical place to seek a loan was with the state of New York; and (5) the dangers from default were not perceived as great, and, should default occur, there might even prove to be some more positive movement for fiscal reform by the city.

Ethically, the president also saw many reasons for not supporting New York City's request for aid. As John Casserly, a speechwriter for the president, mentioned in his memoirs: "He doesn't have to shout it. Mr. Ford simply tells everyone: 'It's absolutely against my philosophy (the way New York has been run).' "[17] A fiscal conservative, Ford believed that rewarding irresponsible practices with federal money was not right and was unfair. Indeed, in his presidential files, he noted that New York "Must do what's right. Bite bullet";[18] and in his memoirs, he said, "To ask us to pay any more simply wasn't fair":

> No longer could New York's officials offer high school graduates free tuition at the city university and expect taxpayers elsewhere to pick up the tab. No longer could they promise extravagant wage settlements and pension benefits without knowing how they would cover costs. They had to start cutting back on nonessential services.[19]

In addition, besides being unfair to taxpayers throughout the nation, Ford felt that such aid would be unfair to other states and cities by setting a "dangerous precedent. If we 'rescued' New York, officials from every city in America would come knocking at our door."[20] "The extent to which the federal government can or should redistribute revenues among the states is limited by standards of equity."[21] Moreover, in a memorandum forwarded from L. William Seidman to the president, it was stressed that "any form of federal guarantee or insurance is objectionable substantively. Among other things, it would be impossible to contain and in effect could result in the federalization of all municipal financing."[22]

Thus, for Ford, "What New York had to do was get its house in order"[23] by behaving responsibly. As the president wrote to the mayor on May 14:

> Fiscal responsibility is essential for cities, states, and the federal government. I know how hard it is to reduce or postpone worthy and desirable public programs. Every family which makes up a budget has to make painful choices. As we make these choices at

home, so must we make them in public office too. We must stop promising more and more services without knowing how we will cover their costs.[24]

In the larger environment, the administrative and political realities and the shifts in the system tended to favor the rational and ethical views of Ford. *Administratively,* there was no workable plan in place, and the piecemeal proposals urged by New York state/local officials were not feasible without further federal legislation, legislation which the president indicated he would not support. With regard to that lack of a plan, the president observed that, well into the summer, he kept asking the mayor and the governor, "What are you going to do?"

> "Are you going to cut down your retirement benefits and your overhead? Are you going to stop giving free tuition to students at the City University?" Beame and Carey had no answers. Nor did they have a plan.[25]

And in the instance of state/local proposals for aid, a White House press release at the time noted:

> There is very little that the Executive Branch can do to meet the current fiscal crisis of the City of New York. The President does not have the legal authority to borrow funds for the City or lend funds to the City.
> The only Federal assistance that can be undertaken, other than specific legislation, is by virtue of action taken by the Federal Reserve Board. The Federal Reserve can, whenever disruption of financial markets might occur; they do have the authority to move in and shore up bank credit by guaranteeing loans.
> . . . the only solution would require legislation . . . and such legislation would be inconsistent with our thoughts.[26]

In fact, as late as November 1975, the *only* piece of federal legislation the president did support to help New York get through its financial woes was one related to the administration of default rather than rescue: a bankruptcy bill (HR 10624) designed to expedite big city bankruptcy procedures.[27]

So there the Ford Administration stood, opposed to unworkable proposals and insistent upon having the supplicants from the Empire State solve their own problems. As L. William Seidman said at the time: "We don't care how they do it. We just don't want to get involved in running the affairs of the city."[28] And there was very little administrative need for the president to do otherwise.

Politically and *systemically,* pressures also favored Ford's inclination not to bail out the city. As the *Congressional Quarterly* observed: ". . . most members of Congress tended to dismiss New York's plight as the price it finally had to pay for living beyond its means. The negative attitude in Washington toward New Yorkers "living high off the hog" took hold years ago."[29] And in Ford's own memoirs he goes on to note that Congress was in turn attuned to a "national mood, which said that inasmuch as New York had got into this jam by itself, it ought to find its own way out."[30] This mood was, of course, also reflected in the financial markets which, according to William Simon, "made the same judgment we have—namely that the City spends too much. Until the city cuts its spending level significantly, there is little likelihood of market access."[31]

Thus, the administration, the politics, and the mood of the larger system remained unswayed by the pleas of Mr. Carey and Mr. Beame, and, in the face of these pressures and perspectives, the two officials were forced to look away from Mr. Ford and find a helping hand at the end of their own arms until environmental conditions, or the president's mind, changed.

GETTING TO YES

Given his own views and the forces in the environment, what moved President Ford later to help New York? First of all, environmental conditions *did* change from May to November. *Administratively,* with little prospect for federal help, the governor and mayor began to help themselves. For example, in addition to advancing the city $800 million in April and May, the state established the Municipal Assistance Corporation (MAC) in June to act as an interim borrowing agency for the city. In that capacity, MAC began to monitor New York's financial reform efforts and restructure the city's short-term obligations into longer-term MAC bonds through borrowings of up to $3 billion. This amount was thought sufficient to carry the city until October, when, it was hoped, it would be able to reenter the bond market on its own.

Unfortunately, the borrowings proved less successful than had been hoped. Despite assurances that MAC's bonds were backed by proceeds from the city's sales and stock transfer taxes and the "moral obligation" of the state, the response of the bond-buying public was lukewarm: only 2 of MAC's projected $3 billion were sold by August, and further offerings proved unmarketable. In large measure, as a Joint Economic Committee report noted at the time, "most of the corporation's market difficulties must be attributed directly to the fact that MAC's securities were perceived by the market to be tantamount to New York city issues,"[32] and investor confidence in the city had far from returned. Indeed, at the time, the White House shared a similar skepticism. In a September 2 memorandum from L. William Seidman to President Ford, devoted largely to preparing for New York's default, one section, entitled "New York City's Actions: Promises and Deliveries," noted a series of actions and "nonactions" that raised questions regarding the city's capacity to manage its crisis and restore market access, including (1) a "deficient" wage freeze; (2) limited and questionable layoffs; (3) a promise to cut expenditures at the City University by $32 million, with no known action on this objective; (4) a 400% increase in the tax on stock and bond transactions which dramatically lowered the volume of bond trading in the city; (5) the rescinding of a promise by the mayor to close a substantial number of fire houses and hospitals; (6) the lack of sound financial data; (7) the need for more direct participation in the city's financial affairs; (8) the lack of a specific three-year budget plan; and (9) the lack of a plan to eliminate expense items from the capital budget.[33]

Thus, with the city's financial affairs suspect and anticipated funds running out by early September instead of October, more aid and more creative administrative approaches were needed to keep the city afloat. Once again, necessity proved an inventive parent, and on September 9, the New York State Financial Emergency Act for the City of New York was signed by Governor Carey. Through this legislation, a complex $2.3 billion financial package was passed to meet the city's cash requirements through early December; and, perhaps equally significant, a more demanding administrative mechanism, the Emergency Financial Control Board, was created which, in essence, allowed the state to take over much of the financial management of the city and, in the words of Shalala and Bellamy, "eliminated the last vestiges of fiscal home rule."[34]

Still, despite this latest legislation, the reaction from the White House was once again one of skepticism. As L. William Seidman was later to note:

> In September, the New York State Legislature approved a plan that would enable the city to meet its financial obligations through early December. For the first time, city pension funds were tapped. Cuts in municipal expenses were begun. But this was a temporary bandaid remedy, and everyone knew it. The plan committed the State of New York and the City, but the plan was clearly short term. At the end of three months, it was probable that both the State and the City would need to be bailed out. Could the Federal Government resist such an urgent plea from a "debt addict"?[35]

In fact, just such a "plea" was put to the test long before December. On October 17, one portion of the $2.3 billion package almost unraveled when Albert Shanker and his teacher's union pension fund trustees resisted purchasing $150 million in MAC bonds. Without that purchase in place, the $449 million in debts due that day would not be met and the city would surely default. As the prospects for a resolution of this dilemma grew dim and the hour grew late, New York officials called Washington for help, only to receive the following response from Mr. Seidman:

> Predictably a crisis materialized in October and I received a 1:00 A.M. call requesting that I advise the president immediately that unless Federal help was forthcoming New York City would default the next day. No Federal help was offered.[36]

Once more left to their own devices, the city and the state went back to the drawing boards and soon solved the problem themselves, by finally pressuring a reluctant Shanker into providing the necessary pension funds late in the day. As Seidman observed:

> It was so close that the New York banks stayed open an extra hour to await funds to avoid default. New York City rescued itself for the moment with a loan from the City pension funds. New York officials began to believe what the president had been saying—there would be no bailout.[37]

And with that belief, further reinforced by an October 29 National Press Club address by the president stating he would "veto any bill which had as its central purpose a Federal bailout of New York City in order to prevent a default,"[38] state and city officials set about making even more comprehensive administrative reforms.

By late November, a workable plan did take shape which, according to President Ford, reflected "a concerted effort to put the finances of the City and State on a sound basis" and included "steps—adding up to $4 billion—[that] are part of an effort to provide financing and to bring the City's budget into balance by the fiscal year starting July 1, 1977."[39] Among those steps were the following:

1. More than $200 million in new taxes had been voted.
2. Additional personnel reductions of 40,000 beyond the layoffs of 22,000 city employees already made were mandated.
3. A partial wage freeze and deferral was imposed.
4. The city reduced its subsidy to the City University by $32 million. The trustees were told to make it up by charging tuition.
5. The transit fare was increased from 35 cents to 50 cents.
6. Municipal employees would be required to contribute $107 million per year to pension systems. The city had been directed to stop the practice of using, for budgetary purposes, income of pension systems in excess of 4 percent per annum. Designated business leaders had been asked to report on the actuarial soundness of such systems. Outrageous abuses of the pension system through improper use of overtime in computing pension levels were terminated.
7. Extensive management changes including a new deputy mayor for finance and a new chief of planning were instituted.
8. The Emergency Financial Control Board developed a three-year plan to produce a modest surplus in the city's expense budget by fiscal year 1977–78.
9. Payments to the city's note holders would be postponed and interest payments reduced through passage of legislation by New York State.
10. Banks and large institutions agreed to postpone collection on their loans and accept lower rates.
11. The city pension system would provide up to $2.5 billion in additional loans to the city.[40]

In further commenting on those steps, the president noted that he was "surprised that they have come as far as they have. I doubted that they would do so unless ordered by a Federal Court." "Only a few months ago, we were told that all these reforms were impossible and could not be accomplished by New York alone. Today they are done. This is a realistic program."[41]

And yet, according to state and city officials, one final step remained in order to make this "realistic program" complete: federal seasonal loans of up to $2.3 billion a year over the next two and a half years. Because the bulk of the city's tax receipts came in the spring, there was an imbalance between revenues and expenditures during the course of a fiscal year; that is, the city would have deficits in some months and surpluses in others which, by year's end, would come into balance. For example, as was noted in a White House press release at the time (November 1975):

> According to information furnished by New York City, for the balance of the current fiscal year, the City will run a deficit of $141 million in December; $324 million in January; $310 million in February; and $500 million in March. In the April through June

period, however, it will run monthly surpluses of $334 million, $345 million and $596 million respectively, leaving receipts and expenditures in balance for the fiscal year.[42]

In order to cover the current deficits to ensure that day-to-day services would be provided throughout the year, the city would normally resort to short-term seasonal borrowing in the private credit markets. However, in the current case, because these markets were no longer open, a temporary line of credit was being sought from Washington to allow New York to implement its "realistic program," prove it had mended its ways, and thereby gain reentry to those markets.

Thus, from an administrative standpoint, what one sees over the course of New York's fiscal crisis are a series of progressively more serious financial steps taken by the city and the state, culminating in a workable plan in November, a plan which could save the city from default, bring it back to financial health, and restore market access, but a plan which still required federal seasonal loans in order to succeed.

Politically, there were also changes in the pressures on the president, not the least of which came from the federal portion of the plan just noted. When the state/local participants agreed to take part in that plan, all parties indicated that their participation was contingent upon the other's meeting their commitments *and* the federal government's providing help. Thus, in a November 13 letter from MAC Chairman Felix Rohaytn to Secretary Simon, explaining the plan and supplying letters of intent from the various parties, one sees stressed that "the program referred to in the enclosed materials is conditional upon the availability of Federal government assistance."[43] And the letters from the parties themselves were equally emphatic. Union leaders representing the city's teachers, sanitation men, and clerical workers wrote that they promised to convert $1.2 billion of short-term obligations into ten-year bonds "subject to the completion of a financial package assuring funding of the City government through Fiscal Year 1977–78, including the Federal guarantees of securities, or other Federal funding, required to complete the financial package."[44] The banks too agreed to make money available only if the federal government assisted in the city's seasonal borrowing needs.[45] And in a follow-up letter to Secretary Simon on November 14, Governor Carey also stressed that while "This is a program that has my full commitment as Governor . . . [t]here is still a need, however, which can only be met by Federal assistance."[46] Moreover, all of these comments and enclosures were in turn passed along to the president for his review in a November 14 memorandum from Deputy Treasury Secretary Stephen Gardner entitled, "New York Plan."[47]

In short, the commitments noted above meant that, without federal help, the entire plan could collapse and the near-certain subsequent default could be blamed on the president. Thus, political pressure for his support of the plan, proposed by those who had already agreed to make significant concessions, was very real.

Furthermore, while the president pondered federal help, he also observed that congressional legislative activity was moving forward in the form of "at least eight different proposals . . . to prevent default."[48] The political problem with such activity was that it could produce not only an undesirable bill, but also a no-win situation for the chief executive. In commenting on the hazards of a "bad bill," lobbyist and former deputy treasury secretary Charls Walker wrote in a memorandum to the president:

> Politically, there seems to me to be real dynamite here. My conversations on the Hill indicate that the odds of Congressional action are growing. I can therefore envisage your having on your desk by Christmas a bad bill. . . . Then, if you vetoed it in the public interest, NYC defaulted, and the roof fell in—I don't like to think about all of that happening.[49]

And even if a bill came to the president's desk which somehow looked "good" to him, his signing it could be interpreted as "caving in" to outside pressures by supporting legislation which he had previously promised to veto. Consequently, if Congress managed to take the initiative and passed either a "bad" or a "good" bill before the president could act, a no-win condition could result, a condition which could be avoided only if Mr. Ford took action first.[50]

Systemically, conditions were also shifting. The timing, and the "times," were changing. As Deputy Treasury Secretary Gardner noted in his November 14 memo on the "New York Plan":

> As a practical matter, time is of the essence: (1) the U.S. Congress, which may need to act on this matter, is planning to recess November 21; and (2) the restructuring of the short-term debt must be accomplished by December 10. Because of the complexity of the restructuring arrangement, at least two weeks will be required for this to take place.[51]

Besides, to further quote Mr. Walker, since Christmas was approaching, "I think this needs your earnest attention. A bad bill to save NYC on your desk around December 25 would be a lousy Christmas present."[52] Moreover, beyond Christmas, an election year loomed large; and since the president had decided to run for office, that too was on Mr. Walker's mind when he observed that the president's inclination to veto any "bailout" legislation "might represent the 'big mistake' that could cost him election in his own right."[53]

In addition to timing, the "times" or mood of the country toward New York was changing as well. After the city's well-publicized near-default of October 17, and the president's equally visible no-bailout speech of October 29, a Harris poll was taken in early November "to assess public reaction to President Ford's speech." Interestingly, among the findings, the survey said:

1. By a massive 69–18% margin, the American people favor the federal government's guaranteeing loans to New York City if the city balances its budget and such a plan would not cost the taxpayers any actual money than for New York City to default and go bankrupt.
2. By 50–37%, the American public disagrees with President Ford's announced intention of vetoing any legislation providing a guarantee from the federal government to New York City.
3. Backing for federal aid to New York City is not confined to cities, people in the Northeast, or a single, particular segment of the population. Instead, it is spread throughout the United States.[54]

Other polls also reflected this qualified shift in attitude toward federal help for New York. For example, in a memorandum sent from Jim Cannon to the president on October 18, he was informed that, in a poll of the officers and directors of the National Association of Counties, most favored federal assistance for New York City under stringent conditions.[55]

The nation's mayors were concerned as well. In a fall session before the Joint Economic Committee, thirteen mayors came to Washington to support aid legislation and express their worries about a New York City default. As Denver Mayor William H. McNichols noted at the time regarding the systems consequences of such a default:

> Every city in the nation is like a tenant in the same building. . . . If somebody says the third floor is going to collapse, you can't say that's not going to bother me because I'm on the second floor.[56]

In sum, by late November, what one sees in the environment surrounding the president are changes in conditions, changes that reflect administrative, political, and systems movements toward helping New York, most likely brought on in large measure because the city, and the state, had tried to help themselves.

In the face of these changes in the environment, it was not so hard for the president to change his mind. After all, *ethically,* city and state officials had "bitten the bullet" and produced major reforms to demonstrate they could bail themselves out and act in a fiscally responsible manner. Indeed, they had further proved their character by overcoming several brushes with default. And the painful crises and concessions they had experienced could hardly create a precedent to be willingly followed by other cities around the country.

Federal help could also be more readily justified *rationally.* The proposals for fiscal reform had come from the logical governmental levels: the state and the city. Through their efforts, a "realistic," workable plan had been devised which would go beyond stopgap measures, balance the budget, and provide long-term financial stability for the city. Furthermore, that plan would cost Washington less because it would involve federal loans that would cover only current seasonal cash flow imbalances rather than past or future city deficits, a circumstance which, in the president's words, had not been present even a few months before:

> . . . when the Governor and the mayor were asking for any kind of help, short-term or long-term, there was the anticipated deficit for the current fiscal year in New York City of $4 billion. In the meantime, the mayor and other public officials in New York City, along with the help of private citizens, have reduced that fiscal deficit for this current year to zero. So there is quite a different circumstance.[57]

And, to further cite the president, to ensure that there would be not only responsible behavior but also "no cost to the rest of the taxpayers of the United States," the loans themselves would be subject to stringent conditions:

> Funds would be loaned to the State on a seasonal basis, normally from July through March, to be repaid with interest in April, May and June, when the bulk of the city's revenues come in. All Federal loans will be repaid in full at the end of each year.[58]

. . . we include . . . a lien for the Federal Government, so that the Federal Government has a priority claim against any other creditor for the repayment of any seasonal loan made by the Federal Government. The net result is the Federal Government will be held harmless and the taxpayers won't have to lose a penny, and the city of New York will straighten out its fiscal situation.[59]

Thus, with these considerations in mind, on Wednesday, Thanksgiving Eve of November 26, 1975, the president announced that he had "decided to ask the Congress when it returns from recess for authority to provide a temporary line of credit to the State of New York to enable it to supply seasonal financing of essential services for the people of New York City"[60] in an amount not to exceed $2.3 billion per fiscal year through June 30, 1978. On December 9, 1975, after having been rushed through Congress in five days, the New York City Seasonal Financing Act of 1975 was signed by the president into law.

WEIGHING THE PRESIDENT'S DECISION: HALF EMPTY OR HALF FULL?

Having analyzed the New York City fiscal crisis from the presidential perspective, it would be useful, at this juncture, to ask how well Mr. Ford performed. Were his decisions foolhardy or prudent, half empty or half full? Did he "sell out," "bail out," or "tough it out" with a municipality which has hardly been known for its soft edges?

From the materials this author has uncovered, a "sellout" was not the likely case. If it had occurred, it would have been in May rather than November, long before the city had been compelled to push ahead with fiscal reforms. As concerns a "bailout," that too was a questionable depiction because, in a very real sense, the city, along with the state, had been required to devise a plan to bail itself out and behave responsibly. And the reason why New York pushed ahead to "heal itself" was that President Ford had chosen to "tough it out" by withholding aid and risking, indeed planning for, default in the process.

A decision favoring early aid for New York before November would have been counterproductive. As one administration official said at the time, "Once we start giving them money, they've got us over a barrel."[61] Consequently, the White House strategy instead assumed "that the prospect of federal money and the threat of default would do more to put the city fiscal house in order than the guarantee of that money itself."[62] As the president observed during his Thanksgiving Eve news conference:

. . . we have always felt that they could do enough, but only because we were firm have they moved ahead to accomplish what they have done now, which is a bailout of New York City by New York officials. If we had shown any give, I think they would not have made the hard decisions that they have made in the last week or so.[63]

Thus, what one sees throughout this crisis is a presidential willingness to hold fast, to stand firm and thereby extract concessions and a plan from the city of New

York. In his so doing, environmental conditions adjusted to the ethical and rational convictions of the president far more than he did to them. And in the end, it was not so much a change of Mr. Ford's mind as a meeting of the minds that led to New York's return to solvency.

NOTES

1. "Remarks and a Question-and-Answer Session at the National Press Club on the Subject of Financial Assistance to New York City, October 29, 1975," in *Public Papers of the Presidents: Gerald R. Ford,* Book II (Washington, D.C.: Government Printing Office, 1977), p. 1733.

2. "The President's News Conference of November 26, 1975," in *Public Papers of the Presidents: Gerald R. Ford,* Book II, p. 1904.

3. For further discussion of the background of the crisis, see, for example, U.S. Congress, Joint Economic Committee, *New York City's Financial Crisis: An Evaluation of Its Economic Impact and of Proposed Policy Solutions,* 94th Cong. 1st Sess., November 3, 1975, and U.S. Congress, Congressional Budget Office, *New York City's Fiscal Problem: Its Origins, Potential Repercussions and Some Alternative Policy Responses,* Background Paper No. 1, 94th Cong. 1st Sess., October 10, 1975.

4. Text of letter from President Ford to Mayor Beame, May 14, 1975, folder "NYC Finances: May–August, 1975," Box 23, James Cannon Papers, Gerald R. Ford Library.

5. See, for example, Donna E. Shalala and Carol Bellamy, "A State Saves a City: The New York Case," *Duke Law Journal* (1976), pp. 1119–1132; Martin Shefter, *Political Crisis/Fiscal Crisis: The Collapse and Revival of New York City and the Liberal Experiment* (New York: W.W. Norton, 1980); and Fred Ferretti, *The Year the Big Apple Went Bust* (New York: G.P. Putnam's Sons, 1976).

6. "Ford to City: Drop Dead," *Daily News,* October 30, 1975, p.1.

7. Memo, L. William Seidman to the president, May 8, 1975, folder "New York City: 8/9/74–6/13/75," Box 9, White House Central Files, Gerald R. Ford Library.

8. Memo, Jim Cannon to the president, May 13, 1975, folder "New York City: 8/9/74–6/13/75," Box 9, White House Central Files, Gerald R. Ford Library.

9. Draft statement to the president, May 12, 1975, folder "New York City: 8/9/74–6/13/75," Box 9, White House Central Files, Gerald R. Ford Library.

10. Gerald R. Ford, *A Time to Heal* (New York: Harper and Row, 1979), p. 315.

11. Text of letter from President Ford to Mayor Beame, May 14, 1975, folder "NYC Finances: May–August, 1975," Box 23, James Cannon Papers, Gerald R. Ford Library.

12. Ibid.

13. Ibid.

14. Ibid.

15. Proposed Comments on the Consequences of a Default by New York, May 13, 1975, folder "New York City: 8/9/74–6/13/75," Box 9, White House Central Files, Gerald R. Ford Library.

16. Ford, *A Time to Heal,* p. 316.

17. John J. Casserly, *The Ford White House: The Diary of a Speechwriter* (Boulder: Colorado Associated University Press, 1977), p. 207.

18. Presidential memorandum, May 13, 1975, folder "New York City: 8/9/74–6/13/75," Box 9, White House Central Files, Gerald R. Ford Library.

19. Ford: *A Time to Heal,* pp. 315–316.

20. Ibid., p. 315.

21. Draft statement by the president, May 12, 1975, folder "New York City: 8/9/74–6/13/75," Box 9, White House Central Files, Gerald R. Ford Library.

22. Memo, L. William Seidman to the president, August 8, 1975, folder "New York City: 6/14/75–8/31/75," Box 9, White House Central Files, Gerald R. Ford Library.

23. Ford, *A Time to Heal,* p. 315.

24. Text of letter from President Ford to Mayor Beame, May 14, 1975, folder "NYC Finances: May–August, 1975," Box 23, James Cannon Papers, Gerald R. Ford Library.

25. Ford, *A Time to Heal,* p. 316.

26. Memo, with press releases, from John G. Carlson to Roger Porter, May 15, 1975, folder "New York City: May-October, 1975," Box 78, L. William Seidman Files, Gerald R. Ford Library.

27. See Daniel J. Balz, "If a City Goes Bankrupt," *National Journal,* November 29, 1975, p. 1631.

28. Daniel J. Balz, "There's No End in Sight for New York's Money Problems," *National Journal,* November 19, 1975, p. 1630.

29. "New York's Plight Stirs Little Federal Response," *Congressional Quarterly,* September 27, 1975, p. 2056.

30. Ford, *A Time to Heal,* p. 316.

31. Memo from William E. Simon and James Cannon to Economic Policy Board, July 1975, folder "New York City: May–October, 1975," Box 78, L. William Seidman Files, Gerald R. Ford Library.

32. U.S. Congress, Joint Economic Committee, *New York City's Financial Crisis,* p. 8.

33. Memo, L. William Seidman to the president, September 2, 1975, folder "New York City: September, 1975," Box 140, L. William Seidman Files, Gerald R. Ford Library.

34. Shalala and Bellamy, "A State Saves a City: The New York Case," p. 1128.

35. L. William Seidman, "Rediscovering Fiscal Responsibility," transcript of a speech delivered before the Detroit Economic Club, Detroit, December 15, 1975, p. 4, folder "Economic Policy Board," Box 6, Margeta White Files, Gerald R. Ford Library.

36. Ibid.

37. Ibid.

38. "Remarks and a Question-and-Answer Session at the National Press Club," p. 1733.

39. "The President's News Conference of November 26, 1975," p. 1903. For a more comprehensive explanation regarding the entire financial plan, see the "Carey Plan," in Balz, "There's No End in Sight for New York's Money Problems," p. 1629.

40. Seidman, "Rediscovering Fiscal Responsibility," pp. 6–7.

41. "The President's News Conference of November 26, 1975," p. 1903.

42. Press release on New York City's Fiscal Situation, Novebmer 26, 1975, folder "New York City: 11/26/75," Box 141, L. William Seidman Files, Gerald R. Ford Library.

43. Letter, Felix Rohaytn to William E. Simon with attachments, November 13, 1975, folder "New York City: November, 1975–July, 1976," Box 79, L. William Seidman Files, Gerald R. Ford Library. The following points regarding the necessity of federal assistance were also included in the "Federal Role," in Balz, "There's No End in Sight for New York's Money Problems," p. 1630.

44. Ibid.

45. Ibid.

46. Letter, Governor Carey to Secretary Simon, November 14, 1975, folder "NYC Financial Crisis (3)," Box 4, John G. Carlson Files, Gerald R. Ford Library.

47. Memo, Stephen Gardner to the president with attachments, November 14, 1975, folder "New York City: November, 1975–July, 1976," L. William Seidman Files, Gerald R. Ford Library.

48. "Remarks and a Question-and-Answer Session at the National Press Club," p. 1732.

49. Memo, Charls Walker to the president, October 7, 1975, folder "New York City: 10/21/75–10/31/75," Box 9, White House Central Files, Gerald R. Ford Library.

50. This point was originally included in Lawrence Portnoy, "The Ford Administration and the 1975 New York City Financial Crisis," unpublished University of Michigan Honors Thesis, 1985, p. 73, Gerald R. Ford Library.

51. Memo, Stephen Gardner to the president with attachments, November 14, 1975, folder "New York City: November, 1975–July, 1976," Box 79, L. William Seidman Files, Gerald R. Ford Library.

52. Memo, Charls Walker to the president, October 7, 1975, folder "New York City: 10/21/75–10/31/75," Box 9, White House Central Files, Gerald R. Ford Library

53. Memo, L. William Seidman, with Charls Walker, to the president, November 8, 1975, folder "New York City: 11/8/75–11/10/75 " Box 10, White House Central Files, Gerald R. Ford Library.

54. Special In-Depth Survey of the American Public on the Subject of Federal Assistance to New York City, Louis Harris and Associates, Inc., November 1975, folder "New York City: 11/21/75–11/23/75," Box 10, White House Central Files, Gerald R. Ford Library.

55. Memo, Jim Cannon to the president, October 18, 1975, folder "New York City: 9/15/75–10/20/75," Box 9, White House Central Files, Gerald R. Ford Library.

56. "Aid to New York," *Congressional Quarterly,* September 27, 1975, p. 2060.

57. "The President's News Conference of November 26, 1975," p. 1908.

58. Ibid., p. 1904.

59. Ibid., p. 1906.

60. Ibid., p. 1904.

61. Balz, "There's No End in Sight for New York Money Problems," p. 1628.

62. Ibid.

63. "The President's News Conference of November 26, 1975," p. 1908.

CHAPTER 5

Bill Clinton:
Leading a Troubled Presidency

JOHN ALOYSIUS FARRELL *

It was getting on toward midnight. The society writers had long since rushed to the White House pressroom to phone in accounts of the night's state dinner. Russia's president, Boris Yeltsin, red-faced and sweaty, had been packed off in his motorcade. Guests were searching for their coats. And still the Clintons danced. The young president looked tall and trim in a black tuxedo. His wife glowed in red chiffon. He held her close as they circled the floor, there in the great north hall. The orchestra played "It Had to Be You," and as he grinned down at her beaming face, she sang him a verse from the Gus Kahn lyrics: "For nobody else gave me a thrill / With all your faults, I love you still / It had to be you, wonderful you / It had to be you. . . ."†

It began with such promise: the reign of Bill and Hillary Rodham Clinton. "We force the spring," Clinton said in his inaugural address. "We pledge an end to the era of deadlock and drift." He promised to govern as a "New Democrat"—a president not beholden to his party's sclerotic barons and doctrine. Indeed, as he neared the second anniversary of his election on that late September night of the Yeltsin dinner, Clinton could look back with satisfaction on a number of important triumphs. He had worked

---

* Reprinted courtesy of *The Boston Globe:* "The Troubled Presidency of Bill Clinton," by John Aloysius Farrell, Jan. 22, 1995, *Boston Globe Magazine.*

† "IT HAD TO BE YOU," words by Gus Kahn, music by Isham Jones © 1924 Warner Bros. Inc. (Renewed). Rights for Extended Renewal Term in USA controlled by Gilbert Keyes Music and Bantam Music Publishing Co. All Rights Reserved. Used by Permission. WARNER BROS. PUBLICATIONS U.S. INC., Miami, FL 33014.

hard in his time in office to reduce the budget deficit, restore progressivity to the tax code, boost exports and high-wage jobs, make a dent in the size of government, and end a six-year impasse between liberals and conservatives over legislation to fight crime. But as the Clintons danced that autumn night, the voters were preparing to give them and their Democratic Party allies a historic repudiation.

There was anger in the land—anger rooted in deep-set economic anxiety, the turbulent times of the post-Cold War era, and Clinton's own failures as president. He is a great politician, with all the flaws the term implies. From Little Rock, he had watched the fall of the Berlin Wall and understood, better than most of his peers, its portent. The old clarities—East and West, left and right—had grown muddled. There was room for what he called a "third way." And so he had challenged the formidable George Bush, running on a platform of change, offering the voters a leaner but activist government that would champion their cause in the new world economy. He won in a three-man race with 43 percent of the vote, and there were Republicans in Washington, Newt Gingrich among them, who feared that Clinton had beaten them to the next paradigm—that he, not they, would overthrow the old order and lead his party to the spoils of the next New Deal.

It didn't happen. Clinton, the man who tempered his resistance to the Vietnam War with his desire "to maintain my political viability in the system," quailed at the role of rebel. He tried to finesse a revolution. Neither he nor his inexperienced staff was up to such a task.

And so the voters, impatient with his vacillation, sent Clinton a message on Election Day, awarding him Gingrich and Bob Dole as partners and sending him on a search for answers—so much so that he dug out the speech he made when announcing his presidential candidacy, scanning the text for clues to what went wrong.

Clinton's resilience is legendary—as are his will to power and his almost shameless facility at changing his political spots. He still holds the presidency; as with a prizefighting champion, someone will have to wrest it from him. He could yet win reelection. But there's a sense of tragedy about the Clinton White House, a bitter taste of chances lost and fear that the torch of revolution may have passed for good to more audacious hands.

Indeed, a *Globe Magazine* poll of those who vote in the New Hampshire Democratic primary conducted for this article found that, even among loyalists, Clinton's leadership was suspect. Only 53 percent approved of his moral values and strength of character. Only 41 percent called him strong or decisive. Only 40 percent felt he had kept his promises.

More than 40 percent of those Democratic primary voters agreed with the notion that Clinton "tries to be all things to all people, and insincerely says what he thinks people want to hear." When voters were asked what it was about Clinton that had caused their opinion of him to drop, the top three answers were that Clinton was "wishywashy," was "not assertive enough," and had "not accomplished what he said he would."

"Clinton blew it—totally, totally blew it," says Republican pollster William McInturff. "He had a chance to redefine the Democratic Party and create a stable governing authority. And he blew it."

The story of Bill Clinton's blown opportunity begins with the economy. Candidates and their hired guns came away from the midterm election struck by the corrosive effects of economic dislocation. In governing, Clinton failed to heed the slogan that had ruled his own presidential campaign. Sure, unemployment dropped, and the bond- and stock-market dealers were humming. But average income slumped, and below the rosy surface, real families felt real pain. It was still the economy, stupid.

Stanley Greenberg, the president's pollster, says, "There are a lot of college-educated, blue-collar, particularly younger, men who have watched their incomes decline, who are angry about the economy and indeed angry even about *talk* of a good economy when they have so much difficulty seeing rising living standards. It leaves them disconnected from the elite, disconnected from the political parties, willing to express their anger."

Americans fought for 45 years to win the Cold War, only to find that economic unrest, not a prosperous homecoming, was one of the fruits of victory. "I was a child of the Cold War," says Democratic Senator Bill Bradley of New Jersey, a former Rhodes Scholar and professional basketball player who grew up in smalltown Missouri. "I used to keep a little diagram of my own personal bomb shelter: where I'd keep my cot, where I'd keep my favorite books, where I'd keep my favorite food, and where I'd keep my basketball—the premise being, even after a nuclear holocaust, there would be basketball.

"But all that's over now. There will be 4 million Americans, between 1986 and 1996, who will have lost their jobs in the defense sector. Or, take the information revolution. On one level, it offers us tremendous opportunities for productivity gains, for having a cleaner and more prosperous society and a more efficient economy. Yet if you were a steel worker in 1979, you had about 750,000 fellow steel workers. If you're a steel worker today, you have about 340,000. And yet we produce more steel—export more, import less—because of the application of information to the production process. And this occurs not just in steel but in industry, in sector after sector.

"There are a lot of positive signs out there. But if you are in the midst of one of these big transformations, you don't see them, because you know too many people who've lost their job, might be losing their job, could be losing their job, had to move to get a new job, had to take their kids out of school in order to get a new job in the new place, had to leave their roots in order to be able to feed their family, got demoted, lost their health insurance, had to change their pension plan.

"When you're in the middle of this kind of turmoil, no matter what the numbers say, you don't feel secure," says Bradley. "In the long run, it works out. But as a lot of my friends who have been displaced say, in the long run, we're all dead."

American workers used to fear cyclical downturns, in which they would be laid off in a recession, subsist for a few months on unemployment benefits, and be called back to work on the assembly line when the next cycle of expansion began. But today, corporations announce layoffs in the midst of boom times. The comforting icons of postwar American prosperity—IBM, Pan Am, Bethlehem Steel, Sears—have died off or been transformed by wrenching changes. Robots, computers, and mergers are making industry more productive but at the cost of jobs forever lost. In sharp contrast to the days of cyclical layoffs, some 75 percent of those laid off these days will never get their jobs back, says Labor Secretary Robert Reich. And of those who land new jobs, he says, half have to settle for a cut in pay.

"Other factors obviously influenced the recent elections," Reich says. "But never, never underestimate the political potency of a declining paycheck. Support for Democrats dropped most precipitously between Election Day 1992 and Election Day 1994 among men who lacked college degrees. This group includes nearly three out of four working men.

"They have seen their economic prospects shrivel over the past 15 years. They have suffered a 12 percent decline in average real income since 1979. They voted for change in 1994, just as they voted for change in 1992, and they will do it again and again and again, until that downward slide is reversed."

Economic change has engendered a crisis of faith, says Reich. "This isn't the way it is supposed to be in America. Unlike more fatalistic cultures, Americans have always had a deep faith that efforts will be rewarded, that you reap what you sow. In other words, you can earn your fate. That was the American credo. That was the work ethic.

"Middle-class families tried every means they had of holding on. Spouses went to work. Both parents worked long hours or they took multiple jobs. They decided to have fewer kids. They pushed these coping mechanisms about as far as they can go," Reich says, "and they still feel that they are losing the American dream.

"We are on the way to becoming a two-tiered society composed of a few winners and a larger group of Americans left behind, whose anger and whose disillusionment is easily manipulated," he says. "Once unbottled, mass resentments can poison the very fabric, the moral integrity, of society—replacing ambition with envy, replacing tolerance with hate."

Economic change explains part of the fix that Clinton is in. The country, after all, turned on the Democrats with the same callous swiftness with which it spurned George Bush. After two decades of domination, the Republican share of the presidential vote dropped a whopping 16 percent from 1988 to 1992, a decline unmatched since the Vietnam War. Two years later, the electorate lashed out again, ending the Democrats' 40-year reign in the House of Representatives. Nor is this an American phenomenon. The political status quo has been shattered in Germany, Russia, and Japan. In the last national Canadian election, the ruling Conservatives saw their seats in Ottawa drop from 153 to 2.

These political shifts partly reflect a crisis of purpose at the close of the Cold War. Historians will mark this century as the time when three generations of free men and women fought against totalitarian gangsters of the left and right. Clinton looks back enviously at President John F. Kennedy, who spoke of the honor of waging a "long twilight struggle" against tyranny, and left his audiences feeling proud and special.

Now, that struggle has been won—with a whimper, not a bang. And gone is the sense of noble mission. For fear of raising the electorate's expectations, America's political leaders didn't even give their constituents a moment to celebrate, relax, and congratulate themselves for the long years of sacrifice and tension. Was not the fall of communism worth its own V-E Day? Nor did we emerge from victory unscathed. American democracy still suffers the scars of the Cold War, still bears the divisive legacy of McCarthyism, Vietnam, and Watergate. Like soldiers hardened on the battlefield, so our souls were steeled by the years of drawing diagrams of our own personal bomb shelters, of aping the enemy's tactics, of purging the nonconformist.

"The fight against communism diminished us. That's why we are unable to rejoice at our victory," said author John Le Carré when he spoke before the Boston Bar Association last year. "It left us a state of false and corrosive orthodoxy. It licensed our excesses, and we didn't like ourselves the better for them. It dulled our love of dissent and our sense of life's adventure."

The effect on post-Cold War life is dear, said Le Carré: "The service industries of criticism have almost drowned the magic of creation. Our intellectuals hate too much. Our press revels in public executions. We are poisoning ourselves with malice."

Without a defining foe, the Western democracies are groping for purpose in a time when the old verities of politics, religion, and morality have been challenged by scientific and moral relativism. When accepting the 1990 Nobel Prize for Literature, Mexican author Octavio Paz warned of the "spiritual wilderness" that the survivors would face as they surveyed the post-Cold War landscape.

"It is the end of all utopias . . . the end of the idea of history as a phenomenon whose outcome can be known in advance," Paz said. "For the first time in history, mankind lives in a sort of spiritual wilderness, no longer in the shadow of the religious and political systems that consoled us even as they oppressed us. Ours is the first age that is ready to live without a meta-historical doctrine.

"This is a dangerous experience," said Paz. "It is impossible to know whether the tensions and the conflicts unleashed in this privatization of ideas, practices, and beliefs will end up destroying the social fabric. Men could become possessed once more by ancient religious fury or by fanatical nationalism."

Onto this troubled stage, with his 43 percent mandate, strode Bill Clinton, a relatively unknown governor of a small Southern state, blessed—and cursed—with adaptability. He immediately faced a series of defining choices by which the country would get to know him on the job. His newness was at first an asset, but it also presented his political opponents with the opportunity to define him, and this he let them do.

From the start, it seemed, Clinton miscalculated. Though he campaigned as an agent of change, neither he nor his staff fully appreciated how the end of the Cold War had left the old verities crumbling. Senator Daniel Patrick Moynihan, a Democrat from New York, says Washington still suffers from a case of "gigantism everywhere," the legacy of Cold War bureaucrats who—too busy worrying if the blips on the radar screen were "Canada geese or SS-I 8 missiles"—allowed a runaway growth of government during the Cold War.

Clinton proclaimed himself a "New Democrat," but in his first two years in office, wary of displeasing the Democratic bosses on Capitol Hill, he did little but nibble at the bureaucratic edges—"reinventing" the ashtrays of the federal government—instead of taking the walls apart with a chain saw. The product of a violent home, Clinton admits that he avoids confrontations in favor of mediation, a characteristic that ill suits a rebel. His first concession to the Democratic leaders of Congress was to abandon—in return for their help on the $500 billion deficit reduction bill—the themes of congressional and political reform that he'd campaigned on.

Dulled by their addiction to 30-second TV commercials and the never-ending rounds of special-interest fund-raising needed to pay for them, the complacent Democrats did not grasp what was happening in the land. But the voters knew what they wanted: a cheaper government that offered basic security and equal opportunity—but no special preferences—to its citizens, and a government that would kick the lazy off the welfare rolls, restore safe streets, and stay the hell away from bedrooms, doctors' offices, and gun collections.

"Maybe we needed a bureaucracy to put a man on the moon and win World War II. We don't need it now," says Senator Phil Gramm of Texas, a Republican presidential hopeful. "In the new information age it is freedom, it is creativity, and government constrains that."

In the first few months of 1993, trying to please the factions of his party, Clinton made other defining choices. To the dismay of his fellow New Democrats, the results left him looking like a tax-and-spend liberal. "We got lost. We forgot what message had won," says Democratic Senator John Breaux of Louisiana. "In an effort to be all things to all people, we lost the principles that people had voted for.

"Instead of a stronger military for less money, we argued about the rights of gays in the military. Instead of cutting spending and investing in private-sector growth, we debated a multibillion-dollar, deficit-financed stimulus package. Instead of emphasizing individual responsibility for achievement, we argued over Lani Guinier's concept of quotas as the way to success. Instead of following through on middle-income tax relief for families, we listened to Joycelyn Elders' proposal for condom distribution in our schools and decriminalization of drug use," says Breaux. "And instead of debating the welfare system that everyone agrees serves no one very well, we spent our time on a do-it-all-at-once health proposal that many Americans felt was a take-from-me and give-to-them redistribution regime mandated by Washington."

In each case cited by Breaux, and in a number of other instances, Clinton was forced by popular opinion to back down. Having outraged conservatives with his original positions, he then lost the support of many other Americans by appearing feckless and rudderless.

"There are two sources of anger with Bill Clinton," says William Schneider, a political analyst at the American Enterprise Institute, a Washington think tank. "Ideological conservatives, who make up about one-sixth of the electorate, are deeply devoted, die-hard Clinton haters. They are generally white, over 50, men, Southern, and Republican. To them he's a liberal pretending to be a moderate. He's Hillary. He's a phony. But there is also a much larger group of voters who are deeply disappointed.

Their view is that he is a weak president; he cannot make government work, which was what he was elected to do."

"These guys can't decide where they are," says House Speaker Gingrich about the Clintons. "If they wanted to run as a counterculture socialist party, they could at least turn out their 35 percent. If they wanted to run as a centrist, New Democrat reform party, they would have split the party, but at least it would have been a great fight, and people would have understood why they needed to go vote. Instead, they zigzag wildly: Their left is unhappy with them, the center is unhappy with them, and nobody believes them."

Nor can defensive liberals write off the fall election as the roar of unwashed racism. The same polling samples that reflect anger and impatience with government also show an increased sense of tolerance for gay Americans and interracial relationships. The percentage of Americans who think homosexual teachers should be fired dropped from 51 percent in 1987 to 38 percent in 1994, while support for interracial dating among white Americans climbed from 43 percent to 65 percent, according to a national survey by the Times Mirror Center for the People and the Press.

"With Clinton, what people find so lacking is that he has no strength," says GOP consultant Ed Rollins. "If, a year from now, the American people still think this guy is weak, then I think he loses."

Compounding Clinton's strategic sins were a remarkable string of tactical flubs, gaffes, and controversies. For its first 18 months, the White House seemed to suffer an embarrassment a month. There was the travel office, the failure of the stimulus bill, the $200 haircut on the tarmac in Los Angeles, the Guinier nomination, the suicide of old friend and counsel Vincent Foster, the Whitewater affair, allegations by Arkansas state troopers of infidelity, Hillary Clinton's lucrative commodity trades, the Paula Jones case, the resignation of Agriculture Secretary Mike Espy, a grand jury probe of how Clinton's aides handled Whitewater, and the resignation—and ultimate conviction—of old buddy Webster Hubbell, a former deputy attorney general.

Every president has his ideological enemies. But via what media critic Jon Katz has dubbed the "new media"—that hodgepodge of TV and radio talk shows, single-interest publications, gossip columns, electronic bulletin boards, partisan cable television networks, and the like—a relatively small core of the disgruntled can "distort and exaggerate" public opinion, influence the mainstream media, and cow elected officials, say Times Mirror researchers.

Radio talk shows, right-wing journals, and Internet news groups served as forums of resentment. Conservative activists spun wild conspiracy tales about the Clintons: of drugs, perversions, even murder.

"Part of it is ideological," says McInturff. "Much of it is character, with the problems connected to Whitewater and Paula Jones, which have further eroded the moral authority of government. There is a big chunk of the country who very strongly believe the kind of personal values one looks for in a president are lacking."

The administration found few friends in the media. Did Clinton and his aides alienate the press with their dissembling and arrogance? Or is the president justified in claiming that he suffers from what media expert Thomas Patterson calls a "hypercritical" press? The blame probably rests with both sides, but the initial consequences were felt first by the White House. "A lot of it was their fault," one aide says about the Clintons. "Her fault in particular, for not bellying up to the bar and saying, 'Oh, I get it. We have to disclose this, because if we don't, we'll look suspicious.'

"Earth calling Clintons. Come in, please," says the aide. "They are very bright people with a huge blind spot in how you deal with the press. Her, in particular. I think he has learned a lot more. But think of Gennifer Flowers. That was his first exposure to the national press, when legitimate news organizations used the supermarket tabloids as their primary source. Did he have an affair with her? God knows. Probably. But was the way they went about reporting it right? No, of course not."

Even when Clinton fulfilled his campaign promises—as when he gave a tax credit to 15 million blue-collar working families in 1993—his staff members failed to live up to their own high self-opinion. Taking advantage of Democratic bumbling and what futurist Alvin Toffler, author of *The Third Wave,* calls today's fragmented "mosaic of communications," the GOP won the war of words.

"The Republicans were able to send out a message of a tax increase," says Senator Dianne Feinstein, a California Democrat. "In California, there were 13 million personal-income taxpayers, and we increased taxes on only 163,000. So, for over 10 million people, there were no tax increases. And for 2.1 million people, taxes went down. But guess what? No one believed it. And that was our failure.

"Part of the poor communication," Feinstein says, "lay with the Democratic National Committee, where $35 million to $40 million was raised, most of it spent to promote the health-care plan and to hire consultants. Little was spent to communicate the accomplishments on crime and the economy. It was an egregious waste of money."

Greenberg takes comfort from polling data, which show that the voters haven't written Clinton off yet. "They are still very open to the Clinton presidency," the pollster says, "even as they are enormously critical of his results in the first two years."

Indeed, the Republican "Contract with America" contains many crowd-pleasing distractions and nostrums—but no measures that directly address the economic and spiritual crises that American democracy is facing.

In a handwritten and personal speech to a crowd of New Democrats last month [December, 1994], Clinton admitted that he had lost the support of the very working families he ran for office to help—the ones who elected him to office. In an effort to recapture their allegiance, Clinton has now proposed a series of middle-class tax cuts, funded by cuts in government spending.

"There's still people out there killing themselves, thinking, 'I'm doing everything I can. I'm working a longer workweek. I can't afford a vacation anymore. I'm paying more for health care. I may lose my job tomorrow. My kid could get shot on the way to school. And all my money is going to people who misbehave,'" the president said. "We did a lot of things that they didn't like very much, especially after it was explained to them, as we say back home.

"I think I was right when I opposed discrimination and intolerance, but a lot of folks thought I was just more concerned about minorities than the problems of the majority. I believe we were right when we stood up to the National Rifle Association and said we ought to take these military assault weapons off the streets. But a long way from the battlegrounds of the inner cities, a lot of folks out in the country said, 'My Lord, I'm paying too much in taxes. I can't hold my job. And now they're coming after my gun. Why won't they just let me alone?'

"All my life, ever since I was a little boy, I have seen people like that mistreated, disadvantaged," said Clinton, harking back to his days growing up in the segregated South. "I have seen some of them inflamed in anger and enraged and taken advantage of. We owe it to them to let them know we heard and we're fighting for them, and we're going to deliver."

It's too late, says Gingrich, who has claimed the mantle of change for his own. "I believe I am part of a national movement, part of a band of brothers and sisters in a genuine revolutionary cause," he says. "And I think now we have an opponent who totally personifies everything we are trying to do away with. It's sort of the perfect contest.

"Take health care. They had an opportunity to build from the grass roots up, totally participatory. Instead, they took the ultimate elitist model, to pick 500 people and lie about the number, meet in secret, and produce—as though it were from the head of Zeus—a magnificent nationwide bureaucratic mode. That is the antithesis of where we are going.

"What has happened in a wonderfully ironic way," says Gingrich, "is that the Clintons picked the fight they dreamed of all their life and decided to prove to the country that we should have a debate over the size of government. The country has now had that debate. And discovered we are to the right of Ronald Reagan."

CHAPTER 6

Al Gore:
A Vice President To Be,
or Not To Be, President?

*PETER BOYER**

Inside the home of Albert Gore, Sr., and his wife, Pauline—a marble farmhouse in the rolling hills of middle Tennessee—there is a room (the kitchen, oddly enough) that serves as the family photo gallery. One photograph shows Al, Jr., at the age of ten, wearing a bandage on his forehead after being accidentally hit by a bat in a baseball game. That picture was taken in 1958, on the day that his father won reelection to the United States Senate. In another photo, Al is kissing his mother goodbye as she and the Senator, who is dressed in white tie and tails, leave for a dinner party at the Kennedy White House. (J.F.K., although he was a decade younger than the Senator, was a close pal.) Along one wall, another frame holds a 1991 picture of Al, Jr., and his family at a nearby lake, taken at the time that he announced he would not seek the presidential nomination eventually won by Bill Clinton. If a destiny can be mapped, Al Gore's is on display in this room, whose walls are crowded with the snapshots of a family's life at the center of our recent political history.

But the map is not complete. "You'll notice that all the walls are filled," the elder Gore said to me on a recent visit to his home. Then, pointing with his walking stick, he added, "Except this one. That's reserved for a purpose."

That purpose, Albert, Sr., makes clear, is to memorialize a Gore Administration. "That wall has been empty since we built this house," the eighty-six-year-old father of the Vice President later told me. "I hope to live to see it filled."

---

* "Gore's Dilemma," by Peter Boyer, first published in *The New Yorker,* © 1994 by Peter Boyer. Reprinted with permission of the author.

The starting date for the Gore Administration was penciled in as January 2001, when the famously futurist pol, propelled by the momentum of a two-term Clinton reign, would lead the Democrats into the new millennium. But the electoral massacre of Clinton and his party midway through his first term has nervous Democrats seeing foreshadowings of another Carter disaster. And embedded in that anxiety is the prospect of a double hit: Would a Clinton failure also mean that Al Gore, rather than becoming the first President of the twenty-first century, would become the Walter Mondale of the nineties? The prospect horrifies Gore loyalists, those Democrats who believed that the greatest payoff of the Clinton election was its anticipation of a Gore Presidency. As Leon Wieseltier, of *The New Republic,* who is a friend of the Vice President's, bluntly puts it, "Al Gore is too good to waste on Bill Clinton."

Bob Beckel, the Democratic consultant who ran Mondale's failed 1984 Presidential campaign, four years after Jimmy Carter was turned out of office, discerns in the Vice President's camp a feeling that Gore's political life is endangered. "I've talked to some of Gore's people, his political friends around the country, who are just fretting about this," Beckel says.

The apprehension is warranted. Bill Clinton's first half term, despite its isolated triumphs, was a thudding political failure as measured by the most meaningful test, the ballot box. Clinton's challenge, one that he extravagantly embraced during his campaign, had been to prove that Democrats could govern from the center; but the Democrats either could not or would not, and they were made to pay on November 8. The many preelection explanations of the voters' "baffling" mood—that they were angry at all incumbents, frustrated by gridlock, disappointed by the failure of health-care reform, frenzied by talk radio, turned off by negative campaigns, and so on—skirt the simple truth: voters rejected Democrats (not a single Republican incumbent governor, senator, or representative lost), and the Democrat they rejected most was Bill Clinton. (A *Time/CNN poll* conducted just after the election found that 48 percent of the respondents believed the Democratic Party should nominate someone other than Clinton in 1996.) This was made vividly clear to Al Gore in the most personal way, when his home state's three statewide races—for governor and for the Senate seats once held by both Albert Gores—went to Republicans. So toxic was the president deemed in Tennessee that when Gore went home last month to campaign for his old friend Jim Sasser, a key Clinton ally, he and Sasser managed to give eight speeches in four Tennessee cities without once mentioning Bill Clinton's name.

In the second half of his term, Clinton will be dealing not only with a surly public and a Congress stuffed with Republicans but also with a weakened and alienated centrist branch of his own party—the so-called New Democrats. The New Democrats had been home turf to both Clinton and Gore. But the Administration's political choices and its style of governance appeared to be an abandonment of the New Democratic philosophy—the advocacy of a smaller, more efficient, more entrepreneurial government—as it had been articulated and popularized by the Democratic Leadership Council. Gore was a founding member of the D.L.C., and Clinton was its chairman before he resigned to run for President. The D.L.C. was the Clinton–Gore ticket's intellectual base, providing the ideas—welfare reform, job retraining, national service, youth apprenticeship, the reinvention of government—that defined much of Clinton's candidacy. But Al From, the D.L.C.'s president, is so disheartened by Clinton's first two years that he says he may take the D.L.C. outside the Democratic Party—a powerful revolt that would only further damage the president's re-election chances. Add to this the prospect of a third-party candidacy in 1996 and open speculation about an intra-Party challenge to Clinton, and the picture turns even grimmer. To these next two years, of course, Al Gore's own destiny is also shackled.

"If this is a failed Presidency, it cannot help Al Gore," says Roy Neel, Gore's former chief of staff, who also worked in the White House for Clinton. "There is no way. And I've heard more cynical observers say, 'Well, the best thing for Al Gore would be for Clinton to lose this time, and Gore could run without the baggage of Bill Clinton.' I just think that's total nonsense. Al Gore's political future is, at least in the near future, inextricably tied to Bill Clinton's."

From the moment the Clinton–Gore ticket was formed, some Democrats have longed for a role reversal, and at the depth of Clinton's descent this fall there have arisen wishful murmurs of a Gore-led ticket in 1996. When Gore hears such talk, he cuts it off. "I'm happy to bind my future with Bill Clinton," Gore told me recently. "I'm proud to do it, I'm happy to do it. I've invested everything I have, heart and soul, into the success of this Administration. And I think that anyone who looks at temporary poll numbers not even halfway through his first term will be badly misled about the place of Bill Clinton in history. I believe that he will be regarded by historians as one of the greatest Presidents this country has ever had. I believe that. I believe it."

That hopeful assertion, like Gore's Election Day prediction that Democrats would prevail, is the political equivalent of whistling past the graveyard, which is littered just now with Democrats tied to Clinton. "There are a lot of obvious lessons from the elections," Gore told me last week. But he said he had not yet considered the implications that the debacle held for him. Others, however, have. "Oh, Gore has a very serious problem," says Oklahoma Representative Dave McCurdy, who was a rising Democratic star until his career crashed on November 8. McCurdy had embraced Clinton's promise of "a new way," worked hard for his nomination, and delivered a seconding speech at the Democratic National Convention. But McCurdy, like many Democrats, became disillusioned and publicly broke with the president. His campaign for Oklahoma's open Senate seat was a run against Clinton and his policies. Yet McCurdy could not expunge his past alliance with the president. "And if it sticks to me," McCurdy says, "it's all over Gore."

Al Gore's dilemma is implicit in the Vice Presidency, which can be defined as an indeterminate period of waiting, with one's fingers crossed, for the President to leave. As Roy Neel notes, "It's nobody's ambition to be Vice President," and it is certainly not Al Gore's. The gamble resides in the chance of a President's failure, and Gore's wager on Clinton was extraordinarily high. Unlike Dan Quayle, who was plucked from relative obscurity to be installed down the hall from the Oval Office, Gore invested in Clinton his own national stature as well as a lifetime's preparation for the top job.

"He has been groomed from childhood to be President," Nathan Landow, a prominent Democratic fundraiser and a Gore enthusiast, says. From his birth (which was announced on the front page of a leading Tennessee paper), Al Gore's life has been framed by exalted expectation, his political prospects cast not simply as ambition but as something more like fate. That sense is embedded in the family lore, such as the story about the time when Al's father, believing that a boy needed to know the rigors of real work, asked his son, then a teen-ager, to plow a field with a particularly treacherous slope. Pauline Gore worried that the task, requiring the use of an unwieldy hillside plow, was too much to ask of the boy, and she and her husband argued about it. Finally, she yielded, with the sarcastic note, "Yes, a boy could never be President if he couldn't plow with that damned hillside plow."

A values lesson was the only serious use that Al Gore, Jr., was ever likely to make of a plow. Gore was a son of politics, a child of Washington, where his father served for thirty-two years as a congressman and a senator. The family residence was an apartment in the elegant Fairfax Hotel, which was owned by a Gore cousin; young Al walked across the street every morning to the Cosmos Club, where a bus picked him up for the ride to Washington's most elite prep school, St. Albans, on the grounds of the National Cathedral. Drop-ins at his parents' home were men like J. William Fulbright and Clark Clifford and J.F.K., the totems of power, and for young Al the lesson was always made clear: his purpose in life was to lead. Gore's father, a breeder of champion bulls, has said of his son's rendezvous with the White House, "We raised him for it." Gore's mother, although she frowns at such talk—"People take it the wrong way"—helped to set the expectations for her son. Mrs. Gore, who is a lawyer, says, "I always told Al that there was so much more room at the top than there was at the bottom or in the middle," and Gore took it to heart. He was captain of the St. Albans football team and an honors student at Harvard, and, at twenty-eight, he won his father's old congressional seat. At thirty-six, he went to the United States Senate, and in 1988, before his first term was over, he ran for President.

What motivated this high-speed tear up the ladder, apparently, was Gore's awakening to a profound sense of his own destiny. "He could lead, and if he could, he *should*," Pauline Gore says. "He really does believe that he was born to lead," Leon Wieseltier says. "He believes he is a historical figure. And in American politics a sense of destiny doesn't hurt."

But in 1988 Gore's sense that his purpose in life was to lead was not matched by any such sense among voters, and when his campaign floundered he pulled out, a badly beaten third. His sense of mission, however, did not ebb; he embraced environmentalism with religious fervor, and made the Green cause his own. Despite his defeat, Gore's stature was such that in 1992 his decision not to take on George Bush was a key to opening the Democratic field to the Party's lesser-known long shots, such as Bob Kerrey, the Nebraska senator, and, of course, Bill Clinton of Arkansas. When Clinton approached Gore about the Vice Presidency, in July of 1992, it could be seen more as a negotiation between equals than a tryout for Gore. Clinton, though he'd locked up the nomination, was still plagued by questions about Gennifer Flowers and the draft; he was in third place in the polls, trailing Ross Perot and Bush. Gore provided the lift that Clinton needed, and after the choice was announced (and Perot temporarily left the race) Clinton surged to a ten-point lead, and never fell back. Although Gore is nineteen months younger than Clinton, he lent weight to the ticket: Clinton was inexperienced in foreign policy, Gore was a recognized expert on such matters as arms control; Clinton had finessed serving in the military, Gore saw duty in Vietnam; Clinton had troubling image problems regarding his character, Gore was a foursquare family man. Indeed, the "double date" matchup of Al and Tipper Gore, whose publicly affectionate marriage is a kind of Beltway model, with Bill and Hillary Clinton, who'd been obliged to acknowledge their marital difficulties on national television, had a distinctly softening effect on the eventual First Couple's campaign image.

In risking his political capital in Clinton, Gore officially assumed the role he had occupied, in a way, for much of his life—that of President-in-waiting. A friend of Gore's says, "I always thought it would be great if Al could just be appointed President," and that is what Bill Clinton came close to doing when he chose Gore as his running mate. For Gore, the potential payoff was irresistible. Every Vice President in the last forty years (except for Agnew, who resigned in disgrace, and Nelson Rockefeller, who served in Gerald Ford's abbreviated term) eventually earned his party's Presidential nomination; four have become President.

As Clinton neared his nadir last month [October, 1994], with Democrats running away from him and the midterm disaster looming, I asked Gore whether Clinton's difficult two years had given him second thoughts about seeking the Presidency. "No," he said. "To the contrary. Some of the uncertainties I had about the job of President have been dispelled."

When Clinton was deciding on a running mate, a particular character trait of Al Gore's emerged as a recurring theme in the candidate's discussions with advisers. The Democratic consultant Bob Squier put it most directly: "He will not stab you in the back, even if you deserve it." Clinton could not have known then just how grateful he would have reason to be for this aspect of Gore's character once the two were in office. He surely knows now, with his policies repudiated, his party reeling, and Democrats openly speculating about whether the president will, or should, head the Democratic ticket in 1996. Gore, the one Democrat besides Clinton with most at stake, is also the surest to remain steadfast. Martin Peretz, *The New Republic's* owner and editor-in-chief, who was a mentor of Gore's at Harvard and has been his friend for nearly thirty years, is not surprised by Gore's unassailable loyalty. "He has never in my hearing said a churlish word about the president," Peretz says. "Now, I'm not saying he hasn't had a churlish thought."

If he has, Gore has kept it private. Like George Bush, of Andover and Yale, Gore, of St. Albans and Harvard, is a political aristocrat for whom loyalty is a requisite of an immutable personal code. As Bush suppressed his differences with Ronald Reagan to the point of attracting ridicule, and then stood by Dan Quayle to his own detriment, Gore betrays no hint of anything but utter fealty. In a casual conversation with friends following last month's visit to Washington by the South African President Nelson Mandela, Gore remarked that Mandela was the world leader that he most admired. He quickly added, "After Bill Clinton." When Washington social chatter turns, as it inevitably does these days, to the question of just how Al Gore will manage to distance himself from Clinton, or possibly replace him in 1996, people who know Gore well demur. "There's no possibility that somebody like Gore will set his own course," Squier says. "He would stay there and try to make this thing work. And you wouldn't think of even suggesting it to him." Actually, Gore does hear such speculation, and when he does, he orders it stopped cold.

Yet Gore has been distancing himself, willy-nilly, from Clinton from the moment they were inaugurated. In being the Good Vice President, Gore has been a good Vice President, easily the biggest success story of the Administration. When Ross Perot threatened to kill the North American Free Trade Agreement, Gore vanquished the troublesome Texan on Perot's proven turf, "Larry King Live." In a White House forever recruiting some new "old Washington hand" to provide adult supervision, Al Gore is the resident grownup. Even the enduring knock against him that he is wooden has the effect of making him seem, compared with a President who muses about his underwear on MTV, startlingly Presidential. When Clinton told workers at a General Motors plant that he used to drive an El Camino pickup with AstroTurf in the back, no one doubted him. "There are some things that the President does that we can't imagine Al doing," Peretz says.

As a team, Clinton and Gore, despite their much noted similarities—they were the Boomer-Baptist-Bubba ticket—are the more remarkable for their differences, not the least of which is background. Gore is no Bubba. "Bill came up in a very provincial atmosphere," Pauline Gore says. "And even though he went to Yale, and he went to Oxford, you don't undo or move out of that provincial atmosphere that has influenced you in your early life."

Background is not wholly determinate, but it is clear that Gore—the son of a Southerner who risked and lost his political career by fighting for civil rights and opposing the Vietnam War—became the sort of politician he is because of it. The sense of destiny that Gore's friends speak of may be preposterous, but it has the effect of giving him spine. Cautious and methodical, Gore agonizes over decisions, but he decides. Both Clinton and Gore are admired for their intellect, but they are starkly different sorts of thinkers. Clinton is circular, a lover of the debate but not the terminus point—a characteristic that suggests indecisiveness. Gore is linear, a listener and speed reader who devours information in order to reach a conclusion, and to act.

Before they took office, Gore got Clinton's promise of access and influence, and the Vice President enjoys an unprecedented autonomy and top ranking among Clinton's advisers. The famous bonding that was said to have occurred during their campaign bus trips may or may not have resulted in the buddy picture that aides painted, but Gore is trusted and heard. It is a complementary relationship, not least because of the focus Gore brings, although he is sometimes frustrated by the chaos. *The Agenda,* Bob Woodward's 1994 chronicle of White House disorder, told of a meeting with Clinton, Gore, and some aides in which Clinton, complaining of some long unresolved aspect of his economic program, asked Gore, "What can I do?"

Gore, exasperated, blurted, "You can get with the goddam program!" The lack of discipline in the White House—so many voices urging so many different directions—was dismaying to Gore. Eventually, he was instrumental in persuading Clinton to replace his friend Mack McLarty, the chief of staff, with Leon Panetta, thus imposing some measure of order in the White House. A Presidential adviser says that Gore is "very careful not to overstep his boundaries, but he does step in on things when he thinks that there's a need, and makes it happen. And that's a damned rarity."

Gore, of course, didn't share the allergy to foreign policy that Clinton and his corps of advisers brought from the campaign into the White House. It was Gore who led the secret negotiations with the Ukrainian President Leonid Kravchuk that resulted in Ukraine's surrender of nuclear weapons, and his ongoing relationship with the Russian Prime Minister Viktor Chernomyrdin is our main channel to Moscow. Gore believes in a firm assertion of American strength when needed, and has urged decisive action in Bosnia (calling for air strikes) and Haiti, where he was a key force in pushing Clinton to change policy and eventually to intervene. "I think he helps the President to arrive at a conclusion that the President knows he has to make, and to do it a lot quicker," one former White House aide says. A foreign-policy adviser who has seen Gore skillfully work Clinton in countless meetings says, "He's very good at forcing decisions, at bringing issues to closure. His stock-in-trade, in part, is that he does not like to let things linger. He likes to get things done and move on, for better or worse. He may make mistakes, but he does like to get it done. In meeting after meeting where I've been with him, his role is wrapping things up at the end and saying, 'We need to get this done here. You've got to make this decision. It's time for a decision.' I think there is a tendency in a lot of meetings with him, when others are in the room, to look to him to sort of do the benediction and bring it to conclusion. He has that relationship with Clinton to make it happen." It was Gore who, somewhat surprisingly to many of his friends, was Jimmy Carter's conduit to the White House during the former President's freelance foreign-policy excursions in North Korea and Haiti; but it was also Gore who kept Carter at bay when Carter wanted to negotiate a deal with Fidel Castro.

There is probably no better illustration of Gore's light-beam-in-a-fog function at the White House than the work he undertook with the National Performance Review, which came to be called "reinventing government." Before taking office, Gore had Clinton's assurance of a key party role, but which of the high-profile projects would he get? Hillary claimed health care, and no one argued. Gore wanted welfare reform—a bell-ringing New Democratic issue that had been central to the campaign and would, if accomplished, help to define Clinton's Presidency—but several people in the President's circle worried that it was too good an issue to give away, telling the President, according to one staffer, "No, you can't give this to Gore, you lose your identification with it." So Gore didn't get welfare reform, and, as it turned out, the issue that might have saved Clinton's first half term was ignored for a year, and ultimately got lost in the shuffle.

What the White House had in mind for Gore was something a little more *Vice*

Presidential, a worthy but unexciting chore that seemed, at the time, to hold almost no box-office appeal. As events have proved, it was a dramatic, and quite characteristic, political miscalculation. Reinventing government was a bedrock New Democratic idea and was based on a 1992 book—*Reinventing Government,* co-authored by David Osborne, a fellow at the D.L.C.'s think tank, the Progressive Policy Institute—that advocated bringing the private sector's entrepreneurial spirit to government by decentralizing it. But in the early days of the Administration nobody was particularly enthralled by reinventing government, including Al Gore. Health-care reform and welfare reform—those were the big, bold initiatives that would give the Clinton Administration its own New Frontier identity, and Gore was deeply disappointed not to get the leadership of either. But, characteristically, he embraced his new assignment with enthusiasm. "It took him about thirty minutes to get excited about it," Roy Neel, who was then Gore's chief of staff, recalls. "Light bulbs just started popping off. He said, 'Now, let's do A, B, C, and D, let's get these people together, let's get a working group, we need to do this,' and he was operating at light speed."

Inside the White House, Gore's project was the ugly stepchild, and it was given no people and no money from the president's staff budget, forcing Gore and his team to scrounge for staff and resources. Gore brought in Elaine Kamarck, from the Progressive Policy Institute, to be project manager, and populated the project with government employees borrowed from federal agencies. He set a six-month deadline for the team to come up with detailed recommendations of ways to make government work better and cost less. Gore got the assignment in March of 1993, and by August the work was nearly done.

Gore was proud of his team's effort and downright giddy about the project's prospects. His reinventing-government task force identified efficiencies that could reduce government costs by $108 billion and cut the federal workforce by 252,000 over five years. Early one Saturday morning in August, Gore went to the White House to sell the president on it. He arrived with props, including ashtrays (which, he had discovered, were subject to their own set of government specifications) and huge rolls of paper to show the unnecessary paperwork that bureaucracy generates, and generally played the eager salesman. And the President was sold. But Clinton's enthusiasm was not shared by the senior Presidential adviser George Stephanopoulos or by four outside consultants—the pollster Stan Greenberg, the media adviser Mandy Grunwald, and the campaign consultants Paul Begala and James Carville. They didn't believe that reinventing government would "resonate" politically. "David Gergen liked it a little more," one former White House staffer recalls, "but all those other folks thought, this is bullshit, nobody cares about any of this stuff, this is insider stuff. Procurement reform? Who cares about that stuff?" Gore argued for a splashy rollout for the project, asking two weeks of White House attention and a major investment of the President's time. Clinton's advisers said no, and Hillary Clinton's team, already annoyed because the NAFTA debate had pushed aside health care, worried that too much attention to Gore's project would just be more background noise distracting from the Administration's signature undertaking.

Instead of the two-week rollout that Gore wanted, reinventing government got a few days, and although Gore later made a small splash by going on "The Late Show with David Letterman" with his ashtray-smashing routine, his project quickly fell between the cracks of the White House's and the public's attention. Health care became a beast whose shadow covered all else, even though there was early evidence that neglecting Gore's undertaking was a mistake. In September of 1993, the Democratic pollster Peter Hart had conducted a survey testing which issues the public most wanted the Administration to address, and, since Gore's reinventing government had just come out, Hart decided to throw that into the mixture, too. He was stunned by what he found. When Hart's respondents were asked which issues people most wanted Congress and the White House to address in the coming months, they overwhelmingly cited "reforming government and making it more efficient" as the top priority, *ahead* of crime. Health care was a distant third. "It was a winner," Hart says. "It just hit, surprisingly. I mean, it was just one of these things that we just threw in and when we looked at it we said, 'Wow, he's done the right thing.' I distinctly remember saying, 'There is a guy who sort of chose the right issue at the right time and in the right way.'"

A year later, with the defeat of health care, and the White House searching for a winning issue, reinventing government was rediscovered. It is now loudly touted by the President, and will be given high priority in the second half term—a development that prompted Elaine Kamarck to remark dryly, "It's amazing what polls will do for you." The government efficiency project was a major score for Gore, and, what was most significant, it was a vital, if lonely, connection to the neglected New Democratic theology, which Clinton now desperately needs in order to survive.

There has been no more disaffected group than the New Democrats, who see the Clinton Presidency as a self-destructive denial of the source of his campaign success—namely, them. The D.L.C. was founded in 1985, after Ronald Reagan's landslide reelection, at a moment when it was clear to many Democrats that the Party might not win the White House again unless there were dramatic changes. If Republicans hated government, Democrats loved it too much, and the New Democratic idea was, at its core, simple pragmatism: to forge a centrist politics by holding that government should solve problems but first had to win faith by showing itself efficient and clean. As the ideology emerged, it acquired other tenets, such as mainstream cultural values and an emphasis on personal responsibility, which, in practical terms, gave conservative-to-moderate Democrats a reason to stop voting Republican, as they had with Reagan and Nixon. The new movement's center of gravity was the South, where the national party's leftward tilt had rendered local Democrats an endangered species, and among the D.L.C.'s earliest members was Al Gore. This politics of pragmatism was also ideally suited to the young Arkansas governor with national aspirations.

To launch his 1992 campaign, Clinton gave a series of speeches at his alma mater, Georgetown University, that were designed to frame his candidacy as a mission of the New Democratic faith. The speeches, which collectively bore the Biblical title "New Covenant," were prepared with the help of the economist Robert J. Shapiro, a vice president of the Progressive Policy Institute, and they emphasized the "new way"—the ideas of reduced, more efficient government and personal responsibility. It was in one of these "New Covenant" speeches that Clinton revealed his plan for a middle-class tax cut.

The New Democratic identity energized Clinton's candidacy by distinguishing him from the disastrous failures of such Old Democratic nominees as Michael Dukakis and Walter Mondale, and at key moments during the campaign Clinton beat back creeping doubt with a striking gesture. His formation of a Vice Presidential search committee comprised one Wasp male, one Jewish woman, and one black man. Fears arose that Clinton might yield to Old Democratic identity-politics pressures, possibly even choosing Jesse Jackson as his running mate. But he picked a fight with Jackson when he criticized the rap singer Sister Souljah. He also made an effective TV commercial about welfare reform, in which he simply looked into the camera and declared, "In my state, we've moved seventeen thousand people from welfare rolls to payrolls. It's time to make welfare what it should be—a second chance, not a way of life."

But after the election Clinton almost immediately began emitting Old Democratic signals. Fearing a repeat of Carter Administration mistakes, which had resulted in the threat of a challenge from the left and no communion with Congress, the Clinton team sought to appease its traditional base on cultural matters and align itself with the Party leadership in Congress. The D.L.C.'s Al From, who had helped shape Clinton's campaign and took a justifiable portion of credit for its success, wondered how his New Democratic President had vanished. "Just take gays in the military and add diversity," From said, "and, after just weeks of being in the White House, if there's a divide between Old and New Democrats, between cultural liberalism and mainstream values, Clinton is on the other side of that divide." Oklahoma's Dave McCurdy, reflecting on his election loss, squarely blames Clinton's quick turn away from centrism. "There were two things early on that killed them," McCurdy says. "One was gays in the military. And the second was assigning the First Lady and Ira Magaziner to health care. One became the symbol of 'You don't hold our values,' and the second became the symbol of big government."

Clinton's alliance with the congressional leadership led him into the morass of his stimulus program, a proposed spending spree that failed, but not before the battle over it had identified Clinton as more of the same Old Democrat. "I think he believed in the basic stuff that we developed here and worked with him on," From said. "I just think he was ill-prepared, because I don't think he's strong enough, in a lot of cases, to deal with this town. And when Tom Foley said, 'I don't want the line-item veto,' he said, 'O.K.' When George Mitchell said, 'We're not having a 25 percent staff cut in Congress, we've already done it,' he said, 'O.K.' When Robert Byrd said, 'You've gotta have a stimulus and let's not let any Republicans in on it,' he said, 'O.K.'"

Clinton was on a course to failure, and most maddening to From and other New Democrats was the prospect that if Clinton failed they would pay the price. For many in Congress, the term New Democrat was another way of saying what folks back home in conservative districts considered "Barely tolerable Democrat," and they were by definition the most vulnerable members of the Party. The more Clinton became an Old Democrat, the more the New Democrats, such as McCurdy and Tennessee's Jim Cooper, resisted him, until, finally, they were obliged to openly oppose the President in their campaigns for the Senate. (Both McCurdy and Cooper lost, along with a lot of other New Democrats.) Welfare reform was sidetracked in favor of the Clinton health-care proposal, which eventually managed to completely identify Clinton and the Democrats as big-government, liberal-elite federalists—exactly the thing voters were repulsed by. As the midterm storm gathered, many Party strategists were near despair. In the campaign, every time that Clinton got trapped in the Old Democratic mold, his campaign got into trouble," Al From said. "And every time he's done it since he's been President, he's got in trouble. I mean, it should be obvious. Why does he keep going back to it? That's the question. It's got to be that he squares all circles. In a sense, he doesn't see conflict. His brain doesn't allow him to see conflict from inconsistencies."

New Democrats had elected one of their own, and he was going down, which meant that it was their failure too. In the days before the midterm election, From had come to feel that maybe the Democratic Party was constitutionally incapable of change. "What I've basically decided I want to do with this operation is to operate extra-Party," he told me. "I mean, everybody knows I'm a Democrat . . . but what I want to do is get beyond the restraints of my party."

The election was a cold bath for Clinton, and although New Democrats lost at the polls, their ideas may have finally won in the White House. In the aftermath of the election, when the White House was trying to figure a new course for Clinton, Al Gore argued that the president should return to his New Democratic roots, pushing for a new emphasis on welfare reform and reducing government. There were arguments against it (led by Hillary Clinton), but Gore's side, supported by Mack McLarty, who is now counselor to the President, seems to be winning. Two days after Election Day, Clinton returned to Georgetown, where he slipped back into his New Democratic persona, inviting Republicans "to join me in the center of public debate, the place where the best ideas for the next generation must arise." And Gore, through the act of goodsoldiery, now owns the New Democratic franchise at the White House.

Many New Democrats are more than a little wary of Gore, whose inclination to cast issues, particularly those related to the environment, in apocalyptic terms—"an environmental holocaust," "An ecological Kristallnacht"—is seen by some as clouding the debate. His *Earth in the Balance,* published in 1992, became a bestseller and was cheered by environmentalists, but it came across to many others as a militantly New Age, squishy recast of industrial West-bashing. In the book, Gore equated industrialized society's need to "consume the earth and its resources" with the motivations that plunged Germany, Italy, and China into totalitarianism. We are, Gore postulated, a "dysfunctional civilization," whose drive to plunder the earth arises from an emptiness within (caused partly by an unhealthy adherence to the ideas of Plato and Descartes).

This strain of thinking, and the urge to employ the metaphor of mental illness, is not new. When Gore was at Harvard, in the late sixties, he wrote a remarkable series of letters to his father, who was working on a book, *The Eye of the Storm,* about his controversial career as a liberal Southerner. In these letters, the young government-studies major offered editorial advice, as well as his own opinions on such matters as our anti-Soviet containment policy and the Vietnam War. "We do have inveterate antipathy for communism—or paranoia as I like to put it," young Gore wrote to his father. He went on to consider the policy implications of this American Cold War obsession. "My own belief is that this form of psychological ailment—in this case a national madness—leads the victim to actually create the thing which is feared the most. It strikes me that this is precisely what the U.S. has been doing. Creating—and if not creating, energetically supporting—fascist, totalitarian regimes in the name of fighting totalitarianism. Greece, South Vietnam, a good deal of Latin America. For me, the best example of all is the U.S. Army."

At that time, Cambridge, Massachusetts, was a hothouse of political revolt, and Gore's letters reflected that influence. But he soon enlisted in the Army and served in Vietnam, partly to blunt attacks on his father for opposing the Vietnam War—a stance that cost Gore, Sr., his Senate seat in 1970.

What is most interesting about the letters, though, is Gore's response to them now. After an initial expression of dismay when I asked him about the letters ("Oh, good Lord! Oh, God! Is that a private letter? Did he share that with you? Good Lord!"), Gore quickly recovered and attempted to put the 25-year-old musings into mature perspective.

"Well, obviously, that's a college kid's silly language in the midst of a very intense period for the country," he said. "I went into the Army right after that. And I found out better. Being in the Army was one of the most important growth experiences I ever had. And it certainly allowed me to shed that nonsense. But . . . I would think that would have sounded grating to me even then. I'm surprised, I'm surprised to hear that language, really."

Of America's "national madness" and "paranoia" regarding Communism, Gore said, "That's dead wrong, too. I have very strong, inveterate antipathy myself for Communism. But in the context, as you will recall, the debate about the nature of the conflict between North Vietnam and South Vietnam was one that was defined by one side as purely a struggle against Communism, with very little appreciation for the colonial history and the nationalist dimension of the conflict. And, in that context, we certainly did have a lack of perspective on the true nature of that conflict. But Communism is an evil ideology that is enslaving and doesn't work.

"I went through changes of my view of the Vietnam conflict when I went to it. Because I found I made a lot of friends among the South Vietnamese, who were genuinely terrified of losing their freedom to Communism, for reasons that didn't fit at all into the black and-white ideological debate back home. They wanted their freedom. . . . And those of us who were opposed to the war were just wrong in not appreciating the extent to which that was a motivating cause for American policy. Now, those who supported the war were just wrong for not understanding the significance of nationalism and the colonial history that we walked into. And I still think it was a mistake for us to get into the Vietnam War. But I certainly changed my view of the country's basic motivations of getting into it."

Those letters, and Gore's response, are relevant because the arrival of the Vietnam generation at the first tier of political leadership also brought a time-warp version of the old, unresolved debates. The divides of the sixties—hawk and dove, Silent Majority, and Woodstock Nation—became the lens through which that generation is seen in middle age, and the view is kaleidoscopic. The Vietnam generation came to be judged not only by whether or not it was in the military but by the circumstances of its service or avoidance. Did Dan Quayle pull strings to enter the National Guard? Did Bill Clinton deceive in order to avoid the draft? (The ideal seems to be the experience of Bob Kerrey, who served heroically and then returned home to protest the war.) Because the Commander-in-Chief puts other people's children in harm's way, it is reasonable to question his own response to the military call. Al Gore was the son of a senator when he believed that the United States Army was "the best example" of "fascist totalitarianism"; it is worthwhile to hear his explanation of those views, and how they have changed. It is also useful to weigh politicians' current responses to questions about their actions and attitudes from that passionate time. Quayle and Clinton equivocated, and their questions linger. Gore confronted his question, and settled it.

In the days before the midterm election, when the storm could be sensed but the skies had not yet opened, I asked Gore how tightly bound his own fortunes were to those of Bill Clinton. Should future voters judge Gore on Clinton's performance? "Absolutely," he said. "Absolutely. If I decide to run for President at some point in the future, I will be happy and honored to be judged by the accomplishments of Bill Clinton's Administration. And I *ought* to be judged on that basis if I ever run, in significant measure because I've worked so hard as a part of this team."

But Gore also noted, in his careful, measured way, a distinction between himself and the president. "My principal goal is to help the President do the best that he possibly can," Gore said. "And so my own record as Vice President is necessarily obscured, in significant measure because so much of my energy goes into trying to help him. And I take pride in his accomplishment and the accomplishments of his Cabinet, and the others around here that I help out. But inevitably there are some things that he asks me to play a particularly prominent role in helping to handle, like the environment, or reinventing government, or the information superhighway, or the empowerment zones, or violence prevention, and others, that, I think, will have an identifiable record of accomplishment associated with them." In other words, Gore hopes to perform the hard trick of laying down his own record as Vice President, but to do it quietly—to be distinct from Clinton without being seen as trying to distinguish himself from his boss.

It is one of the curious features of this Administration that the Vice President, whose job has little inherent purpose, has managed to be perceived as successful while the President has not. Any open rift would sour the relationship that made Gore's success possible. "The main thing that makes it click is the acknowledged level of confidence that the President has in the Vice President," Roy Neel says. "If the president went south on Al Gore, and started saying to some of his top advisers, inside or out, something that represented disapproval of Al Gore, or a lack of confidence, or something that suggested that he was working on his own agenda, then you would see the Vice President's resources just dry up overnight. You would see him getting bad-mouthed by the insiders and by the consultants and people like that in print."

Friends of Gore hope that the free rein given their man by Clinton may prove Gore's political salvation. "If you have one defining event in your entire Vice Presidency, you're lucky," Carter Eskew, who was Gore's media adviser during the 1988 Presidential run, says. "What was Bush's? Iran–Contra. What was Quayle's? Was it 'potatoe' or just getting chosen? But Al has had this series of huge successes. I mean, the Perot debate—unbelievable, he slew the dragon, and Perot's never recovered. The reinventing government. Dealing with Ukraine. And I said to him, 'You only need one a year.'"

As it happens, Gore is most identified with the one Clinton Administration policy that is most attuned to the national voter mood—reducing government. And he has not been identified with health care, the Clinton undertaking that represented the paternalistic style of governance that strikes an antipathetic chord.

But, ultimately, Gore may find distance from Clinton in the fact that much of the antagonism directed toward the President is personal, reflecting lingering doubts about the draft, his personal life, and his honesty. "The nature of Clinton's problems is such that Gore's sort of protected," Al From suggests. "Gore didn't have anything to do with Whitewater. He hasn't had anything to do with any of the womanizing stuff. You didn't see Gore out there on the hustings for health care. So he's sort of untainted by the stuff that has made Clinton the most vulnerable."

Back in Carthage, Tennessee, Pauline Gore, who raised her boy to be President, is candid about her fears that a Clinton failure will hurt her son's chances. But Al Gore, she reminds us, is not Bill Clinton. "He will be damaged politically," Mrs. Gore says. "But the important things about Al will not be damaged. His character, his ability, his honesty, his integrity."

Last week, Gore, still digesting the midterm-election disaster, said he wasn't focusing on his own political future just now. "There are too many contingencies," he said. "There are too many uncertainties." With the president and Mrs. Clinton out of town on business in the Far East, Gore called a series of meetings with advisers at the White House to help chart a political course for the next two years. "I'm not going to belabor a case that this election has made everything easier," the Vice President said. But it is clear that he believes the case for Al Gore was not decided by the rebuke of Bill Clinton on November 8. "I would like," Gore said, "to be President one day."

CHAPTER 7

Tip O'Neill:
Lessons for Leadership
from the "Man of the House"

RICHARD A. LOVERD[1]

As I look back on my career, I would love to claim that my rise from humble member of Congress to Speaker of the House followed a natural and easy path, and that my political and legislative abilities were so self-evident that I was everybody's first choice by acclamation.

But politics doesn't work that way. If I was talented, so were a hundred other guys who served with me. Why, then, did I become Speaker whereas they didn't?[2]

—Tip O'Neill

By the time Thomas P. "Tip" O'Neill entered the U.S. House of Representatives in January of 1953, he was hardly a newcomer to the game of politics. He was, after all, a product of Boston, a realm well-known as a spawning ground for legendary public figures since the start of the republic.

Born and bred in the highly political working-class Irish Catholic neighborhood of North Cambridge and voted "class politician" by his 1936 senior class at Boston College, this "work and wages" New Deal liberal entered the Massachusetts House in 1937 and, by 1948, had engineered a Democratic majority to become the first Democratic Speaker in the history of the state.[3] Little wonder, then, that during his fifty years in public life[4] he might rise to even greater stature as the Speaker of the House[5] in our nation's capital and serve in that capacity for ten years—"the longest continuous term for any Speaker since Congress first met in 1789."[6]

Not to say that such ascension was a certainty. For, as Mr. O'Neill notes in his memoirs, "The answer [to my becoming Speaker] has to do with a combination of factors, including timing, fate, money, personality, and even tragedy—not to mention the usual list of human frailties, feuds and jealousies."[7] And while some of these factors were under his control, others were not.

In fact, throughout his political career, it was as much the moves of others as those of his own that played key roles in propelling his rise to Speaker. For example, in 1952 it was Representative John F. Kennedy's move to the Senate that created the House vacancy he was to fill. Later on, once having arrived in Washington, the presence of another Massachusetts politician, seasoned House leader John McCormack, proved pivotal in providing him with a mentor who could help move his career along. And still later, in October 1972, the untimely disappearance of majority leader Hale Boggs in a plane flight over Alaska provided yet another key vacancy for him to fill en route to becoming Speaker. Moreover, during the bulk of his years in office, the presence of a general public attitude which was supportive of a more expansive and active governmental role[8] provided the perfect complement for this New Deal liberal legislator who promoted public policies reflecting his belief that "the government has a moral responsibility to help people who can't take care of themselves."[9]

Therefore, while some of his success could be attributed to his own hard work and talent, other circumstances beyond his direct control did much to further his career. Nonetheless, the fact that Mr. O'Neill was able to recognize such events as opportunities and obtain the necessary support to take advantage of them provides ample testament to the effectiveness of his leadership skills.

How did Mr. O'Neill approach the task of leadership? What sorts of strategies and tactics did he use to rise to power and make effective use of his public office? As a start toward answering these questions, a review of a number of his perspectives will be presented as a series of "lessons" to be learned from this "man of the house."

APPROACHING THE LEADERSHIP TASK: LEARNING HOW TO PLAY THE GAME

Tip O'Neill loved sports about as much as he loved politics, and both involved learning how to work with the rules and the players of the game. In fact, his very nickname, "Tip," was derived from a late nineteenth-century St. Louis Browns baseball player by the name of Edward O'Neill, who knew the rules of the game very well, so well in fact that in 1887 he used them to generate the remarkable batting average of .492. Because the rules allowed walks to be counted as hits in those days, this player would keep on foul tipping pitch after pitch until the pitcher would miss the strike zone four times and produce a "hit" for him. It was those shrewd foul tips that earned him the name of "Tip" O'Neill, an altogether fitting moniker for both the early sportsman and the latter-day politician as leaders who patiently found ways to play the game to their advantage.

As we will see in the lessons that follow, in Speaker O'Neill's case, he learned how to work with the rules and players of the game of politics and increase his "batting average" by patiently pursuing a leadership approach which involved (1) taking a local, inside view, (2) getting to know, and becoming known, to the players, (3) exchanging favors for support, and (4) learning how to count.

LESSON 1: TAKE A LOCAL, INSIDE VIEW

In a very real sense, this first lesson, reflecting the Speaker's oft-cited phrase that "All politics is local," provides the basis for the O'Neill approach to leadership and helps frame all the other lessons to follow. Indeed, perhaps as a way of emphasizing just such a point, the only other book the Speaker wrote beyond his memoirs was one entitled, *All Politics Is Local and Other Rules of the Game.*[10]

At base, this perspective stresses that a leader should never lose touch with his or her followers, the constituents. Tip learned this lesson all too well early in life when, in his first race for Cambridge City Council, he lost by 160 votes "because I took my neighborhood for granted."[11] He never did so again, making certain to keep his voters informed and tending to their needs as directly and effectively as possible. As he later observed:

> A politician learns that if a constituent calls about a problem, even if it's a streetlight out, you don't tell them to call City Hall. *You* call City Hall.
>   Members of the House learn this quicker than anyone else because they only have a two-year term. They learn that if you don't pay attention to the voters, you soon will find yourself right back there with them.[12]

Perhaps this viewpoint helps to explain why, as a congressman, he consistently won his elections, running unopposed in five of them and never dropping below 69 percent of the two-party vote.[13] And perhaps as a way of reminding people and public servants of its continued importance, in the election year of 1994 the *New York Times* observed that the O'Neill phrase "All politics is local" appeared in newspapers and magazines across the country a total of 588 times.[14]

The significance of this local perspective helps to explain why those legislators who take a "wholesale" view of their leadership roles by addressing larger national, international, or generally more grandiose concerns without first paying attention to the more "retail," individual parochial needs of their constituents do so at their own risk.[15] According to Christopher Matthews, Speaker O'Neill's former chief spokesman, several well-known figures in American politics, including J. William Fulbright of Arkansas, Frank Church of Idaho, and Albert Gore, Sr., of Tennessee, experienced rejection because they had taken the wholesale approach and "had caught a bad case of Potomac fever, becoming more familiar in the salons of Georgetown than in the meeting halls back home."[16]

And in another, less fatal but equally compelling instance, Mr. Matthews relates how House Republican leader Robert H. Michel of Illinois learned that the "All politics is local" lesson is just as relevant in Peoria as it is in Cambridge. It seems that during the latter part of the 1982 congressional election year, Speaker O'Neill brought a $1 billion jobs bill to the House floor which the Republicans, through majority leader Michel, roundly criticized as the worst sort of election year boondoggle. In response, the Speaker, armed with information about Michel's own backyard of Peoria, took to the House floor and "began reading the names and street locations of the bridges in Peoria that were below Illinois state safety standards, each of which would be eligible for repair under the proposed jobs bill the Republicans had been attacking as 'make-work,' another damned New Deal leaf-raking bill."[17] In so doing:

> As the Speaker read his litany of hazard areas into the record, his words were carried via cable TV directly into the Republican leader's district. Minutes before, Michel had been playing the grand and dutiful role of national party spokesman. Now he was in a local damage-control mode. Red-faced, he stood in the back of the House chamber giving frantic instructions to his press secretary.[18]

Therefore, as a way of avoiding such embarrassing and debilitating circumstances which place large-scale over local interests, the Speaker recommends that legislators lead by taking the parochial, retail approach first:

> . . . pay attention to [your] own backyard and take care of [your] folks. . . . Keep them informed and you will find that they will like and respect you and allow you to be a "national" Congressman and vote for things that are good for the country but may not have a direct impact on your district."[19]

Of course, for O'Neill, these same local views were just as applicable to leading the "backyard" of Congress as the district back home. A master of the "inside game," he made a point of focusing on how the people and processes of the legislative system worked, so that he could work with them in moving desired legislation forward.

The Speaker was particularly baffled by those leaders choosing to play an "outside game," by not only campaigning against the Washington establishment but *also* attempting to govern without working with its players once in office. As spokesman Matthews mentions: "It is one thing to run against institutions. It's another to declare war against the very people you are going to have to work with."[20] In this regard, one of the Speaker's earliest encounters with a newly elected outsider, President Jimmy Carter, particularly comes to mind. In their very first conversation, O'Neill recalled, "[President Carter] told me how he had handled the Georgia legislature, by going over their heads directly to the people. I said, 'Hey, wait a minute, you have 289 guys up there [the House Democrats] who know their districts pretty well . . . and they wouldn't hesitate to run against you.' He said, 'Oh, really?' "[21] Obviously, there was a difference in viewpoint between the outsider president and the insider Speaker, a difference which tended to foretell many of the problems in governance the president would encounter in the months to come.

From the Speaker's perspective, instead of attacking or avoiding the players, the president, or any leader, for that matter, should follow the rules of the inside game by working with those players and, as the next two lessons suggest, (1) getting to know, and becoming known, to them, and (2) being willing to exchange favors with them.

LESSON 2: GET TO KNOW, AND BECOME KNOWN, TO THE PLAYERS

Tip O'Neill enjoyed getting to know people, as individuals as much as in group settings, and this trait undoubtedly helped provide him with the social networks needed to enhance his leadership and move his career forward. People of all stripes enjoyed being around him and the feeling was mutual, except perhaps for an occasional Republican or a contentious member of the press.

Of course not all politicians were as good at building personal relationships as he. For example, former Speaker Sam Rayburn once described President Woodrow Wilson as a "cold snake. . . . No, snake's not the word—cold fish. He'd look at you cold and steady through those thick glasses. He loved people in the mass, but I don't think he gave a damn about them as individuals."[22] And somewhat ironically, Speaker Rayburn himself was exclusive in his encounters, choosing to deal with only a select few in Congress while generally ignoring the rest. Of course, the context of Congress for leadership was different in those days, more readily allowing such behavior. As majority leader (and future Speaker) Jim Wright noted:

> In Mr. Rayburn's day, about all a majority leader or speaker needed to do in order to get his program adopted was to deal effectively with perhaps 12 very senior committee chairmen. They, in turn, could be expected to influence their committees and their subcommittee chairmen whom they, in those days appointed. . . .
>
> Well, now that situation is quite considerably different. There are, I think, 153 subcommittees . . . basically about all the leadership has nowadays is a hunting license to persuade—if we can.[23]

As part of that process of persuasion, current contexts suggest that leaders should reach out, get to know, and become known by their prospective followers much more than in the past.

Interestingly, during his early years in politics, even John Kennedy had his problems in meeting people in one-on-one encounters. According to one account:

> When O'Neill and Jack Kennedy once appeared together at a firemen's breakfast in East Cambridge, O'Neill was surprised to see Kennedy sneak out the back door after his speech. O'Neill knew you didn't win votes that way. "[Kennedy] hated the part of politics of the shaking of the hands. He just hated it."[24]

However, by the time Mr. Kennedy reached the Senate, his views about getting to know people must have changed somewhat, because the one piece of advice he passed along to newly elected Representative O'Neill was: "Tip, don't do what I did down there. Be nice to [Democratic leader] John McCormack."[25] Obviously, Kennedy's appreciation of the need for politicians to cast a wider net and get to know a wider range of individuals had grown over time.

And cast a wide net O'Neill did. With his family remaining in Cambridge while he lived in Washington, he had plenty of time to reach out and get to know the capital's players. Unlike Speaker Rayburn, he made a point of meeting and conferring with a wide range of legislators, Democrats and Republicans, on and off the job. In addition to seeing them at work, as one loathe to cook a meal he also dined out with them at breakfast, lunch, and dinner. And on several evenings each week, he played another game with them, poker, which, oddly enough, served to strengthen his hand in the game of politics by providing further opportunities for him to build friendships, trade information, and learn about the strengths and weaknesses of his fellow politicians. In fact, it was one of those poker players from the Wednesday night game, Ohio Democrat Michael J. Kirwan, who in 1970 helped pave the way for Mr. O'Neill's succeeding him as chair of the highly influential Democratic Congressional Campaign Committee.

And then there was John McCormack, a fellow Massachusetts Democrat from a neighboring congressional district who was indeed worth "being nice to." Actually, the two already knew and respected each other long before John Kennedy's advisory, for in 1948 it was McCormack who gave O'Neill the idea of trying to break Republican rule and make the state house Democratic. Obviously, O'Neill's subsequent success could only have warmed the elder Democrat's heart. In McCormack's case, Tip had much to admire as well, starting with his well-earned position as House minority whip (soon to become majority leader and then Speaker in 1961) and all the connections that that implied, connections that McCormack was more than willing to share with the newcomer. As O'Neill recalls, "I knew that he liked me, but I wasn't prepared for the great kindness and generosity that he extended to me from the time I came in until the day he retired in 1970 after serving nine years as Speaker."[26]

With no children of his own, O'Neill became like a "political son" to McCormack, accompanying the leader to all kinds of gatherings where, in addition to legislators, he met "generals, admirals, cabinet members, ambassadors, and other prominent people" who comprised the key players of Washington. At first, people thought "the big Irishman with McCormack" was his bodyguard, but that perception was soon dispelled when everywhere they went, McCormack introduced him as "Tom O'Neill. Tom was Speaker of the Massachusetts legislature. He's in Congress now and I want you to keep your eye on him. Someday he may become Speaker of the House."[27] As O'Neill observed, such introductions from "one of the most powerful men in Washington . . . opened a lot of doors for me. Because of my association with McCormack, not to mention all the people he introduced me to, I was able to get things done a little easier than most of the other junior members of the House."[28] And the doors open to him grew wider still during his second term in office when, with McCormack's help, O'Neill became one of the youngest members ever to secure an appointment from Speaker Sam Rayburn to the powerful House Rules Committee.

Eventually, with McCormack's assistance, O'Neill "knew, or claimed he knew, the names of at least one person he could ask for help in every major government agency," what he called his "happy faculty," which gave him a reputation among his colleagues as one who "had good contacts downtown," contacts which could help to forge friendships in Congress.[29]

LESSON 3: EXCHANGE FAVORS FOR SUPPORT

Of course, contacts alone do not guarantee ongoing support for a leader. For Tip O'Neill, the exchange of favors was also necessary—personal favors which seal connections, build loyalty, and reflect the reality that one hand washes the other in getting elected and being effective once in office.

It was during his first electoral campaign that the importance of the most basic of favors, the favor of asking people for support, was taught to him in a lesson he was to recount for years to come. On election eve his high school elocution and drama teacher from across the street, a Mrs. Elizabeth O'Brien, stopped by and told him, "Tom, I'm going to vote for you tomorrow even if you didn't ask me to."

> This shocked me, to be perfectly truthful. "Why Mrs. O'Brien," I said, "I've lived across the street from you for eighteen years. I cut your grass in the summer, I shovel your walk in the winter. I haul out your ashes. I didn't think I had to ask you for your vote."
> "Tom," she replied, "let me tell you something: people like to be asked."[30]

In the eyes of this budding leader, "She gave me the lesson of my life, which is why I've been telling that story for fifty years. . . . It's true: people *do* like to be asked—and they also like to be thanked."[31]

"Big favors, little favors, medium-size favors. People did not forget them [and] neither did O'Neill. [For example,] he, or the people who helped in his campaigns, kept a list [and] those who owed him favors were eventually called and asked to help get out the vote on election day."[32] Once in office, the trading of favors continued, with both constituents and colleagues. With constituents, favors provided the very essence of public service from O'Neill's perspective: "We run a public service operation here. Every time [constituents have] a problem with the . . . government, they wind up in our office. . . . Public service, personal favors, are the norm, the way politicians operate."[33] And with colleagues, the use of favors also proved pivotal as a way to build alliances to win leadership positions and enact favorable legislation.

A good example of favors in action took place when, in 1948, O'Neill successfully sought to break the long-standing Republican hold on the Massachusetts House and become its Speaker. After a survey was generated pinpointing 40 potentially vulnerable Republican House districts, a campaign war chest of $26,000 was created with the help of such luminaries as John McCormack, John Kennedy, Paul Dever, and James Michael Curley. Next, the most popular, promising Democratic candidates were sought out and encouraged to run in those districts in exchange for having all of their expenses paid by the party's war chest. The strategy worked, with 38 of the 40 seats becoming Democratic and an overall Democratic margin of victory of 122 to 118 seats.[34]

While the margin was clearly a win for the Democrats, it was less clear that a Democratic House Speaker would result. After all, a swing of 3 votes could give the post to a Republican, and with the "proper encouragement," certain Democrats might not show or otherwise defect to the Republican camp. Indeed, right up until the vote on January 5, 1949, there were rumors that as many as eight Democrats might be induced to trade votes for Republican offers of $2,500 (for no-shows) or $5,000 (for outright defections). But the Democratic leadership could trade favors too, and trade they did by producing five individuals from the Republican side who would, if necessary, change their votes in favor of O'Neill, with the promise of judgeships or key departmental posts in the offing. When the votes were finally cast, O'Neill defeated Republican Representative Charles Gibbons of Stoneham by a margin of 122 to 116, and while the "bargain with the five Republicans had not been put to the test and so, of course, there was no need for special favors, . . . the five representatives were thereafter given very particular consideration by both the governor [Paul Dever] and the Speaker."[35]

In 1970, similar sorts of favors were used when Congressman O'Neill succeeded poker partner Michael Kirwan as chair of the Democratic Congressional Campaign Committee (DCCC). As a party organization charged with providing campaign funds to Democratic candidates for the House, it proved an ideal repository for the distribution of favors which could significantly build personal loyalty and strengthen Tip's leadership prospects. And distribute them he did—to his credit, much more effectively than his predecessor. Realizing that money was the lifeblood of politics, he targeted funds with more precision than Mr. Kirwan by discarding the previous practice of automatically providing $500 to every Democratic candidate running for office. Instead, on the basis of studies of districts and polls, he chose to be more selective by "[giving] out money only to candidates who really needed it, and only if they stood a chance of winning,"[36] just as he had done earlier in Massachusetts. And for those who did win, obviously some measure of gratitude could be directed toward O'Neill.

In addition to funding—also unlike Mr. Kirwan, who preferred to stay in Washington—Tip provided more direct personal support in home districts as he traveled throughout the country on behalf of candidates, campaigning for them and meeting local party officials. In so doing, he noted that while ". . . I attended more cocktail parties than I care to remember. . . . I also did a lot of favors and became known as something of a power in the party,"[37] a power based on favors which could be traded to secure desired legislation and/or move up the Democratic Party leadership ladder.

While still serving as chair of the DCCC, a favor from another source came his way which demonstrates how such kindnesses can cut in both directions. With the 1972 elections approaching, the large-scale defeat of presidential candidate George McGovern appeared a certainty. O'Neill was worried that such a loss would diminish the prospects for other Democratic candidates running for the House that year, and on the flight back from the Democratic National Convention in Miami he shared his concerns with Robert Strauss, the treasurer of the Democratic National Committee at the time. Strauss responded by saying that he would help the DCCC by raising a million dollars in ten days through fund-raising events held across the country. Tip's skepticism at such a promise turned to delight when, ten days later, a million dollars was indeed raised. Divided equally between House and Senate candidates, those additional funds helped to elect a good number of Democrats despite the 1972 Nixon landslide.

The next year, Robert Strauss asked O'Neill for a favor in return: an endorsement for becoming chair of the Democratic National Committee. While O'Neill was happy to oblige, his support dismayed some of the more liberal Democrats in his party because Strauss was viewed as no friend of labor. In response to such criticism, O'Neill stressed that his support was indeed justified "Because one hand washes the other. . . . Because when we were stone broke, he's the guy who came through for us."[38] Favors are to be honored and exchange of favors expected—that's what friends are for, and how the game is played.

One further set of favors worthy of mention involved the exchange of information itself. Starting with his days on the Rules Committee, O'Neill had served as a source of informal information for House members, one in the know that others could turn to; and as he moved up to successively more important positions (from majority whip, to majority leader, to Speaker), his need for information grew only greater. Indeed, according to former spokesman Christopher Matthews, the "one failing he would not suffer [was] being out of the know. For a leader and lieutenants not to know what the members were up to was the national equivalent of that worst political sin, losing touch with the people back home in the district."[39] Consequently, he was constantly on the lookout for new information that would keep him abreast of the latest developments.

However, in addition to *receiving* information about House members, this leader went one step further and made a point of *sending* "a constant stream in the other direction," so that the members might have a better idea of what the leaders had in mind, and why. "Whenever the congressional leadership went to the White House for a meeting, I distributed notes to the members. I also made sure that . . . regular information packets were sent out to help the members become more knowledgeable about upcoming legislation."[40] Through such a more systematic, regularized exchange of information,[41] O'Neill expected that followers might be not only better informed, but also more inclined to work together with the party leadership, particularly at a time when Congress was opening up and party loyalty was on the decline.[42]

Of course, not all public officials shared O'Neill's view of this sort of "get along, go along" inside game involving the exchange of favors, and once again President Jimmy Carter particularly comes to mind. An outsider, his approach was clearly different. In part, this difference in perspective was shaped by a difference in backgrounds. As the president's press secretary, Jody Powell, noted at the time, "They're different sorts of folks . . . a rural Southern Protestant outside the system, and an Irish Catholic from Boston who has come up the way you're supposed to come up."[43] To Jimmy Carter, Tip O'Neill represented "the kind of crony-loving, patronage-oriented machine politician he had fought his entire political life," while for O'Neill, Carter "reminded him of the bloodless, moralistic, self-contained Yankees of his child-hood—autocrats and technocrats with no feeling for the human side."[44] Furthermore, as presidential scholar Stephen Hess relates: "Carter wanted to lead by standing above the tangle of normal politics. He wanted to advocate policies solely on merit. He saw himself as 'doing what's right, not what's political,' in the words of Charles O. Jones."[45] Consequently, rather than trade favors with Washington players for support of his policies, he preferred the pursuit of more moral and rational bases for governance.

Such a preference during the Carter years helps to explain why the president's top staff person, Hamilton Jordan, would say that "We don't play the heavy patronage game," and why, in the selection of many top personnel, a selection committee would be formed to seek "the best persons for each position, regardless of political ties."[46] It also helps to explain why Carter's first two major White House appointments from Massachusetts, Pittsfield Mayor Evan Dobelle and former cabinet officer and ambassador to Great Britain Elliot L. Richardson, were both Republicans, and why "jurisdiction over appointments and programs [within departments] was left to cabinet officers, instead of being concentrated in the White House."[47] It even explains why this president would choose "to review [and seek to eliminate] 19 major water-development projects already authorized and funded by Congress and signed into law . . . [projects which] involved jobs and contracts—and, of course, the whole pork-barrel, log-rolling tradition so beloved of Congress . . . calling them 'of doubt-ful necessity now, in light of new conditions and environmental policies.' "[48] But such actions during the early months of Carter's Administration did little to endear him to Tip O'Neill and the other legislators in Congress.

In O'Neill's view, after eight years of having to endure Republicans in office, President Carter was weakening his governance by ignoring and wasting patronage, the favors that lubricate and direct the political system toward policy victories. "We won the election, but you'd never know it,"[49] the Speaker said. "Control of patronage meant control of policy; and the president's failure to make effective use of patronage had undermined party discipline in the Congress," he complained, "preventing the leadership from welding the Democrats into a cohesive group and leaving policy objectives in doubt."[50]

Perhaps, as Speaker O'Neill notes in his memoirs, President Carter "never really understood [or wanted to understand] how the system worked,"[51] particularly with regard to the reality of the legislature. Clearly, "a Congress of 535 men and women, elected on individual merit, divided into two large bodies and subdivided into committees and subcommittees, operates differently than one man in the Oval Office. Of necessity, Congress approaches problems in a piecemeal manner. Various aspects of one major issue may be handled in half a dozen different committees. No one person is in charge of it."[52] As Congressman John Brademas observed at the time:

> Carter tended to think comprehensively and rationally. Not that we think irrationally. But Carter tended to say, "Okay, what's the problem? Let's analyze it, look at the pros

and cons, what's best for the country." Then he'd say, "We're going to have a comprehensive this and a comprehensive that." We don't operate that way and we cannot operate that way. We're piecemeal incrementalists.[53]

Therefore, in such a congressional climate, even if one *thinks* comprehensively and rationally, rarely is one able to *actually produce* outcomes in a similar fashion. For Tip O'Neill, favors, patronage are needed to put together coalitions of legislators to even begin to attain those objectives.

CONCLUDING LESSON 4: LEARN HOW TO COUNT

Former Senate Republican leader Howard H. Baker, Jr., once said, "The most important part of a Senate majority leader's education is over by the third grade; he has learned to count."[54]

Tip O'Neill learned this lesson well. For him, the job of leader involved cobbling together people and favors in order to count the votes necessary to build winning coalitions. As political scientist Randall Ripley observed:

> . . . his ability to talk to all sides on an issue within his party, to help engineer winning compromises, and to assert his preferences in a personal manner that left even those opposed to his positions in agreement that he was a fine person and an effective leader [helped to explain a number of his legislative successes]. He was tireless in visiting with members of the House, lobbyists, the president, and other executive branch officials. He had seemingly boundless capacities for hard work, compromise, and doing a series of personal favors for individuals. Thus, depite the decentralization of power throughout the subcommittee system that had occurred in the previous years, O'Neill could operate as the undoubted central figure of the House.[55]

"As [O'Neill himself] liked to say, you put the people together, job by job, favor by favor, and you get a program, a bill, a policy. Fail in this basic rule of politics and there will be only a hollow ache in an ethically pure heart."[56]

In a meeting with President Carter, the Speaker once recounted the story of a father who tore a map of the world out of a magazine, cut it in small pieces and asked his son to reassemble it. In very short order, the son had put it together. Amazed, the father asked his son how he had done it:

> "Dad," the boy replied, "on the back of the map there's a picture of a boy's face. I just put the boy's face together and turned it over, and the map of the world was there."
>
> "The moral of the story," says Tip O'Neill, "is that if you put the people together rightly, the world will take care of itself."[57]

NOTES

1. The author wishes to thank Leah Weisse, Project Archivist for the Thomas P. O'Neill, Jr., Papers, Congressional Archives at the Burns Library, Boston College, for her comments and suggestions on an earlier draft of this chapter.

2. Tip O'Neill, *Man of the House: The Life and Political Memoirs of Speaker Tip O'Neill* (New York: St. Martin's Press, 1987), p. 147.

3. Ibid., p. xiv. See also "House Speakers: 1780–1980," in Cornelius Dalton, John Wirkkala, and Anne Thomas, *Leading the Way: A History of the Massachusetts General Court, 1629–1980* (Boston: Office of the Massachusetts Secretary of State, 1984), pp. 403–427.

4. See "Thomas P. O'Neill: A Chronology," in Series IIIA, Personal Papers: Biographical Information and Awards, 1973–1974, Thomas P. O'Neill, Jr., Papers, Burns Library, Boston College.

5. See "The Role of the Speaker," in *How Congress Works,* 2nd ed. (Washington, D.C.: Congressional Quarterly Press, 1991), pp. 9–21.

6. O'Neill, *Man of the House,* p. xii.

7. Ibid., p. 247.

8. Interestingly, such a public attitude seems to be in retreat. See, for example, Alison Mitchell, "In New York, the Dying Days of Expansive Government," *New York Times,* May 8, 1995, p. 1, and see the chapter on Speaker Newt Gingrich included in this volume.

9. O'Neill, *Man of the House,* p. xv. See also O'Neill's "Epilogue: What I Believe," in the same volume, pp. 451–454.

10. Tip O'Neill, *All Politics Is Local and Other Rules of the Game* (New York: Times Books, 1994).

11. Ibid., p. xv.

12. Ibid., p. xvi.

13. Robert L. Peabody, "House Party Leadership: Stability and Change," in Lawrence C. Dodd and Bruce I. Oppenheimer, *Congress Reconsidered,* 3rd ed. (Washington, D.C.: Congressional Quarterly Press, 1985), p. 265.

14. "All Politics Is Local," *New York Times Magazine,* January 1, 1995, p. 29.

15. Christopher Matthews, *Hardball: How Politics Is Played by One Who Knows the Game* (New York: Harper and Row, 1988), p. 45.

16. Ibid., p. 47.

17. Ibid., p. 49.

18. Ibid.

19. O'Neill, *All Politics Is Local,* p. xvi.

20. Matthews, *Hardball,* p. 34.

21. Martin Tolchin, "An Old Pol Takes on the New President," *New York Times Magazine,* July 24, 1977, p. 6.

22. Matthews, *Hardball,* p. 44.

23. Christopher J. Deering and Stephen S. Smith, "Majority Party Leadership and the New House Subcommittee System," in *Understanding Congressional Leadership,* ed. Frank H. Mackaman (Washington, D.C.: Congressional Quarterly Press, 1981), pp. 288–289.

24. Paul Clancy and Shirley Elder, *Tip: A Biography of Thomas P. O'Neill, Speaker of the House* (New York: Macmillan Publishing Co., (1980), p. 70.

25. Ibid., p. 85.

26. O'Neill, *Man of the House,* pp. 139–140.

27. Ibid., p. 141.

28. Ibid.

29. Clancy and Elder, *Tip,* p. 86.

30. O'Neill, *All Politics Is Local,* p. 8.

31. O'Neill, *Man of the House,* p. 25.

32. Clancy and Elder, *Tip,* p. 45.

33. Ibid., p. 90.

34. For a slightly different view of this incident, and of Massachusetts Democratic Party politics, see Ted Frier and Larry Overlan, *Time for a Change: The Return of the Republican Party in Massachusetts* (Worchester, Mass.: Davis Press, 1992), pp. 90–91.

35. Clancy and Elder, *Tip,* pp. 62–63.

36. Ibid., pp. 247–248.

37. Ibid., p. 248.

38. Ibid., p. 250.

39. Matthews, *Hardball,* p. 132.

40. O'Neill, *Man of the House,* p. 264.

41. The actual White House meeting notes can found in Series IIA: 2, Legislative/Staff Office Files: Eleanor Kelley's Files, 1954–1986, Thomas P. O'Neill, Jr., Papers, Burns Library, Boston College. In addition, the information packets can be found in Series IIB: 5, Administrative and Party Affiliation Files: Whip and Democratic Study Group Publications, 1971–1986, Thomas P. O'Neill, Jr., Papers, Burns Library, Boston College.

42. O'Neill, *Man of the House,* p. 265.

43. Tolchin, "An Old Pol," p. 6.

44. Ibid.

45. Stephen Hess, *Organizing the Presidency,* 2nd ed. (Washington, D.C.: Brookings Institution, 1988), p. 152.

46. Clancy and Elder, *Tip,* p. 215.

47. Tolchin, "An Old Pol," p. 9.

48. Ibid., p. 6.

49. Ibid., p. 9.

50. Ibid., p. 9.

51. O'Neill, *Man of the House,* p. 355.

52. Clancy and Elder, *Tip,* p. 217.

53. Ibid.

54. Matthews, *Hardball,* p. 33.

55. Randall B. Ripley, *Congress: Process and Policy,* 3rd ed. (New York: W.W. Norton, 1983), p. 221.

56. Clancy and Elder, *Tip,* p. 4.

57. Tolchin, "An Old Pol," p. 43.

CHAPTER 8

Howard H. Baker, Jr.:
A Legislative Leader as White
House Chief of Staff—
Building Leadership Power
in the Senate and the White House

RICHARD A. LOVERD[1]

The presence of Ronald Reagan in the White House was a central factor; the Republican Senators wanted him to succeed, and they knew that it was he who set the Congressional agenda. But the explosive personal and ideological mix in the Senate had to be harnessed, and, for that task, [Majority Leader] Howard Baker was the key.[2]

[As Chief of Staff] Howard Baker may not have been a man for all seasons. But in the seminal political crisis of the Reagan Administration, he proved the right man for the moment.[3]

The oil can is mightier than the sword.[4]

SETTING A NEW COURSE IN THE SENATE

By the time Howard Baker became majority leader in 1981, he was by no means a stranger to the Senate, nor, for that matter, to the ways of Washington. He had had Potomac politics in his veins for quite some time, both by upbringing and by marriage. His father (also Howard Baker) had been a congressman from 1951 until his death in 1964, and his father-in-law was former Senate Minority Leader Everett McKinley Dirksen. Therefore, it was no surprise that this Tennessee trial lawyer would continue the family tradition and run for elective office the same year his father died.

However, what *was* surprising was that he eschewed his father's vacant House seat and sought a Senate post instead. Unfortunately, during his first electoral attempt, time was not on his side and he was buried in the Johnson presidential landslide of 1964. Undaunted, two years later he tried again. This time more seasoned and more astute, he won senatorial office, the first Republican ever to do so from the Volunteer State.

Three years after arriving in Washington, upon the death of his father-in-law, he sought the position of minority leader. That effort, and another in 1971, fell short as Pennsylvania Senator Hugh Scott won, and then kept, the post. However, in 1977, upon Scott's retirement, Senator Baker's experience and persistence paid off. By one vote, he outpolled a new rival (and former Scott whip), Michigan Senator Robert Griffin, and became minority leader. Four years later, the Reagan landslide brought him majority status.

Therefore, given this personal history, Mr. Baker had added much to his power by the time he became majority leader. He had been literally born into the profession of politics by blood and betrothal; and when he arrived in Washington, he had had the benefit of counsel and direct assistance from a highly placed father-in-law to further anoint him and familiarize him with the ways of Washington. In addition, though some might argue that his 1964 Senate campaign and his first two attempts at securing the Senate party leadership post were premature, those losses added to his seasoning by providing opportunities for learning grace in defeat, and proving a certain admirable persistence on his part.

Moreover, Baker's fourteen years in the Senate lent experience and maturity to his stature which made him all the more able, and credible, when he finally took majority office. He had, for example, shown political fortitude and independence of judgment by opposing his father-in-law on the latter's attempts to halt the speedy implementation of the Supreme Court's famous "one-man, one-vote" redistricting decision, and by persuading Mr. Dirksen to drop his continued opposition to open housing civil rights legislation. Furthermore, in 1968 he had endorsed Richard Nixon and been considered as a possible vice-presidential running mate. Five years later, as the vice chairman and ranking Republican on the Senate Watergate Committee, he had attempted to separate that same president from the actions of his subordinates by calmly and persistently asking the well-crafted, lawyer-like, and now-famous question, "What did the president know and when did he know it?" And during the Carter years, much to the chagrin of conservatives, he had helped shepherd the Panama Canal treaty through the Senate.

Throughout all this preparatory period, he developed a very strong reputation as a highly credible master of negotiation and human relations skills. While clearly an individual who tended to lean to the right, he was more a pragmatist than an ideologue, whose "eclectic alignment on issues, ranging from a liberal position on open housing to a hard-line position on military spending, points to the flexibility that helps people get ahead in Congress."[5] Indeed, in 1979 the senator himself stressed that "Government by ideological reflex, left or right, will not bring the unity we need. . . . I can appeal to the broadest range of support."[6] As a consequence, most observers tended to view him as a "conciliator or consensus-builder in a pluralist branch"[7] who pursued "a moderate, stable approach to government"[8] with a "genius for finding the compromise point and pushing it through."[9] The *Chicago Sun Times* noted, "To hear them talk in the Senate, Howard Henry Baker could bring together a boll weevil and a cotton grower if he tried."[10] And perhaps his stepmother, Irene Baker, said it best when she observed: "Henry has never been too overtly conservative or too overtly liberal. He's more like the Tennessee River; he flows right down the middle."[11]

While so negotiating, his human relations skills earned him high marks as one who, much like his father-in-law, tended to "use the oil can more than the sword."[12] He was, for example, a good listener, one who, according to Senator Warren Rudman "had patience and compassion. When Howard Baker listened to you, you had the feeling that all that was going on for him was what you were saying at that moment."[13] Notably approachable, he tried to build coalitions between himself and his colleagues and "disagree without being disagreeable"[14] in the bruising world of politics. As Baker aide James Miller notes: "He spent his whole day on the phone holding people's hands. He knew that if you beat someone, you might need him again. He knew the most important time to stroke some senator was right after you'd beaten him."[15] In short, it is thus not surprising that Senator William Roth could liken Mr. Baker to a "political neutron bomb: one who could overwhelm his enemies while leaving their egos standing."[16]

Interestingly, when Senator Baker took up the tasks of minority leadership, one of his first steps was to prepare for the day when the GOP might be in the majority. Worried that his fellow Senate Republicans were in danger of establishing a "permanent minority mind-set, always opposed to something [and] almost never in favor of something,"[17] he set out to practice more positive thought and action from the start. As Mr Baker recounts:

> . . . in January of 1977, when I was first elected Minority Leader, I set up a regular weekly meeting on Tuesday mornings at 11:30 A.M.—the senior Republicans. Those who would be chairmen if we had a majority. And the first time I got them together I said, now, look, what we're going to do now is practice to be chairmen. And not many people took that seriously because the chance of becoming a majority had not occurred to most of them. And I said we are going to practice that. And every week when we meet in the Minority Leader's office I want you to give me a piece of paper suggesting what you would do if you were chairman, what bills you would try to report, what hearings you would try to conduct, and how you would bid for time on the calendar of the Senate to take up these measures. And it was sort of a game, you know, for a while. But pretty soon it was serious and they liked it.
>
> And then pretty soon we began having Republican conferences which involved all Republican Senators and we started adopting positions—party positions, unanimously, more often than not. And pretty soon columnists—I remember David Broder for the *Washington Post*—wrote a piece that the Republicans are offering a coherent agenda of legislative items as the majority. . . . And then I realized that these people really do want to act like chairmen—they really want to be chairmen. And I've always felt that that

taste, that foretaste of what it would be like to control the Senate, energized a lot of people and helped us to gain the Republican majority of the Senate in 1980.

But that's when it began. As we began practicing, as we began fantasizing about what we'd do if we were the majority, and thus, we were able to hit the ground running in January of 1981. . . .[18]

Therefore, by the time Senator Baker finally did become majority leader in 1981, much of the "majority mind-set" necessary for Republican governing had already been forged through practice, and the skills necessary to hit the ground running were in place.

Still, the question of momentum remained. Who would provide the direction necessary for the majority Republican effort? From the outset, the new majority leader made a conscious choice to "carry the flag" for the president. While he might have chosen to pursue a more independent course and implement his own objectives, Mr. Baker decided, during the president's inaugural address, that Mr. Reagan would set the course for policy initiatives while he, in turn, would help accomplish them by steering the senatorial ship of state to the right:

I heard him say we were over-taxed and over-regulated and . . . at that point, I must confess, sitting there on the inaugural platform, I thought, you know, Baker, you've been around here a while and you've sat on other inaugural platforms, and you've watched other presidents make these inaugural speeches, and you've never seen one, really, who was able to perform, and do you think this man can do any different? And then there was this blinding realization that came over me because I thought, you know, he's not making these promises just for himself, but in a way, he's making them for you, too, because you are the Majority Leader of the Senate. It's something that Republicans haven't done in a long time and you have never done and he's making these promises for you.

And I guess that it was at that moment that I decided . . . I was going to be his man in place in the Senate and carry his flag.[19]

This momentum, promulgated by the president and embraced by Mr. Baker, provided a potent force for both men during the early Reagan/Baker legislative initiatives.

An example of such momentum in action, and the effective use of credible colleagues, can be seen in Mr. Baker's first legislative test as majority leader, a crucial February 1981 period during which the president and he sought Senate approval for the raising of the debt limit to nearly $1 trillion. During that effort, the Democrats, long portrayed by their opposition as wasteful spenders, made clear that they would vote to raise the debt limit only if a majority of the Republicans followed suit. In so stating, the problem for Mr. Baker was that "thirteen of the sixteen Republican freshmen, having campaigned on a hold-down-the-debt platform, flatly refused to reverse themselves, even at the President's request."[20]

In addition to "working on them one at a time and two at a time as we got closer to the vote,"[21] the majority leader turned to credible colleagues, the conservative veterans of his party, including Strom Thurmond of South Carolina, John Tower of

Texas, and Pete Domenici of New Mexico, and asked them to get together with the reluctant newcomers. Mr. Tower told them, "You guys are the rookies on this team and the quarterback has called a play."[22] Mr. Thurmond, a legislator who had never voted to raise the debt during his 27 years in the Senate, was even more forceful. As Senator Baker recalls, the two of them met with the freshmen:

> . . . and Strom started slow and low in that measured South Carolina cadence. He started working up, and at the end of three or four minutes . . . he said: "Now some of you in this room say that you have promised never to vote for a debt limit increase, and I understand that. And you ought to understand that I've never in my whole career voted to increase the debt limit before. But I've never had Ronald Reagan as President before either. And I'm going to vote for the debt limit increase. And so are you."[23]

And in the end, Senator Baker had his votes.

Clearly, if this first intitiative had been lost, momentum for other presidential policies and Reagan/Baker leadership attempts could have been lost as well. As presidential aide Dick Darman stressed at the time, in order to preserve "the appearance of the President's continuing strength and effectiveness, [he needed] the avoidance of association with 'losses,' [and] the association with a planned string of 'successes.' "[24] If the debt ceiling legislation had been defeated, the president and the senator would have lost the first thread in that string. As well, the practice that built the majority mind-set to follow through on the momentum would have been undermined. And the Republican party discipline, which served to build cohesiveness and buffer it from Democratic intrusions, would have been impaired. Moreover, the Senator notes that "to this day, I still think [it was] the most difficult and dangerous point in my career as Majority Leader, because here we were in February . . . a majority that had not really been tested, faced with an issue on the increase in the permissible amount of debt. If I lost it . . . it would be a failure of our ability to govern and maybe validate the claims that Republicans couldn't govern, that we were a permanent minority."[25]

Of course, there were times when presidential appetites, and the congressional capacity to digest them, clashed. In those instances, Senator Baker's leadership skills in relating legislative views to the president proved particularly challenging. Once again, in expressing those views, he made use of credible colleagues to build coalitions which would help bolster his influence with a man representing the more conservative wing of the party. For example, the help of Nevada Senator and Reagan confidant Paul Laxalt proved of particular importance:

> . . . on those tough trips to the White House during which Baker had to inform the President of bad news: impending legislative defeat, threats of mutiny or defection from the faithful, and requests that the White House change its position on an issue. Laxalt served as a counterbalance, so that when the President looked at bad-tidings Baker he didn't say to himself, "Well, maybe Howard still doesn't like me"—Reagan would also see one of his best friends sitting on the same couch, nodding his head in agreement with Baker.[26]

And House minority leader Bob Michel served much the same function. As Senator Baker recalls:

> We acted together and called on the President together more often than not. I remember in many cases we had to, as we say, "bell the cat." Bob and I would get together and say, "We just can't do that," whatever it was the President's people had suggested. And one or the other of us would say, "Who's gonna go tell him," and I said, "*We* are gonna go tell him." Then we went down together and usually the president would respond to that entreaty.[27]

The practical use of all the aforementioned power skills by Senator Baker suggests a high degree of leadership effectiveness during his first year as majority leader. Clearly, his watch as shepherd of the Senate had gotten off to a stellar start. Indeed, according to *Congressional Quarterly,* during this crucial presidential policy period from January to August 1981, its survey indicated that "On the 101 recorded Senate votes on which a majority of Republicans lined up against a majority of Democrats, the average Republican voted with the majority of his party 84 percent of the time . . . the highest party unity score achieved by Senate Republicans since *Congressional Quarterly* began compiling annual scores in 1949."[28] Little wonder, then, that after his first year in office President Reagan would be "frank to say that I don't think we could have had the successes that we've had up there without [Senator Baker's] leadership."[29]

RESTORING CONFIDENCE IN THE WHITE HOUSE

Unlike Mr. Baker's well-charted road to leadership in the Senate, his stint as White House chief of staff proved quite surprising. He was, after all, a creature of the legislature, seemingly unsuited for the executive branch, let alone a staff position. As the senator observed, "I have never, ever in my whole life given any thought to being anybody's Chief of Staff, let alone a President's Chief of Staff. . . I really am sort of an independent personality."[30] Indeed, as a trial lawyer and then a senator, he had always held a line position and never had a boss. As Baker aide James Cannon comments, by moving to the White House he would not enjoy the senatorial role of "independent baron who occasionally talked to the king on his own terms; instead, he would be the king's chamberlain and live in the palace."[31] And in an interview with this author, the senator indicated he was well aware of this difference: ". . . there [in the Senate], I was my own boss, and I was an independent force, and whatever I decided was my policy. Here, I work for the president and what his policies are are my policies. That's the most—that's the biggest difference."[32] In fact, to continually remind him of this difference, his wife Joy presented him with a plaque that read: "I am President and you're not. Signed, Ronald Reagan."[33]

Nonetheless, despite the differences, Mr. Baker officially took the job on March 2, 1987, largely because troubled times were besieging the president and he had asked for his help. As the senator recalls:

. . . the President took me upstairs in the Residence and he pointed out the difficulties he was having and the challenges before him and asked me point-blank to do this. And at that point I had really focused my attention on how I was going to keep him from asking me, because I knew if he ever asked point-blank that I'd probably say yes. But before I could utter a word, he had done the deed, and I was sunk. And I said, "Well, of course I will, Mr. President, if that's what you want me to do."[34]

Chief among the difficulties and challenges for Mr. Reagan were those related to the Iran–contra scandal, a crisis involving charges by Congress that the White House had disregarded laws banning arms assistance to Nicaraguan resistance forces and requiring that there be prompt notification of the covert sale of arms to Iran. In the face of those charges, the president's credibility and confidence had plummeted, he and his staff were in disarray and under investigation, and Congress was talking in tones not unlike in the days of Watergate. Therefore, upon his taking office, Senator Baker's initial mission involved not only establishing his own power base, but also restoring that of a beleaguered White House and a bewildered president as well.

To meet that mission of power building and calming troubled waters, Mr. Baker had much he could bring to restore confidence in the White House; he was able and credible from a variety of standpoints. For example, according to Democratic Senator George Mitchell, the new chief of staff was " 'held in high esteem' on Capitol Hill and benefits from the fact that he was not a member of the Administration during the Iran–contra affair."[35] Furthermore, along with that esteem came legislative expertise and the kind of "quiet relevant Watergate experience"[36] that few individuals could offer in confronting a possible impeachment scenario.[37] Furthermore, with his history as a conciliator and honest broker, as Baker aide Martin Gold noted, he "creates an impression for the public as a whole that there is a competent fellow in there who does not have an ax to grind in terms of protecting the conduct that led to the Iran–contra problem in the first place."[38] Reagan pollster Richard Wirthlin pointed out that he was well-known and liked by the news media.[39] And perhaps most important, the very fact that a Republican of Mr. Baker's stature would willingly take the job with this president under siege signaled a vote of confidence in Mr. Reagan's innocence and continued prospects for positive leadership.[40]

Still, the circumstances under which Mr. Baker took office were far from optimal. Coming in on the heels of an unceremoniously fired Donald Regan, there was no time for anointing. In fact, according to one account, there was no time for preliminary practice either. As Mayer and McManus note, though the senator had expected to begin work officially on Monday, March 2, an unofficial phone call tended to move the date up:

[On Friday, February 27] in deference to the president's request, he remained sequestered, ducking phone calls, particularly from the press. One caller, however, got through: on the line for Senator Baker was the attorney general of the United States.

"Howard," said the voice on the other end of the phone, "I think you better get over to the White House. Don Regan's left."

Baker listened, then tried to put Meese off: "Ed, the problem is that the president doesn't want it out until Monday. I gave him my word."

The attorney general seemed not to hear. "Howard," he said again, slowly, "I think you better get over to the White House. There's no one in charge."[41]

Thus began the new chief of staff's stay in the White House, one in which he had to hit the ground running, with few well-worn practiced paths ahead of him. He would have to pave some for himself.

As he made his inroads, the overall topography of the White House proved challenging too. Unlike the Senate, it was, first of all, a much more confrontative and combative climate, with less room for the kind of conciliation and give-and-take that had marked the senator's style. As James Cannon observes, "In the Senate they fight with boxing gloves, while in the White House they fight with guns and knives."[42] Perhaps, as Mr. Cannon speculates, this is so because "few White House appointees have ever experienced the kind of compromise, the leavening process, that comes with running for office."[43] Instead, what he sees are "many 'despots' seeking their own way, not used to the give-and-take of politics"[44] in "an Administration heavy with ideologues to whom fighting is often more important than winning."[45] In this highly combative, ideological climate of the conservative Reagan White House, it should come as no surprise that "Mr. Panama Canal," the "Great Conciliator" and pragmatist, might not be welcomed with open arms.[46]

Nonetheless, despite the difficulties, Senator Baker moved ahead in his efforts to revive a weakened presidency. At the outset he made clear that he would be representing the president's interests and continue to "let Reagan be Reagan" as much as possible. In so doing, he brought in only a handful of close associates, including his own lawyer, A. B. Culvahouse, and his own communications and planning director, Thomas Griscom. Furthermore, to free himself from the more distasteful traditional staff administrative details and thereby allow himself "to spend most of his time in direct consultation with the president and other key advisers,"[47] he appointed Kenneth Duberstein, a chief congressional lobbyist during Reagan's first term, to serve as deputy chief of staff.[48] And much to the delight of the right (and perhaps reflecting the "conventional wisdom that it is far better to have your enemies inside your tent looking out than outside looking in"[49]), he retained conservative Gary L. Bauer and appointed Meese aide T. Kenneth Cribb as domestic affairs advisors. The result was a coalition staff configuration which included a "handful of aides closely associated with Baker in the past, but . . . by no means dominated by them"[50] and by no means intent on subverting the interests of the Reagan presidency. After all, Mr. Baker had been hired to help save it.

As part of that effort to help save the president, Senator Baker sought the most effective ways to represent the president's interests during the Iran–contra controversy. In particular, he made sure that Mr. Reagan was "well-lawyered" on the issue. With White House counsel Culvahouse, he held numerous sessions with the president to raise questions, observe his body language, and make certain he was not culpable. In addition, Mr. Culvahouse and his staff reviewed every relevant Contragate document and followed every paper trail for possible danger signs. Through these investigations, Senator Baker could inform the president of the sorts of legal questions that might be posed, set the record straight to his own satisfaction, and conclude for himself that Mr. Reagan was indeed innocent. In turn, with this knowledge, the chief of staff could confidently and persistently use his own credibility to defend the credibility of his client. He could, for example, answer his well-crafted Watergate question, "What did the president know and when did he know it" by assuredly saying that "He didn't know anything and he never knew anything."[51]

He could also avoid some of the blunders of the earlier Watergate era by cutting past insular attitudes to a considerable degree. In this regard, with his coalition staff in place, the senator moved from the taut, pyramidal, and insular style of his predecessor to a more circular, open, and collegial one.[52] In addition, he let it be known among his staff that there would be no stonewalling on inquiries, he required that everyone who was asked to go to Capitol Hill should do so willingly, and he stressed that they should tell the truth. In so doing, he gave every appearance of wanting to be as cooperative and forthcoming as possible while protecting his client.[53]

Of course, the client too had a role in the Baker strategy of moving toward a more open, approachable, and confident presidency. As the senator notes, ". . . to make sure that the Watergate analogy did not apply, and by that I mean that Richard Nixon's isolation and relative ineffectuality after the disclosures of Watergate did not [happen] to this man,"[54] he had to make the president approachable. To that end, Mr. Baker worked to eliminate any semblance of a "bunker mentality" by requiring that his communications and planning director, Thomas Griscom, put together a three-month, day-by-day agenda for the president, to be carried out, with the president's approval, after Easter break and through the summer of 1987. While the plan itself brought forth a panoply of presidential policy positions, the main point was to reengage Mr. Reagan and bring him out of the shadows.[55] As Mr. Baker observes: ". . . it was a long list of things. But we knew then for three months what we were going to do. And as the discipline of that plan began to take hold, the president began to be more comfortable, more engaged, more confident, and I think more effective."[56] The press took notice too, and by late May, *New York Times* reporter Steven Roberts disclosed:

> In coming to the White House, Mr. Baker and his aides had a clear plan. Avoiding public contact, as the President had been in the Iran–contra scandal's early days, was neglecting his best political weapon, his own abilities as a communicator. Mr. Reagan has assumed an accelerated schedule of travel, speeches and encounters with the press. The Oval Office is less a prison these days, and more a platform.[57]

Furthermore, besides reducing insulation, the Baker plan had the added benefits of requiring presidential practice through its day-to-day rigor, regenerating momentum, and thereby proving through his goal-oriented behavior "that [Mr. Reagan] was Presidential, that he was in control, and that we had a plan that the President was executing."[58]

Slowly but surely, a presidency previously beseiged began to look like a presidency confidently under control. Little wonder, then, that by late July, after a week at the White House, David Eisenhower would later comment in the *New York Times Magazine* that he "did not see the embattledness of [the Watergate years of] 1973–74. . . . On the second day of Ollie North's testimony, with the President away at a rally in Connecticut, the West Wing was probably one of the quietest enclaves in Washington."[59] And as Senator Baker's strategy for saving the president took hold, so too did his stature with a previously wary White House staff.[60] The public also responded positively; by the time Mr. Baker left office in June 1988, the *Washington Post* observed that the president's approval ratings "stood 15 to 20 points higher than in the dark days after disclosure of the Iran–contra scandal when the White House appeared to be coming apart at the seams."[61]

CONCLUSION: A "MAN FOR ALL SEASONS" AND A "MAN FOR THE MOMENT"

This case has explored the various ways in which Senator Howard Baker sought to build leadership power upon taking office in the Senate and the White House. As has been suggested, the Senate was much more in tune with his style of leadership. Consensus and compromise came more naturally to those elected to the Hill, and the senator used his first ten years well in developing his ability and credibility before taking his first party post in 1977. Moreover, four years later, when he finally rose to the rank of majority leader, he was well established and well regarded on the legislative field of play, more than ready to carry the president's flag.

The White House, on the other hand, provided no such career ladder and on-the-job training. In the face of a firing and a major scandal, the senator had to hit the ground running with an uncertain preparedness and an uncertain path before him. The role of chief of staff was, after all, normally considered an administrative one, and the senator, like his president, had little taste for administrative detail.[62] Furthermore, those who held that post were normally expected to follow the advice of the Brownlow Committee and maintain a "passion for anonymity,"[63] an inclination which a man of Mr. Baker's stature would find impossible.[64] Finally, his consensual style seemed less suited for a staff filled with confrontative ideologues.

Nonetheless, despite his initially questionable suitability for the role of chief of staff, when the president called, the senator took the job, bringing his "immense personal capital—years of Congressional experience and political credentials acceptable across the spectrum"[65] to a beleaguered White House. In so doing, he used his experience where he thought it could best serve the president, as chief counselor, while delegating his administrative tasks to assistants. Furthermore, in this case, Mr. Baker's very lack of anonymity proved fortuitous, for his visible support helped restore legitimacy to a presidency under fire. And his conciliatory skills, perhaps normally a poor fit for White House politics, proved particulary well suited for coping with the Contra crisis. As Mr. Reagan was later to note, the senator deserved high praise "for communicating to Congress and the public 'a tone of cooperation and conciliation in those difficult early months of 1987.' "[66] And as his plan took hold, a formerly wary White House staff began to appreciate his well-earned political skills.

Most likely, if the times had been typical, Senator Baker's talents, well-honed for the Senate, would have proven less effective in the White House chief of staff role. His lack of administrative experience, his visibility, and his nonconfrontative style would have been more gamely criticized. But these were not normal times, and the senatorial "Man for All Seasons" made all the difference as the White House "Man for the Moment." Indeed, history may record that he was the *only* man suitable for that moment. As one pundit records, ". . . if Howard Baker is not the best chief of staff right now, then who is? Except for the far right, the consensus around Washington is . . . Howard Baker."[67] And perhaps the *New York Times* said it best when it noted in its farewell editorial that, "In a lame-duck Administration riven by internal conflict, Mr. Baker did as much as one level-headed man could."[68]

NOTES

1. Research for this study was done under a grant from the Everett McKinley Dirksen Congressional Leadership Research Center, Pekin, Illinois.
2. Martin Tolchin, "Howard Baker: Trying to Tame an Unruly Senate," *New York Times Magazine,* March 28, 1982, p. 17.
3. Lou Cannon, "Baker, Man for the Moment," *Washington Post,* July 4, 1988, p. A2.
4. Roger H. Davidson, "Senate Leaders: Janitors for an Untidy Chamber?" in *Congress Reconsidered,* 3rd ed., ed. Laurence C. Dodd and Bruce I. Oppenheimer (Washington, D.C.: CQ Press, 1985), p. 234.
5. Larry Light, "Baker: Aiming for the Republican Middle," *Congressional Quarterly,* November 10, 1979, p. 2523.
6. Ibid.
7. Gerald Seib and Ellen Hume, "White House Chief Runs into Trouble, But Baker Says Role Is Misunderstood," *Wall Street Journal,* July 31, 1987, p. 40.
8. Tolchin, "Howard Baker," p. 72.
9. Ibid., p. 17.
10. Light, "Baker, Aiming for the Republican Middle," p. 2523.
11. Ibid.
12. Davidson, "Senate Leaders," p. 234.
13. Hedrick Smith, *The Power Game* (New York: Random House, 1988), p. 471.
14. Howard Baker, interview by C-Span Television Network, Series on "The Reagan Legacy," Broadcast January 2, 1989, Washington, D.C.
15. Smith, *The Power Game,* p. 471.
16. Baker, interview by C-Span.
17. Baker, interview by Phil Burton Productions, March 29, 1988, Internal Transcript, The White House, Office of the Press Secretary, Washington, D.C., p. 3.
18. Baker, interview by Burton, pp. 3–4.
19. Ibid., p. 1.
20. Tolchin, "Howard Baker," p. 75.
21. Baker, interview by Burton, p. 5.
22. Tolchin, "Howard Baker," p. 75.
23. Smith, *The Power Game,* p. 459.

24. Ibid., p. 457.

25. Baker, interview by Burton, p. 5.

26. James A. Miller, *Running in Place: Inside the Senate* (New York: Simon and Schuster, 1986), p. 54.

27. Baker, interview by C-Span.

28. Irwin Arief, "Under Baker's Leadership Senate Republicans Maintain Unprecedented Voting Unity," *Congressional Quarterly,* September 12, 1981, p. 1743.

29. Tolchin, "Howard Baker," p. 17.

30. Baker, interview by Burton, p. 10.

31. James Cannon, interview by author, September 28, 1987, Washington, D.C.

32. Howard Baker, interview by author, February 17, 1988, Internal Transcript, The White House, Office of the Press Secretary, Washington, D.C., p. 1.

33. Howard Baker, interview by "Meet the Press," NBC Television Network, May 29, 1988, Washington, D.C.

34. Howard Baker, interview by Burton, p. 10.

35. Dick Kirschten, "The President's Counselor," *National Journal,* May 23, 1987, p. 1333.

36. Patrick Butler, interview by author, October 17, 1988, Washington, D.C.

37. James Range, interview by author, October 18, 1988, Washington, D.C.

38. Kirschten, "President's Counselor," p. 1333.

39. Ibid., p. 1334.

40. Kenneth Duberstein, interview by author, September 28, 1987, The White House, Washington, D.C.

41. Jane Mayer and Doyle McManus, *Landslide: The Unmaking of the President, 1984–1988* (Boston: Houghton Mifflin, 1988), p. 385.

42. Cannon, interview by author.

43. Ibid.

44. Ibid.

45. Barrett Seaman, " 'The Heifer' Takes Some Hits: As Reagan Falters, Howard Baker Gets the Blame," *Time,* October 19, 1987, p. 16.

46. Thomas Griscom, interview by author, September 29, 1987, The White House, Washington, D.C. Also see "Bring Back Don Regan," *Human Events: The National Conservative Weekly,* September 5, 1987, pp. 1 and 17; Patrick J. Buchanan, "How the Baker Boys Toppled Reagan: The GOP Needs Attack Dogs, Not These Compromising Cocker Spaniels," *Washington Post,* November 1, 1987, pp. C1–C2; and David Broder, "Despite Right-Wingers, Conciliation May Ensure Reagan Legacy," *Philadelphia Inquirer,* November 18, 1987, p. 16A.

47. Kirschten, "President's Counselor," p. 1335.

48. A. B. Culvahouse, interview by author, September 28, 1987, The White House, Washington, D.C.

49. Richard Fly, "How the New Right Is Undermining Howard Baker," *Business Week,* September 21, 1987, p. 43. See also Steven V. Roberts, "Baker Courts the Right—And Influences Policy," *New York Times,* May 31, 1987, p. E5

50. Kirschten, "President's Counselor," p. 1335.

51. Butler, interview by author.

52. Kirschten, "President's Counselor," p. 1335.

53. Butler, interview by author.

54. Baker, interview by Burton, p. 11.

55. Griscom, interview by author.

56. Baker, interview by Burton.

57. Roberts, "Baker Courts the Right," p. E5.

58. Baker, interview by Burton.

59. David Eisenhower, "Howard Baker: Fighting the President's Final Battles," *New York Times Magazine,* September 6, 1987, p. 21.

60. Butler, interview by author.

61. Lou Cannon, "Baker, Man for the Moment," *Washington Post,* July 4, 1988, p. A2.

62. Howard Baker, interview with the *National Journal,* May 1, 1987, Internal Transcript, The White House, Office of the Press Secretary, Washington, D.C., p. 1.

63. Samuel Kernell and Samuel Popkin, eds., *Chief of Staff: Twenty-Five Years of Managing the Presidency* (Berkeley: University of California Press, 1986), pp. 195–198.

64. Kirschten, "President's Counselor," p. 1334.

65. "Howard Baker's Selfless Service," *New York Times,* June 16, 1988, p. A26.

66. Cannon, "Baker, Man for the Moment," p. A2.

67. Seaman, " 'The Heifer' Takes Some Hits," p. 16.

68. "Howard Baker's Selfless Service," p. A26.

CHAPTER 9

Newt Gingrich: A Visionary Leader Whose Time Has Come?

DAVID S. CLOUD*

As Newt Gingrich moves forward with his pledge to "rethink government from the ground up," he is rapidly refashioning the House speakership to play a central role in American politics.

Not content to preside as a symbol of the House or to play opposition leader to the White House, Gingrich is turning the speakership into a powerful pulpit from which he hopes to continue to displace Bill Clinton as the primary source of ideas and vision about where the country should be heading.

"We have this accidental moment in history where you have a regime that has, temporarily at least, lost its sense of authority with the country," the Georgia Republican said in an interview. "In that kind of setting, the potential is there to define a new vision."

Gingrich is a figure of fascination right now because of his central role in the 1994 Republican sweep. His ideas seem fresh, even though he has been expounding many of them for years. His ambitions for the speakership and for elevating the role of the House in the national debate—both longtime goals of his—coincide in an almost cosmic alignment with the opportunity for him to carry them out. But Gingrich remains a highly controversial politician, and his star could be eclipsed by a Clinton resurgence or the 1996 presidential campaign.

Still, Gingrich is seizing the opportunity in ways large and small:

*From *Congressional Quarterly,* Vol. 53, pp. 331–335, "Speaker Wants His Platform to Rival the Presidency," by David S. Cloud, Congressional Quarterly, Inc., Washington, D.C. Reprinted with permission.

- At his insistence, Gingrich's daily news conference is now televised nationwide on C-SPAN, so that, as he says, "People around the country can see what I actually say."
- He is putting into practice his belief that charity should replace government assistance, setting up a program funded by private contributions to pay at-risk kids $2 for each book they read this summer.
- Perhaps most significantly, Gingrich has established a support system in the House that leaves him remarkably free from day-to-day management of the legislative process. That enables him to focus on spreading a broader message in speeches, television, college courses, talk radio and other media.

"He's really redefining the Speaker for himself. He has the opportunity combined with his capabilities and drive, which makes it absolutely rare," says Charles O. Jones, a visiting scholar at the Brookings Institution. "I am not certain that he won't be pulled back into the standard parliamentary function of the Speaker, but I kind of doubt that."

Observers say they have never seen a Speaker like Gingrich. Eugene J. McCarthy, a former presidential candidate, Minnesota senator and House member, recently asserted in the weekly newspaper *The Hill* that "Gingrich seems to think of himself as a kind of Prime Minister, chosen by the House of Representatives, as a U.S. equivalent of the British Parliament. Since, under the Constitution, he cannot bring down the government, he appears ready to act as a kind of 'counter government.'"

In Gingrich's view, American society is in crisis: "It is impossible to maintain civilization with 12-year-olds having babies, 15-year-olds killing each other, 17-year-olds dying of AIDs and 18-year-olds receiving diplomas they can't read," he says. With a conservative hostility for federal programs, Gingrich rejects governmental assistance on the grounds that bureaucracy destroys everything it touches. Instead, he wants to create a decentralized but activist society, spread technology to improve lives, and stimulate volunteerism, charity and civic responsibility.

Where he runs into difficulties is in articulating how to get from here to there—and getting people to listen to a Speaker with no national electoral mandate in the same way that they listened to President Franklin D. Roosevelt during the Great Depression. Gingrich is at a particular disadvantage because he is not offering government help. "Trying to get a free people to freely decide in the absence of a depression or a war to make decisive changes is incredibly hard," he says.

THINKING AHEAD

While the House focuses on passing the "Contract with America" in its first 100 days, Gingrich already has moved on. He has left Majority Leader Dick Armey, R–Texas, with almost complete responsibility for overseeing action on the contract bills. "I suspect I have delegated more authority to Armey than probably any Speaker in modern times," he insists.

Gingrich, meanwhile, is chairing a task force that looks to the next challenge. The task force is responsible for constructing a budget, to be presented later this year, that he claims will balance the federal books by 2002 and present "a vision of a renewed American society where power has been returned from Washington to local communities and where voluntarism has largely replaced bureaucratism."

To be sure, Gingrich seems convinced that the only way the country will listen to his ideas about redesigning government is if voters first perceive the GOP House is responding to their demands for changing the way Washington operates. To him, that means passing the bills in the contract. Thus he misses no opportunity to point out that Congress is moving swiftly to do so. But Gingrich is thinking ahead.

The idea of the Speaker competing with the White House in laying out a vision for the country is one sign of how dramatically the 1994 elections have changed politics. That Gingrich takes the task so seriously is an indication of his concern that the Republican gains may be fleeting unless the party can sustain its momentum beyond the completion of the Contract with America.

This approach raises some questions: Can the speakership, an office that traditionally has revolved around managing the flow of legislation, function as a platform for spreading a worldview? Can a government official energize private sector charity and volunteerism as well as give away government power? Moreover, can Gingrich transform himself from a divisive politician into a Speaker able to persuade people to accept ideas that challenge accepted notions about government and society?

By his admission, Gingrich can sometimes sound bizarre when he tries to put his vision into concrete proposals, such as a recent offhand proposal that the way to help the poor was to give them a tax break to buy laptop computers. "It was a dumb idea," he conceded recently. "But somehow there has to be a missionary spirit in America that says to the poorest child in America, 'Internet's for you. The information age is for you.'"

When he is trying to apply his concepts to the problems of urban decay, crime and welfare, Gingrich can often sound like a technocrat groping to impose business principles on policy problems. One recent evening, he invited eight chief executives of Fortune 500 companies to brief him on "the lesson they have learned in downsizing their companies that I can apply to the federal government."

The challenge Gingrich has given himself is immense. Not only is Clinton often an effective communicator and the White House an almost unchallengeable pulpit, but Gingrich, despite his successes, remains a widely unpopular figure. A recent *Los Angeles Times* poll showed that only 26 percent of those surveyed have a favorable impression of Gingrich, compared with 39 percent who view him unfavorably. A *Washington Post* poll showed similar results.

Gingrich's ambitions for the speakership, in a sense, challenge the structure of the U.S. political system. He is, after all, just a House member, elected from a suburban, conservative district outside Atlanta. While he campaigned for many House Republicans and tried to use the contract to nationalize the elections, he was not on the ballot in the same way a parliamentary leader would be.

Republicans blame recent attacks by House Democrats for Gingrich's low popularity, but they also concede that his agenda of dramatically scaling back government and his combative political style are also to blame. "Newt is going to be a polarizing figure if he pursues his vision. I don't think you can get away from it," says Rep. Robert S. Walker, R–Pa., a close Gingrich ally. "The question is can he manage that polarization in a way that allows us to move our agenda. He's been through several trials by fire already."

CONGRESS AS A PLATFORM

Gingrich's attitude toward the speakership is one of the seeming paradoxes of his life. Longtime friends and political associates report that Gingrich has spoken since before he was first elected in 1978 about one day becoming Speaker—a personal ambition that led to his long march to elect a Republican majority. (He also has mentioned the presidency.) They say he has a respect for the office, as well as the House, that is close to reverential.

Yet no member of Congress has been more public about his disdain for recent Democratic Speakers—or, critics say, more ruthless about denigrating the reputation of the institution under their control. And even after pursuing the speakership for years, Gingrich is unabashed about insisting that he will continue to have an identity as a "movement leader" in addition to his job running the House.

Those close to Gingrich say there is really no paradox if you understand his worldview, a set of ideas influenced by sources as diverse as nineteenth-century social critic Alexis de Tocqueville, management guru Peter F. Drucker, and futurists Alvin and Heidi Toffler. As he has developed his critique of the "liberal welfare state," Gingrich has developed a conception of the Congress and of the speakership that incorporates his ideas about leadership, technology and communication.

"Newt sees himself as a vehicle for a set of ideas, and he has seen the speakership and sees the speakership as a means to advance those ideas," says Jeffrey A. Eisenach, a close Gingrich adviser and president of the Progress and Freedom Foundation, a conservative think tank.

From early in his career, Gingrich has conceived of Congress as a powerful platform to pursue his goal of overthrowing the liberal mentality that he says is crippling U.S. society. In 1979, six months into his first term, Gingrich said in an interview with *Congressional Quarterly:* "The Congress in the long run can change the country more dramatically than the president. One of my goals is to make the House the co-equal of the White House."

To some extent, such ambitions made Gingrich unique among Republicans during the 1980s, when Congress seemed a permanent Democratic bastion and the presidency looked like the office from which the party could effect the most change. Gingrich's goal as Speaker is to tilt the balance more toward the House, because he believes that the power to make laws and the responsiveness of the body to public opinion will give him the best opportunity to achieve the scale of change he wants.

"Each generation produces its own style of being effective," he says. "The most accurate statement of how I see the speakership [is] somebody who could somehow combine grassroots organizations, mass media and legislative detail into one synergistic pattern."

In the scale of leadership values, Gingrich says that a leader must first be "a visionary definer, agenda setter and value articulator for the community." Next comes symbol of community power and recruiter of talent. Only after fulfilling those functions does the political leader become "an administrator and manager of government." With characteristic disdain, Gingrich blames the "liberal welfare state" for skewing the way political leaders operate.

With the possible exception of Texas Democrat Jim Wright, a man whose fall Gingrich helped to engineer, no Speaker in recent years has risen to the job with such a view of it. Thomas S. Foley, D–Wash., the man Gingrich replaces, operated on the idea that a Speaker should be above partisanship. Thomas P. O'Neill Jr., D–Mass., looked backward to embody the Democratic Party and its New Deal principles.

Wright's ambition for the job rivaled Gingrich's. But the Texan saw his job principally in legislative terms, and he picked a few issues—aid to the Nicaraguan rebels and the federal budget deficit, for example—on which to oppose the Reagan administration. Gingrich dwells in the realm of ideas, not legislative detail.

Ironically, Gingrich appeared to be following the Wright model as he set up his speakership after the election. Gingrich rewrote the GOP rules to pull power back into the leader's office, much as Wright did, giving himself more control over committee assignments and seemingly preparing to exert personal control on the content of the legislative process. So far, though, Gingrich has largely stayed out of the drafting process, and when he has gotten involved, such as in welfare reform, he has proven more pragmatic than doctrinaire.

"I don't think he is going to end up being a strong Speaker in terms of micromanaging legislation," said Rep. Peter Hoekstra, R–Mich. "In the short term, he may be consolidating power, but it's only as an interim step to accomplish so much of the work that needed to be done."

Showing his passion for delegating work, Gingrich has given Hoekstra the job of running a task force to resolve splits within the Republican Conference so that they do not end up sullying the party's message. For example, Hoekstra said that the panel will search for a tax reform proposal that somehow reconciles Majority Leader Armey's proposal for a flat tax with the fondness fellow Texas Republican Bill Archer, Ways and Means Committee chairman, has for tax breaks.

An idea-driven former college history professor, Gingrich often reaches back into the past for models. He admires Henry Clay, who as Speaker in the early 1800s forcefully laid out his "American System" for building the nation's economic strength. But Clay's vision was easily reduceable to legislative specifics such as a high tariff and support for canals and highways. And it was built around the premise of expanding the reach of government, hardly Gingrich's direction.

FROM GADFLY TO STATESMAN

Gingrich's transformation of the speakership is as much personal as institutional. He has openly conceded that he is trying to restrain his acid tongue and his penchant to attack first and explain later. For all of Gingrich's remarkable abilities as a communicator, he has struggled at times since the Republicans have taken power to convey his goal of "literally replacing the welfare state" in a way that does not alienate the very people he is trying to inspire.

"He's working at it, and I think he's making progress," says Vernon J. Ehlers, R–Mich., a Gingrich ally. "It's difficult to make the transition from gadfly to statesman, but he's trying."

Gingrich, for example, recently conceded that his call following the election to eliminate the federal subsidy for public television backfired because it "maximized the fear level" and "broke down the dialogue." He says he should have made it clear that while he was interested in eliminating the subsidy—$315 million this year, or about 18 percent of the public broadcasting industry's $1.8 billion budget—the popular programs on public television would continue. "We're going to have 'Sesame Street,' " he said. "We're going to have 'Barney.' "

In a way, Gingrich's attempts to change his public persona are nothing new. Longtime associates report that he continually talks about changing himself in one way or another. "You almost always have a 'New Newt' once every six months. Sometimes you can actually see a difference," says Carlyle Gregory Jr., a former top aide.

But this time may be different. Gingrich has urged his colleagues to adopt the mind-set of a governing party and restrain their attacks on the Clinton administration, advice that is diametrically opposed to Gingrich's strategy while in the minority of aggressively seeking out opportunities to start a fight. His explanation? Picking fights with the Democrats is now secondary to the challenge of defining the Republican vision. "You have to have a clash of ideas until a new paradigm breaks through. We're there," he says.

As for his penchant for fomenting controversy, such as commenting after the election about drug use in the White House, Gingrich says, "I wish I could tell you that the more off-the-cuff comments were somehow central to my beliefs, but the truth is they were all too often unnecessary. It's sad to admit this."

After years of attacking the Democratic leadership, Gingrich has found himself the main target of House Democrats during his first month as Speaker because of a book deal. It appears not to have broken any ethics rules, but it raised questions about Gingrich's judgment. Democrats have reveled in fanning the controversy, using tactics that Gingrich perfected in the minority. Democrats think they may have bloodied Gingrich. "One of the great surprises to me, in the argot of the sports pages, is that Newt's a bleeder," says Barney Frank, D–Mass.

Gingrich, who once described Wright as the "most corrupt Speaker in the twentieth century," says he is not worried that the Democrats will use the same tactics to cripple his speakership. "What I said [about Wright] was fundamentally true. What they're saying is fundamentally false, and I think that, over time, people get the difference," he said.

As he made himself the symbol of attack politics during the GOP's slow rise to power, it was clear that Gingrich always cared more about big ideas and grand strategies than the minutiae of the legislative process.

It was Gingrich, more than any other Republican in the late 1970s and 1980s, who stressed the goal of getting to a majority in the House, then went about building the tools, both inside and outside Congress, that finally accomplished the task. He became chairman of GOPAC, a Republican political organization that trained hundreds of candidates in Gingrich's ideas. He began teaching his college course, "Renewing American Civilization," to spread his ideas. He campaigned against ethical lapses of the House under the Democrats, and he gave lengthy floor speeches carried by C-SPAN denouncing the Democrats.

His obsession with gaining a majority culminated in Gingrich's strategy of nationalizing the issues of the 1994 election through the Contract with America.

Gingrich concedes that much of the attention to his ideas and power he now wields as Speaker could be a temporary phenomenon, owing to the unique honeymoon he and other Republicans enjoy in the wake of their electoral sweep. If Clinton rebounds or if a Republican president is elected in 1996, even Gingrich will have trouble dominating the political debate from the speakership.

FLESHING OUT THE VISION

Gingrich could find himself on the defensive in coming months when the obligation to govern forces him into politically unpopular positions that drown out his vision of a renewed, less bureaucratic society.

One such divisive issue is Medicare. Gingrich on January 30 told the nation's hospital administrators that "we are going to rethink" Medicare, the government health insurance program for the elderly and disabled and one of the most fiercely defended middle-class entitlement programs. Saying that "we will make every decision within the context of getting to a balanced budget" seemed to be laying the groundwork for cuts in the program. But Gingrich provided no details.

Anticipating such difficulties, Gingrich is launching a number of projects to flesh out his vision and offer evidence that he stands for more than merely cutting the federal budget. His solutions are unconventional, sometimes challenging accepted notions of what a politician should be doing. And they exemplify Gingrich's goal of making the speakership outward-looking, grass-roots and anti-government.

For example, Gingrich is using his notoriety and the fundraising contacts he had developed through GOPAC to set up what amounts to a private charitable organization, called Earning by Learning. The program, expected to be in at least six cities, will pay $2 to youths in inner cities or those performing poorly in school for every book they read this summer. He is adamant that his experiment is distinctly different from Clinton's AmeriCorps, in which volunteers earn money for college through community service.

"We're trying to put second and third graders through a transformational experience," he says. "I think low-paid government bureaucracies are not the same as voluntarism. . . . I don't think big government is good at transformational experiences because it requires a level of interaction that big governments do very badly outside of basic training in the military."

Gingrich's friend, Mel Steely, a professor at West Georgia College, has been running the Earning by Learning program since 1990 on a shoestring budget. Now Gingrich wants to take it national by setting up a charitable organization. He has put Steely in touch with one of GOPAC's biggest donors, Don Jones, president of Cyberstar, a telecommunications company in Wisconsin, to set up the national organization and raise money.

Gingrich is equally insistent about finding ways to use information technology and other means to break down the barriers that make government and the bureaucracy less accountable.

His latest idea is "corrections day." The House, Gingrich says, will spend the first Tuesday of every month on narrowly drawn legislation to correct "stupid things the bureaucracy is refusing to stop doing."

His idea is to encourage frustrated citizens to bring possible examples to Congress, setting up an electronic mail address to facilitate easy access.

While such a system easily could become captive of lobbyists and narrow interests—not the groups that Gingrich claims to want to empower—he sees it as a way to create "the sense of a genuine partnership that changes the whole ballgame."

Gingrich's ambition to change the speakership will rise or fall with such efforts. If he is able to transform himself into an outward-looking, presidential style leader, he would create a new role in leading the country by his own example. But even if he cannot permanently elevate the speakership, Gingrich insists he still will be working to "didactically move the system by the power of ideas."

CHAPTER 10

From Nancy Hanks to Jane Alexander: Generating Support for Art's Sake at the National Endowment for the Arts

MARGARET JANE WYSZOMIRSKI

With the establishment of the National Endowment for the Arts (NEA) in 1965, the federal government took an important, albeit tenuous, step toward developing a federal policy of direct support for the arts. The potential of this initiative was successfully developed under the leadership of Nancy Hanks, who served as chairman of the NEA from 1969 to 1977.

Hanks' policy efforts were effective in part because of the repertoire of leadership skills she brought to the effort and in part because the circumstances at the time created a window of opportunity. No subsequent chairman of the NEA has brought the breadth of leadership skills nor encountered such propitious circumstances. Instead, successive NEA chairmen had specific—though more limited—leadership abilities. In some cases these were suited to the apparent needs of the moment. In other cases, a chairman's leadership skills seem to have been less sufficient to the task of setting and executing a strategy for advancing and adapting the agency to a changing policy environment.

Increasingly, NEA chairmen have found themselves with fewer political resources and an eroding policy system, while confronting new challenges and concerted opposition. This shift in leadership styles and resources has now progressed to a point where little besides symbolism remains, as an earnest, well-intentioned actress recasts the chairmanship as an exercise in celebrity endorsement.

THE HANKS LEADERSHIP RECORD

When Nancy Hanks took office in October 1969, the NEA was a small, threatened, drifting agency teetering on the brink of its initial survival threshold. By the time she resigned eight years later, the NEA had become institutionalized and could claim both programmatic and political successes. The endowment itself had grown, the number of artists and arts organizations in the country had proliferated, the American arts audience had expanded both numerically and geographically, and official and public attitudes about the arts, as well as the opinion of artists about government patronage, had undergone a positive transformation.

During her tenure, the agency's budget increased by 1,200 percent and its staff by nearly 600 percent. This increase sustained an expansion of both administrative workload and federal arts patronage. The number of applications coming to the NEA jumped from about 2,000 to nearly 20,000, while the number of grant awards rose from 584 in 1969 to over 4,000 in 1977. The agency had fostered programs in all fifty states and six territories and engaged in cooperative efforts with other federal entities. The scope of activities that it supported had come to embrace a wide range of grantees, creative styles, and art forms.

Programmatically, Hanks' NEA had played a significant role in nurturing an arts boom throughout the nation. With the agency's support, the number of artists and arts institutions in America grew tremendously. The number of artists in the labor force nearly doubled—to over one million individuals.[1] The number of professional orchestras and opera companies each increased by 400 percent, while dance companies proliferated by 1,100 percent.[2] Geographic dispersion increased as artistic institutions were established in communities across the nation, especially outside the old urban centers of the Northeast. And quality was the hallmark; by the late 1970s the United States had "for the first time moved to the first rank in world terms in almost every major art form."[3]

Concomitantly, the arts audience expanded. Theater audiences grew from 4 million to 13 million, opera attendance increased from 2.5 million to 11 million, and the dance audience exploded from 1.5 million to 16 million.[4] Other funding also expanded: between 1970 and 1978, state appropriations rose by over 900 percent, corporate contributions quintupled (from $40 million to $210 million), and foundation support doubled (from $114 million to $289 million).[5] By 1980 a nationwide Harris poll discovered that 81 percent of the public wanted "more and better arts facilities" and that 65 percent of those surveyed would be willing to pay ten dollars more in taxes to help support arts activities.[6]

Along the way, the historical mutual wariness of artists and government officials had abated. Artists and arts administrators came to regard the NEA as a source of "hope and encouragement" and credited government funding with having "greatly raised the self-appreciation and self-understanding of artists throughout the country."[7]

And finally, within a decade a core group of strategically positioned, bipartisan congressional supporters had coalesced while advocates at the state level had been mobilized around the establishment and annual legislative funding of state arts councils. By 1977 House majority whip John Brademas (D–Ind.) could declare the arts to be "politically saleable,"[8] with general congressional opinion changed from viewing federal support for the arts as a suspect and risky political venture to seeing it as a legitimate and effective role for government.

The leadership of Nancy Hanks at the NEA was crucial to these transformations. For an appreciation of her leadership skills, an understanding of the ingredients with which she worked is required, ingredients that included bureaucratic resources, political tactics, her personal style, and the environmental context.

NANCY HANKS: ENVIRONMENTAL CONTEXT

When confirmed as the second chairman of the NEA, Nancy Hanks assumed the leadership of a nascent organization that was riding a tide of political, economic, social, and esthetic change. Throughout the 1960s the vitality and quality of the arts in America were surging, even as the financial condition of arts institutions remained precarious. The postwar period had given rise to an increasingly better educated, prosperous, and leisured citizenry that was more likely to become arts consumers. Concurrently, international conflict between the East and the West had extended beyond the military, diplomatic, and economic realms to include a competition between ideologies, ideas, and cultures. In the Cold War struggle for the minds and souls of the world's people, the arts were a key component of public diplomacy. Excellence in the arts was held to be an indication of the virtues of democratic civilization as well as a refutation of the charge that the United States had an excessively materialistic culture devoid of an appreciation of things intellectual and esthetic.

These conditions propelled millions of Americans into the arts audience. Such interest was, however, a mixed blessing for museums and performing arts organizations, since the costs of expanding their labor-intensive activities were greater than the revenues available. Indeed, many arts institutions had outgrown the private patronage of individuals and foundations. Corporate philanthropy was limited and governmental support was meager. In 1969 the federal government contributed only $8.5 million through the NEA, while the total of state government aid added a mere $4–$6 million. Municipal governments (when they did anything) generally helped to support a local museum. Meanwhile, arts organizations also confronted limits on the amount of additional income they might earn from raising prices for fear that they might discourage actual as well as potential arts consumers if tickets became too costly. Indeed, 1969 found American art in the paradoxical position of attracting substantial international acclaim and domestic interest even as it faced an economic crisis.[9]

The Kennedy administration had made several attempts to establish a federal arts program, and these helped to prepare the ground for the creation of the National Endowments for the Arts and for the Humanities.[10] Casting arts policy as part of Kennedy's unfulfilled legacy, Lyndon Johnson combined the needs of the arts and of humanities scholars and linked them onto the educational agenda of his Great Society policies to secure easy passage of the National Foundation for the Arts and Humanities Act in 1965. Under this act, each of the national endowments was directed by a presidentially appointed and Senate-confirmed chairman serving a four-year term. The chairman in turn was to consult with and be advised by a 26-member National Council on the Arts (NCA) whose members served staggered six-year terms and were composed of prominent private citizens engaged in or knowledgeable about their respective disciplines. Furthermore, the chairmen of the two endowments were to be members of and consult with a Federal Council on the Arts and Humanities, which was to include seven federal officials from other government agencies that administered projects in the arts and humanities.[11]

The first NEA chairman had been Roger Stevens, who brought a flamboyant, personalistic, and partisan leadership style to the new agency. A New York real estate developer as well as one of Broadway's busiest theatrical producers, who had backed such hit plays as *Cat on a Hot Tin Roof, The Four Poster,* and *The Bad Seed,* Stevens was a man of great personal presence who possessed a gambler's willingness to take risks but the successful speculator's knack for carefully assessing potential gambles.[12] Politically, he had served as finance committee chairman for the Democratic National Committee during Adlai Stevenson's 1956 run against the Eisenhower-Nixon reelection ticket. In 1961 President Kennedy had appointed Stevens to the board of trustees for the development of a national cultural center. In 1964 Congress named the proposed center the John F. Kennedy Center for the Performing Arts and appropriated $15.5 million toward its completion; Stevens became chairman of the board and continued in that position for over twenty years. Given such combined partisan and artistic credentials, President Johnson asked Stevens to become his special assistant on the arts and to pilot the administration's cultural legislation to enactment. In early 1965, when the National Council on the Arts was created as a preliminary step toward an arts funding agency, Stevens was appointed its first chairman. Six months later, this position carried him into the chairmanship of the newly created NEA, where for a while he continued as presidential assistant and Kennedy Center chairman.

As head of the NEA, Stevens had a philosophy of "not believing in democracy—that is, giving everybody a little money. Instead he tried to create an impact where a small sum could make a difference." He also worked closely with the National Council on the Arts. With Stevens, the NCA functioned virtually as NEA staff, originating project ideas and carefully reviewing individual grants.

For both practical as well as philosophical reasons, the initial emphases of the agency were modest.[13] Indeed, throughout Stevens' tenure, the agency seemed stalled at an appropriations level too low to allow it to do much more than sponsor a handful of demonstration projects or make an occasional rescue grant to an arts organization in financial danger (for example, the very first award given by the NEA was an emergency grant of $100,00 to the American Ballet Theatre, for which the agency was applauded as "having saved a national treasure"[14]). After a 1966 start-up appropriation of $2.5 million, the budget averaged approximately $8 million for each of the next three years. For fiscal year 1970, an incremental increase of 7 percent raised the budget slightly, to $9 million. Clearly, the agency could do little to alleviate the growing economic crisis in the arts with a mere $9 million, when the 1968–1969 combined deficit for professional nonprofit theater, opera, dance, and symphony orchestras was expected to be nearly $100 million.[15]

Politically, congressional support for the arts was uncertain and tended to be liberal Democratic in character. Reauthorization hearings in 1968 revealed that there was little legislative consensus concerning the agency. Considerable criticism focused on grants made to individual artists. Indeed, the House voted to revoke the agency's authority to award such grants, although this bill was amended in conference to allow for grants to persons of "exceptional talent." Furthermore, suggested appropriation levels and reauthorization terms varied widely throughout congressional debate that year.[16] And the very future of the young agency under the new Republican administration of Richard Nixon was uncertain.

When Stevens' term expired in March 1969, his deputy, Douglas MacAgy, became the caretaker chairman. For six months the NEA drifted as a number of the staff and National Council resigned, and Congress was reluctant to appropriate funds for an agency without a leader. Although at least 50 possible appointees were considered, each proved to be either unavailable or unacceptable to key congressmen and senators. Indeed, one observer noted that the position seemed to require "a political virgin who can produce political results."[17] As subsequent events would demonstrate, Nancy Hanks proved to be just the person to meet those specifications.

NANCY HANKS: PERSONAL EXPERIENCE AND LEADERSHIP STYLE

In naming Nancy Hanks to become the second chairperson of the NEA, President Nixon chose neither an artist nor a politician. While Hanks was "almost . . . a lifelong Republican,"[18] she had not been involved in partisan electoral politics. Although she was not a stranger to Washington when she assumed direction of the endowment, neither was she a member of the Washington establishment or even an "in-and-outer." Although she had a long association with the Rockefeller brothers (especially Nelson), they were not her mentors, nor was she their protégé. Born in Florida to Texan parents, she attended high school in New Jersey, earned a Bachelor's degree in political science at Duke University in North Carolina (1949), and spent a summer in Colorado and another at Oxford. A single, attractive, middle-aged woman who combined femininity with a sense of traditional propriety, Hanks became one of only a handful of female federal executives, but she was no feminist.

Hanks had been a philanthropic administrator concerned with the arts, but she was neither an artist, an arts patron, nor even an arts administrator. Esthetically eclectic, she was an aficionado of no specific art form or style, but rather was "open to sampling and enjoying everything."[19] In a field filled with imposing, sometimes bohemian, public personae, she was seen as an accessible, down-to-earth, and very private person. A workaholic who paid meticulous attention to detail, Hanks was neither an artful writer nor a captivating formal speaker. In describing her own particular talent, she once said: "My one art is budgeting. I'm an administrator and a good listener. . . . I'm creative in putting a program into a political context."[20]

Clearly, up to this point the pre-NEA Nancy Hanks had been on the margins—politically, artistically, and even socially—just as the agency itself was. In moving the endowment to the center of the arts world and establishing its social and political support, she forged a particular niche both for herself and for the agency.

Hanks came to lead the NEA as a generalist with experience in the arts; as someone who was politically skillful but not a politician; as one familiar with most of the leading artistic individuals and institutions but taking no side or holding no strong opinions in the wars of taste, style, and school that sweep the arts.[21] In the early 1950s she had worked for Nelson Rockefeller in Washington, and thereafter the Rockefeller connection had carried her into the art world. At the Rockefeller Brothers Fund she coordinated the pathbreaking and influential study *The Performing Arts: Problems and Prospects,* which helped to build support for the creation of the NEA. This project accorded Hanks a broad overview of the major issues and personalities in the worlds of theater, dance, opera, and symphonic music. Later she served as a member of the search committee for a new director for the Museum of Modern Art, in the process becoming acquainted with virtually every important figure in American museums. Then, in 1968, as a member of the Belmont Committee, she became familiar with the conditions, needs, and possible solutions to the critical problems then confronting museums. Finally, as president of the Associated Councils of the Arts (ACA) in 1969, she expanded her network to individuals involved in state and regional arts activities, to other philanthropic and corporate patrons of the arts, to representatives of unions, public arts officials, and public opinion pollster Louis Harris.

The cumulative effect of this record was to make Hanks a generalist who was also "an authority on the arts," "politically skillful" but not a politician, and familiar with most of the leading artistic individuals and institutions but identified with none.[22] And while others might have been more expert in a particular art form, few of these would have had as wide a range of artistic contacts or tastes so catholic. While others might have been more politically worthy, few could avoid at least presumed partisanship. Thus Hanks brought many relevant assets to the job but carried little political baggage.

During her pre-NEA career, Hanks had also acquired various working habits and operational skills that proved to be useful in piloting the agency. First, she had been thoroughly schooled in the consultative, networking style of foundation work. As coordinator of special projects for the Rockefeller Brothers Fund, she was experienced in convening expert panels, coordinating advisory committee decisions, integrating diverse viewpoints, and distilling bountiful information and opinion into an acceptable and practical product. Furthermore, in working for the Rockefellers, she had worked with individuals who had the means, methods, and ability to implement their projects. Hence, much of Hanks' administrative perspective was shaped by a sense of the possible rather than a concern with obstacles. She "believed that there wasn't anything that couldn't be done." Indeed, one of her favorite statements to staff members was, "I'm sure you'll find a way."[23] These experiences and the skills they sharpened were directly transferred to her performance at the NEA.

As a matter of law, the NEA chairman was to consult with an advisory committee (the NCA), just as the Rockefeller Brothers Fund special projects coordinator had had to. In so doing, Hanks maintained that she "never attempt[ed] to make statements that [we]re not based on Council thinking."[24] Also, under her direction, the NEA came to rely increasingly upon panels of art experts to review applications and to maintain close contact with the artistic community. Hanks would frequently sit in on panel meetings and just listen. She would even occasionally have her deputy chair the quarterly NCA meetings so that she could pay closer attention to the views being discussed. Throughout, as Lawrence Reger, her former director of planning and management, observed, she showed "an uncanny ability to take into account incredible amounts [and] variety of opinion and really react to them in what ultimately works out to be the best way. She synthesizes and she sympathizes." In fact, Janet Gracey, one of her former assistants, thought that part of Hanks' charm stemmed from her ability to make others feel "that when she listened to you, you had absolutely her full attention."[25]

As an administrative assistant to the Rockefellers, Hanks had been accustomed to working behind the scenes and leaving the spotlight to others. When this apparent modesty was combined with her equally apparent ambition to do the best job possible at the NEA rather than treat it as merely a stepping-stone to other opportunities, she quite readily and genuinely gave others much of the public credit for designing and furthering federal arts policy. Such generosity not only helped her to win political friends and bureaucratic loyalists but, in the long run, may have accorded her some insulation from the inevitable criticism that occurs in any policy arena.

First and foremost among those whom Hanks applauded was the president himself. For example, she praised President Nixon's announcement that "one of the important goals of my Administration is the further advancement of the cultural development of our nation."[26] She persistently gave the president credit for being the originator and motivator of expanding federal support for the arts and for seeking to make the arts more available to more Americans, particularly youths and minorities. By crediting the president as the pace-setter of federal arts policy, Hanks helped President Nixon get some of the best press of his administration. For example, a 1971 *New York Times* article praised Nixon for making "the most solid contribution to the arts of any President since FDR" while *The Washington Post* speculated in 1972 that Nixon might "go down in history as the nation's most enlightened presidential patron of governmental architecture and design as well as a great patron of the arts."[27]

Hanks was also willing to share the role of agency spokesperson with her deputy chairman, Michael Straight, the former editor and owner of *The New Repub-*

lic. Indeed, Straight himself had been a possible candidate for the NEA chairmanship, but as a liberal Democrat, he was not wholly acceptable as a replacement for that other liberal Democrat, Roger Stevens. In accepting Straight as her deputy, Hanks made a clear statement about the bipartisan character of federal arts support and at the same time improved her ability to cultivate congressional support for the agency. Straight was also a charming and proficient public speaker, always ready with an illustrative tale or a notable quotation, citing anyone from Aeschylus to Thomas Wolfe. In contrast, Hanks was uncomfortable as a public speaker, being at her best in small or informal settings. Therefore Hanks could and did delegate many of the public address tasks to Straight. As a result, the agency gained not one but two artful and persuasive spokespersons, each skilled at a different type of communication.

Hanks also paid attention to detail and was known for her meticulous preparation. One former associate recalled that Hanks "never went into a meeting without knowing the outcome that she wanted" or "without being aware of everyone's view on the subject" and having taken steps to try to defuse "troublemakers" "so that things didn't get out of hand at [the] meeting." Such a personalized and detailed administrative style was time-consuming—so much so that "much of her social side was business," and she was "inclined to work herself into exhaustion."[28] But it also allowed her to assemble and retain a capable, stable, loyal staff and to develop a distinct and positive image for the young agency.

A final significant ingredient of Hanks' administrative style came from the relatively small, intimate, and highly personalistic settings in which she had gained her pre-NEA experience. Such environments prevailed when she was with Nelson Rockefeller at the President's Advisory Committee on Government Organization or at the White House staff, as well as in the philanthropic world and in the arts. Everyone knew everyone else in these circles. Influence was as likely to flow from personality, access, and information as from formal position and tangible power. Such environments both required and responded to extensive networking, proficiency in consensus management and coalition building, informal as well as formal consultation, follow through, and personalized management. All these habits were appropriate to the administration of federal arts policy in the 1970s and, indeed, characterized Nancy Hanks' style as chair of the NEA.

Among other qualities, one can clearly see her reliance on the personal touch at all levels of the agency. In dealing with the Nixon administration, Hanks had impressive and direct personal access to key actors: to presidential assistant Leonard Garment and, through him, to the president and to the directors of the Office of Management and Budget (OMB). She would also reinforce these ties through personal service, such as helping Tricia Nixon host a White House pumpkin-carving contest or getting a monumental modern sculpture that the president disliked moved from the lawn of the Corcoran Gallery.[29] Similarly, Straight reinforced this personal touch by buying a box at Kennedy Center and each Tuesday night inviting two congressmen and their wives to dinner and a concert.[30]

At the bureaucratic level, Hanks went out of her way to visit even the secretarial pool and to get to know all of the staff at the NEA. This personalized networking underpinned Hanks' ability to get things done and also cultivated organizational co-hesion. The fact that "she never lost contact with anybody" fostered a returned loy-alty from her associates and enhanced her ability to call upon many people for assistance. Furthermore, she gave her staff "a lot of authority," expected them to be "generalists" with a shared "approach to problem solving," and kept them well in-formed about what was happening and what was pending. Such a staff system not only gave the impression of competence but fostered both internal and external com-munication by minimizing bureaucratic red tape. Finally, such a staff, since it was also loyal, was likely to be able to head off, if not anticipate and avoid, problems at an early stage.

THE POLICY PLANNING, STRATEGY, AND TACTICS OF NANCY HANKS

The effective leadership of Nancy Hanks was not simply a matter of appropriate per-sonal style. It was also the result of her astute policy planning, strategy, and tactics.

While it is not unusual to find explanations of strategy in the annals of battle-field conduct or of athletic team competition, the statement of a strategy for public policy, complete with an articulation of general goals, methods for securing adequate resources, project programs for implementation, and an assessment of political feasi-bility, is quite rare. Yet just such a master plan for federal arts policy was drafted by Nancy Hanks and endorsed by President Nixon at the very beginning of her tenure as chair of the NEA.[31] Indeed, Hanks had made basic agreement upon the general out-lines of the plan a precondition for her acceptance of the appointment.[32]

Secure in the promise of presidential support, Hanks embarked on an overall strategy, laid out in an October 1969 memo, which involved proposing substantial budget increases for the next three to four years and working for congressional ap-propriations which would build a supportive policy system for the NEA. This long-term financial growth strategy would allow the agency to develop a three-pronged artistic policy aimed at the following goals:

1. *Cultural resources development*—which regarded major nonprofit arts organizations such as theater, dance, and opera companies, as well as symphony orchestras and mu-seums, to be cultural resources and targeted for federal financial assistance through the award of competitive grants

2. *Availability of artistic resources*—which sought to encourage a wider distribution of artistic activities throughout the nation, making them accessible to more citizens and thereby demonstrating the public benefit to be gained from federal arts support

3. *Advancement of our cultural legacy*—which was to encourage new creative opportuni-ties for artists and new artistic experiences for audiences through the provision of fed-eral grant money.[33]

These goals would give the agency a policy focus as well as wed the interests of the arts community to those of the audience/public. While their realization needed clear and sustained White House support to acquire the necessary resources, they also required the strengthening of congressional and constituency support. In addition, the successful implementation of new grant programs to demonstrate the benefits of arts policy was imperative. To obtain and retain these strategic objectives, Hanks employed a repertoire of tactics, the most notable of which were the following:

1. Establishing momentum quickly
2. Securing substantial increases in agency resources—both money and personnel
3. Mobilizing constituency support and cultivating political allies
4. Building a capable, committed, stable administrative staff
5. Adopting pretested program initiatives

Each of these tactics could be seen in Hanks' executive actions discussed below.

Like many a strategically minded executive, Hanks realized that she needed to generate rapid momentum for her agency by creating a positive image for it, setting its agenda, and defining its policy problems and solutions soon after taking office. Consequently, within three months of taking the helm on October 2, 1969, she signaled that the agency was literally on the move by moving it into new and larger quarters. More important, working with presidential assistant Leonard Garment (and through him with OMB), she presented the president with a request for an immediate doubling of the budget for the endowment. She argued that such action would both have a discernible impact on the financial problems confronting arts organizations and serve as an extremely cost-effective way for the Nixon administration to demonstrate dramatically "its commitment to 'reordering national priorities.'" In addition, this initiative would "be a high-impact move among opinion leaders" and would draw enthusiastic endorsement from a strong constituency that was "waiting in the wings" to endorse such a policy. Moreover, Hanks and her NEA staff had also scouted the legislative terrain and ascertained that key bipartisan congressional actors were ready to back such a budget proposal without seeking any major revisions.[34]

In other words, a full game plan and policy rationale were presented to President Nixon for his approval, ready to be put into action. Doubling the agency's meager funding had a low budgetary cost but promised a high political yield. For his part, the president not only acquiesced but gave the initiative a full send-off, complete with a December Special Message to Congress on the arts and humanities and the inclusion of a substantial increase for the endowments in the budget that he sent to Congress the following January.[35]

Meanwhile Hanks was helping to organize a campaign in the arts community to support the president's proposal. First she enlisted the assistance of the American Symphony Orchestra League in getting a letter and telegram wave started.[36] Throughout the spring, as appropriations hearings proceeded, persistent efforts were made to raise public and official awareness regarding the imperiled state of U.S. cultural institutions, especially orchestras. Major metropolitan newspapers ran stories about the difficulties facing orchestras. In Washington the National Symphony Orchestra (NSO) illustrated the plight of orchestras nationwide, as it teetered on the brink of insolvency and President Nixon himself appealed to corporate representatives to support the NSO's fund-raising drive.[37] Congressional testimony by orchestra representatives argued that they were "starving" for funds. In March, Endowment grants of $706,000 to assist twelve beleaguered orchestras only served to illustrate the inadequacy of available governmental support.[38]

In the end, this orchestrated lobbying campaign proved effective when the Senate approved an appropriation that was double the previous budgets of the endowments (for $40 million) and the House followed suit with broad bipartisan support, thus "offering strong endorsement of the validity and continuity of Federal support on the arts and humanities."[39] Soon thereafter the orchestras began to reap the rewards for their political activism as the agency announced the award of more than twice as much money to nearly three times as many orchestras as had been possible under the prior budget.[40]

This first "battle of the budget" illustrates a number of ingredients that would be used repeatedly by Hanks to leverage major increases in the budget for her agency. These were to

1. focus on one or two distinct issues to justify a large-scale funding increase;
2. link these primary issues to particular segments of the arts constituency capable of mobilizing effective lobbying with Congress;
3. offer suggestions of other possible benefits and new programs that more funding might also support;
4. follow a distributive policy strategy of offering more benefits to all arts constituents in reward for lobbying efforts and their consequent increase in appropriations (thus avoiding a redistributive strategy that would reward some constituents only at a cost to others);
5. secure a firm White House Office of Management and Budget commitment to, and publicly involve the president in, support of budget increases;
6. build a bipartisan congressional coalition in support of the proposed budget increase; and
7. deliver immediate "rewards" to the arts constituency in the form of more and bigger grants once increased appropriations have been obtained.

In subsequent years Hanks would advance a series of rationales for increasing the NEA budget. For a number of years the economic crisis of the arts was the general rationale, but each year different arts constituencies were highlighted as worthy and needy recipients of increased support. The music and museum communities, being both numerous and widely distributed, were targeted as more orchestras, then opera companies and choral groups as well as museums, secured substantial federal assistance. Minorities were the focus of new program support for jazz projects, and the development of the Expansion Arts program directed at inner-city, neighborhood, and culturally specific groups. Successively, dance, theater, literature, film, architecture, and folk arts support was expanded and routinized. Each of these initiatives prompted the arts community to greater advocacy efforts through letters, telegrams, telephone calls, and personal visits to members of Congress.

Hanks also took advantage of interagency initiatives and special events to justify other budget increases. The NEA assumed leadership of a presidentially endorsed and government-wide Federal Design Improvement Program. The nation's Bicentennial in 1976 provided a unique opportunity to secure additional funding to sponsor cultural activities as part of the celebration. Even general administrative devices became rationales for increased funding. The change in federal budget procedures and schedule that followed from the passage of the Budget and Impoundment Control Act of 1974 afforded Hanks the chance to secure an added $10–$13 million during a transition period into the new fiscal calendar. And finally, the development of a new category of funding—the challenge grant, which required an extraordinary three-to-one match of private money for every federal dollar awarded—helped boost the NEA's budget.

While the foregoing rationales served to justify increases in the NEA's financial resources, securing these increases required greater efforts to mobilize political support both inside government and from the arts community. Within government, successful coalition building was pursued with presidential staff and agencies, as well as among congressmen on both sides of the aisle (especially Appropriations Subcommittee Chair, Congresswoman Julia Butler Hansen, Authorization Committee members John Brademas (D–Ind.) and Frank Thompson (D–N.J.), and Senators Claiborne Pell (D–R.I.) and Jacob Javits (R–N.Y.)). Hanks also built alliances with various bureaucratic agencies. Thus the NEA became a partner with the Department of Education in arts education programs, as well as an advisor to the U.S. Information Agency on its artistic exchange programs and to the General Services Administration on its program of commissioning works by contemporary American artists for inclusion in new federal buildings.[41]

Outside the government, the organization of a diverse, diffuse, and initially unorganized arts community into a coordinated political interest group was cultivated through the building and/or strengthening of arts service organizations. Under Hanks' leadership, the agency became a "patron of political action," attempting to politically mobilize a constituency from the top down by encouraging groups that could "promote new legislative agendas and social values." These groups were arts service organizations—nonprofit associations that provided services (whether artistic, technical, managerial, or informational) to their respective fields and engaged in political advocacy.[42] In the 1970s the NEA annually awarded between 5 and 9 percent of its combined program and treasury funds to the support of such organizations and their activities. Furthermore, the agency often accorded these organizations special treatment by exempting them from the general eligibility requirement for all applicant organizations: a two-year record of independent existence before they could qualify for federal assistance. Instead, the NEA not only supported relatively untried groups but also promoted the establishment of completely new organizations, including the National Opera Institute, Opera America, and the National Assembly of State Arts Agencies.[43] Thus in a spiraling pattern of cause and effect, the NEA patronized the political action of a constituency, which in turn supported the agency's quest for more resources that could be channeled back into the very constituency the agency had helped to expand and organize.

Two techniques Hanks used to manage the administrative expansion that accompanied such subgovernment evolution involved adopting pretested program initiatives and cultivating a capable and loyal staff. To implement the rapid budgetary and programmatic expansion as well as to preside over the artistic diversification of the NEA, it was necessary for Hanks to increase the staff, with an eye toward both recruiting capable administrators and promoting organizational cohesion. Hanks brought to these tasks a wide pool of acquaintances in the art world. She also had the opportunity to appoint virtually everybody on staff as the agency's personnel quadrupled during her first term and nearly doubled again soon thereafter. Typically, program directors were not only dependable but artistically informed and, in a number of cases, either journalistically or politically experienced as well. By directing staff recruitment and cultivating both personal and institutional loyalty, Hanks succeeded in molding a capable, committed staff that not only enhanced the NEA's operational capabilities but extended and complemented her own political and programmatic capacities.

Hanks also gained a reputation for emphasizing "programs that could demonstrate results."[44] Contributing to this record of programmatic effectiveness was Hanks' practice of adapting ideas that had already been piloted elsewhere. Knowledge of such experiments was constantly flowing into the agency via the program staff, panels, and Council members, who were closely connected to the arts community and its private and state government patrons. Meanwhile, information about projects undertaken by other federal agencies or by prior administrators came to Hanks through her political network, as well as through those on the administrative staff who had work experience elsewhere in the government bureaucracy.[45] Thus in arts policy, as in many other domestic policy areas, programmatic innovation was seldom a matter of inventing new ideas. Rather, it was more often a case of capitalizing on ideas that had incubated for years, slowly amassing public interest and political support.

In a very real sense, therefore, Hanks was fortunate to serve when the times and public sentiments were ripe for her arts policy initiatives. Conversely, the times were also fortunate that a policy leader of Hanks' caliber was in place who was aware of the programmatic options available and who could match them to the opportunities that circumstances presented.

A TRILOGY OF AGENCY LEADERS: BIDDLE, HODSOLL, AND FROHNMAYER

Nancy Hanks succeeded in politically institutionalizing the NEA, yet during her last years as chairperson she found it increasingly difficult to maintain momentum in the face of changing political circumstances. The resignation of President Nixon in the summer of 1974 meant that she lost the cachet of presidential endorsement. The subsequent installation of Ford staff meant that key allies on the White House staff and at OMB were replaced by different and less interested officials. Even continuing arts advocates in Congress became more demanding as a more assertive, post-Watergate legislature sought to exercise greater oversight over executive agencies and, in the case of the NEA, began to call for a less elitist emphasis in the agency's grant activities.

Consequently, each of the next three chairmen led an administratively developed and politically maturing agency through a changing—and increasingly challenging—political environment. In doing so, each chairman brought a different set of leadership skills to the task, although none seemed to have quite the range and versatility of Hanks. Each of these three chairmen pursued a specific strategy, exhibited a particular policy emphasis, and faced a different set of contextual circumstances. Each also found himself dealing with the consequences of his predecessor's actions or inactions.

The first of these was *Livingston Biddle,* who served from 1977 through 1981. Biddle was the scion of a distinguished and well-to-do Main Line Philadelphia family; his skills were primarily political, although he also possessed a set of relevant artistic credentials. A former college roommate of Senator Claiborne Pell, Biddle had served as Pell's staff director on the Subcommittee for Education, Arts and Humanities, while drafting the legislation that had created the NEA and NEH in 1965, and again in 1973–1974 and in 1976. In 1966–1967 he served briefly as deputy to the first NEA chair, Roger Stevens, and later returned to the agency as its first congressional liaison in 1975. In between such public service, he had pursued a career as a novelist, as chairman of the arts division at Fordham University, and as chairman of the board of directors of the Pennsylvania Ballet Company.

Senator Pell had urged President Carter to make the appointment, noting that Biddle had "more experience in dealing with relations between the arts and the Federal Government" than anyone else.[46] Given his clear connection to Senator Pell, Biddle's appointment was criticized by some as evidence that the NEA was becoming politicized. However, as an adept politico, Biddle always maintained that he saw no problem in the chairman's mixing politics and arts. Indeed he asserted that he "disagree[d] with the premise that the arts and the political process, the democratic process—do not mix."[47] This position marked a shift from the Hanks leadership style. Hanks was avowedly nonpartisan while being explicitly bipartisan, whereas Biddle practiced partisan politics. Hanks maintained that the arts were not political even as she was politically adept in the leadership of arts policy; in contrast, Biddle combined art and politics, leading policy with a more explicit political style.

Certainly Biddle's appointment marked a change in the agency's political environment in more than one way. It reflected the resurgence of the legislative branch in the aftermath of the imperial presidency and Watergate. It was also a recognition that an arts policy subgovernmental system had developed, reliant on the alliance of congressional subcommittee authority, the agency, and its organized clientele.[48] During most of her time in office, Hanks had premised her policy strategy and bureaucratic growth on executive alliances while also cultivating legislative support. Now, in contrast, Biddle looked to Congress as the touchstone of his political strategy while also developing executive allies, particularly via the Federal Council for the Arts and Humanities, led by Joan Mondale, and through it, collaborative projects with other federal agencies and departments.[49]

Biddle assumed leadership of an Arts Endowment that faced a changed policy environment in the late 1970s. Hanks' tactic of mobilizing the major cultural organizations in each discipline and of co-opting the leaders of the various arts disciplines into the agency's decision-making processes through the peer panels had helped project an elitist and special interest image. On Capitol Hill, artists and particular arts organizations were seen to be the major concerns of the Endowment, and NEA staff was dedicated to excellence, not "art for the masses."[50] By the time Biddle became NEA chairman, friendly congressional critics were objecting to such apparent elitism and instead were championing a more populist orientation. There was concern that decision-making authority had gravitated toward peer panels that had become closed circles of artistic cronies. Others complained that the geographic dispersion of awards was inequitable and skewed toward a few states, particularly New York. Indeed, whereas Hanks had faced the necessity of establishing the legitimacy of federal support for the arts with both artists and elective officials, Biddle found himself in a philosophical debate over how that support should be administered. Biddle's politically skillful response to the elitist–populist debate was to declare it a nonissue while seeking to combine and transcend both perspectives though a pluralistic approach that promoted programs to broaden public access to artistry of the highest quality. Rather than accepting such polarization, Biddle combined the goals of quality and access, making "access to the best" his rallying cry and overarching policy goal.[51]

Politically, Biddle also had to negotiate a changing arts constituency and administer a comparatively different agency. Hanks had incrementally and sequentially mobilized various aspects of the arts community and orchestrated them into a harmonious coalition of mutual interests—a feat aided by a constantly growing budget. In contrast, Biddle led the NEA during a period with a slower rate of budget growth even as the eroding purchasing power of appropriated funds became more evident. He also faced a restive National Council, an entrenched bureaucracy at the agency, and a more competitive and diversified constituency. To each of these problems, Biddle applied the political skills he had honed during various stints as a congressional staffer—the brokerage skills of negotiation, compromise, and accommodation—and often used congressional action as a catalyst for bureaucratic change.

He used the leverage of a request from the new House Interior Appropriations Subcommittee chairman Sidney Yates (D–Ill.) for a five-year plan outlining agency priorities as a way of initiating changes in the agency. The National Council began working in committees and was engaged in the planning process. This provided the NCA with a renewed sense of participation and validity in the life of the agency.[52] It also set a new tone for relations with the new chairman; it was welcomed by a council that had begun to feel restive in what some felt was a rubber-stamp role to the more entrepreneurial Hanks, and it was congenial to Biddle, who was accustomed (from his congressional staff days) to working in deliberative committee structures. Indeed, Biddle regarded the Council "more as a board of directors than as a council of advisors."[53]

A similar tactic can be seen in Biddle's coordinative work with a reactivated Federal Council on the Arts and Humanities (FCAH), which served both as a special project of the vice president's wife and as a channel to White House support. Working with the FCAH also brought new resources and bureaucratic allies to the NEA through interagency agreements concerning labor, education, international exchanges, transportation, and community development.[54]

The search for additional financial support for the arts also led Biddle to cultivate the business of the arts in a number of ways. The NEA worked with the Small Business Administration to organize a set of meetings in New York, Los Angeles, and Chicago to advise artists on how better to manage their artistic businesses; these meetings resulted in the publication of a widely sold manual, *The Business of Art.*[55] The agency's small Research Division also began to work with economists and arts advocates to develop economic impact analysis as an argument that would appeal to businessmen and community leaders. Biddle himself worked to strengthen cooperation between the corporate world and the Arts Endowment, met frequently with small groups of CEOs and corporate philanthropists, worked with the Business Committee for the Arts, and took pride in pointing out that corporate support for the arts increased to close to $450 million—more than twice the NEA's annual appropriation.[56]

Although Biddle had worked with many of the NEA's staff over the years, as chairman he nonetheless felt a need to put his own stamp on the operation of the agency by seeking to "make the endowment more fully responsive in every way."[57] Again Congress was both the spur to the search for greater responsiveness as well as a specific catalyst. Biddle initiated a series of administrative and programmatic changes. Administratively, he moved from a single deputy to three: one for administration, budget, and planning; another for discipline programs, and a third for partnerships with state and community levels. He sought to institute a five-year rotation system for program directors; this was objected to by some as an attempt to get rid of "dead wood," and others feared this was a way of politicizing the agency by bringing in political cronies. It was also seen by some of the arts disciplines as a challenge to the access and working relationships that had developed between organized arts interest groups and Endowment staff during the previous growth years. Biddle also sought regular rotation in the membership of peer review panels that had become integral to the work of the agency. That each of these reforms could be characterized as an effort to ensure greater responsiveness, fairness, and participation helped make them more palatable within the agency, and in 1979 an investigative report by the House Appropriations Subcommittee that was highly critical of the NEA provided an external justification for such efforts.[58]

In the quest for more pluralism, Biddle established a number of new programs and offices. The Offices of Minority Affairs and of Special Constituencies were created. Opera activities were separated from the music program and expanded to include the more populist musical theater activities. Folk arts, long a special project, was upgraded to full program status, and more support was channeled into festivals, public television and film, and minority-based organizations. The formula for support to state arts agencies was revised to take account of need (based on population), effort (based on state appropriations), and per capita differences. The chairman worked incrementally to reshape funding allocations in a way that preserved the agency's support base among large arts institutions while also distributing awards more broadly. Thus Biddle lowered minimum applicant budget thresholds in some programs (e.g., symphony orchestras), awarded more, smaller Challenge grants, and in his first five-year plan emphasized support for individual artists and for emerging institutions rather than established ones.[59] He also presided over the recruitment of more diversified panelists, substantially increasing the numbers of women and minorities.[60]

The arts constituency that Biddle dealt with as NEA chairman was a more differentiated and competitive group than the one Hanks had helped nurture. By the mid-1970s all states had established a state arts agency, and together these had begun to develop an independent identity. Recasting themselves as policy partners rather than simply agency clientele, the state arts agencies wanted their new role reflected in policy planning and programmatic structure.[61] As the various arts fields became better organized and mobilized through arts service organizations, Chairman Biddle needed to transform their relationship with the agency—expanding advocacy to being one of the agency's highest priorities[62] rather than just the responsibility of its constituency. Here again, the newly instituted planning process afforded opportunities for greater coordination and integration of arts policy stakeholders. And such collegiality was familiar to the chairman and consistent with his skills and experience in the legislative arena. Urging unity of purpose, he warned against the danger of fragmentation, criticizing some in the arts for "concentrat[ing] too narrowly on their own particular interests . . . [and bickering] over resources and relative status."[63]

At the end of his tenure, Biddle faced his greatest political challenge as the new Reagan administration and the Republican-controlled Senate sought to cut, restructure, or even eliminate the NEA. In one electoral sweep, Biddle's senatorial sponsor, Claiborne Pell, lost his power base as oversight subcommittee chairman; Joan Mondale and the network of interagency allies were gone, and key congressional allies like John Brademas (D–Ind.) and Frank Thompson (D–N.J.) failed to win reelection. Employing all his political skills as a carryover term appointee, Biddle orchestrated a budget strategy that fought off draconian budget cuts advocated by the new OMB director, David Stockman, worked to persuade a presidential task force to endorse the structure and record of the NEA, and helped mobilize the arts constituency to new advocacy effectiveness in the face of a serious challenge.[64]

In summary, Livingston Biddle practiced an explicitly political leadership style at the NEA. He both represented and responded to congressional concerns about the Endowment in particular and about executive oversight in general. He understood the policy process and was familiar with many of the key legislative and executive players and could be considered an "uncle" to the agency since its founding. He used his knowledge and standing to monitor the external political environment and to design administrative ways to adapt to changes. His strength was essentially as a political broker among varying policy philosophies, interests, and organizations. He was not the grand strategist that Hanks had been, nor was he particularly concerned with administrative management. He did not attempt to radically transform the agency he had inherited, nor was he interested in presiding over a period of consolidation or reorganization after the ad hoc growth of the early 1970s. Rather he was content to tinker administratively in response to perceived political necessity. He was an able advocate of the agency, although he played that role differently than had Hanks. Hanks had been a goodwill ambassador who was the hidden-hand strategist, orchestrating other advocates. Biddle, in contrast, shared the cultural ambassadorship with Joan Mondale while himself assuming more of a front-line position as chief advocate and defender of the agency and its mission.

When *Frank S. M. Hodsoll* assumed the leadership of the NEA in late 1981, he was the first chairman who had no historic connection with the agency's founding and the first to lack significant artistic credentials. A career political executive and former Foreign Service officer, Hodsoll was an experienced public administrator and bureaucratic politician. An ally of Vice President Bush rather than a Reaganaut, Hodsoll sought to avoid White House opposition toward the Arts Endowment while also appearing less political than Biddle-Carter-Mondale.[65] To perform this role effectively, Hodsoll needed to win the trust of a constituency that considered him a stranger, to lower the profile of the agency to keep it off the president's agenda, and to quietly and effectively manage the NEA while bringing it into line with the administration's general philosophy. In other words, unlike his predecessors, who brought networks with them, Hodsoll had to build his own set of professional relationships while chairman, pursue an inside, internal political strategy, and still exert policy influence.

Drawing on his bureaucratic skills, Hodsoll became a master of administrative detail and practice. He sought to centralize greater authority in the chairman's office—asserting the decision-making authority of the chairman while emphasizing that other players (National Council, panels, and staff) were advisory. He made an early example of the chairman's decision-making power when he took the virtually unprecedented step of reversing panel and/or Council recommendations concerning specific awards—both on procedural grounds and because of inappropriateness for public funding.[66] He organized and enunciated policy through a series of reports submitted to Congress: these included five five-year reports, the first state-of-the-arts report, a panel study report on the grant review system, and *Toward Civilization,* the first national study of arts education policy in nearly a decade. He strove to regularize and formalize the grant review process by requiring staff documentation of panel reasoning and a system of staff communication to the chairman about potentially controversial grants. Indeed, during his first year in office, Hodsoll personally read nearly 5,000 grant applications that had received panel endorsement; he also went on the road, hosting a series of discipline field meetings to meet and listen to the arts community. Later, having established his authority as chairman and his command of detail and information, Hodsoll surprisingly became a champion of experimental and cutting-edge art as well as an effective protector of the Arts Endowment from rising congressional criticism of individual grants that were alleged to be offensive or pornographic.[67]

Programmatically, Hodsoll sought to make innovations that built on the Reagan administration's philosophy of public-private partnerships and encouraged greater private sector initiative. Thus he established a Local Arts Agencies Program and experimented for a time with a director of private partnerships. He was instrumental in persuading the White House to create the President's Committee on the Arts and Humanities, which was to stimulate more private sector support. He emphasized the Challenge Grant Program for established institutions, a planning and advancement program for developing organizations, and a community foundation initiative to help minority-based cultural organizations. He also pursued active collaborations with corporations and private foundations to co-finance programs that were Endowment administered, including new choreography commissions and work in interdisciplinary art forms.

Significantly, Hodsoll could pursue an administrative strategy because the circumstances matched his particular skills. After initial budget cutbacks, the NEA regained its previous fund level by 1984 but secured little in the way of additional funds throughout Hodsoll's tenure. With relatively little new money, the feasibility of an ambitious program agenda was precluded; initiatives could come about only through better management practices, incremental reallocation, or public-private partnerships. Thus Hodsoll could pursue only a limited program agenda. Furthermore, this bureaucratic strategy was appropriate for a chairman who could command little political capital and sought to avoid "politicizing" the agency. Unlike previous NEA chairmen, Hodsoll had no special White House allies like Leonard Garment or Joan Mondale. Nor could he rely on intimate congressional proponents: working too closely with Democratic supporters like Representative Sidney Yates or Senator Claiborne Pell could jeopardize his perceived reliability to President Reagan while retaining credibility with House Republican critics like Dick Armey, Steve Bartlett, and Thomas DeLay (all of Texas). Nor could he too strenuously encourage the arts community in its advocacy for larger budgets if he was to be a loyal member of the administration team and a spokesman for its budget proposals.

In the process, Chairman Hodsoll held a relatively steady, low-keyed course through strong and effective administrative leadership, masterful chairing of the National Council, and attention to planning and expanded public-private partnerships. As a skillful bureaucratic politician and a member of the Reagan administration's team, he also sought to protect his agency from legislative micromanagement or explicit partisanship. Further, he used his administrative skills to reassure an initially suspicious arts constituency while avoiding being thoroughly co-opted by it.

Biddle had pursued change and a broad philosophical agenda and thus generated controversy within the arts community, but he found allies and proponents both in Congress and in the White House. In contrast, Hodsoll pursued good management, process-oriented adjustments, and a limited policy agenda. The long-term costs of such a strategy became evident only later: the Hodsoll years saw less attention to the cultivation of congressional support, the agency drew back from the active advocacy role that Biddle had practiced, and it did little to spur the advocacy efforts of the arts community. Nor did the agency adequately reposition itself in response to monitoring significant changes in its economic, social, or even artistic environment. In other words, the bureaucratic strategy worked during an administration whose priorities

were focused elsewhere, for a limited agenda, and when practiced by an adept bureaucratic leader. Yet the slow atrophy of political support and energy progressed; the
unperceived ossification of structure and operations meant missed opportunities for
agency adaptation, and a limited programmatic agenda weakened the policy imagi-
nation of the arts community even as it lulled it into a sense of entitlement[68] and false
stability.

Hodsoll left the NEA early in 1989 to take up a new post as deputy director for
management at OMB in the new Bush administration, leaving a deputy as acting
chairman at the NEA. In October of 1989, *John Frohnmayer* became the fifth chairman of the agency. During the interim, a crisis of historic proportions had gathered
over the NEA, touched off by controversy concerning two NEA grants—one to the
Southeastern Center for Contemporary Art involving Andres Serrano's photograph
of a crucifix immersed in urine and entitled, "Piss Christ," and the other support for
a traveling exhibition of the photographs of Robert Mapplethorpe, which included
homoerotic and sadomasochistic portraits. When Frohnmayer took office, the controversy was thoroughly inflamed, threatening not only the agency's annual appropriation but its upcoming reauthorization as well. Thus Frohnmayer became
Endowment chairman at a trying and precarious time.

The son of a prominent political family in Portland, Frohnmayer was a lawyer
who had headed the Oregon Arts Commission, had been a director of the Western regional arts organization, and was a singer. He felt that he brought state and national
experience in arts issues, "some empathy for the artist . . . the skills of a negotiator,
energy and enthusiasm, and contacts in all the states."[69] Hoping to mediate a path
through the charges of pornography, blasphemy, and censorship, Frohnmayer was
given no time to settle into the chairmanship, was "bewildered by the intensity of
press interest,"[70] and was attacked by the Religious Right. With the agency facing serious and vocal opposition for virtually the first time in its institutional life, Chairman
Frohnmayer vacillated before awarding a grant to an organization in New York City
called "Artist Space," for an exhibit about AIDS that included images of homosexu-
ality and whose catalogue ridiculed public figures such as Senator Jesse Helms, John
Cardinal O'Connor, and Congressman William Dannemeyer. This fumble alarmed
proponents in the arts community and in Congress. As a result, the arts constituency,
legislators, agency staff, and the White House never trusted his judgment, principles,
or commitment.[71]

Unlike previous NEA chairmen, Frohnmayer never found an advocate at the
White House staff; instead he felt confounded by powerful and influential critics like
John Sununu [President's Chief of Staff], Richard Darman [White House Budget Di-
rector], and William Kristol [Vice President's Chief of Staff].[72] Furthermore, he had
difficulty developing interagency allies, even with his counterpart at the National Endowment for the Humanities, Lynne Cheney, and he felt he got no explicit support
from former Chairman Hodsoll at OMB. Within the agency, Frohnmayer felt that his
deputy, Al Felzenberg, who had close connections to the White House, was spying on
him; he eventually fired Felzenberg, ostensibly over leaking confidential application
information to the political columnists Evans and Novak concerning pending grants

to controversial performance artists Karen Finley, Holly Hughes, Tim Miller, and John Fleck.[73] Furthermore, Frohnmayer antagonized the arts community by instituting an "anti-obscenity pledge" as a requirement of all grant recipients, a move that was widely regarded as an overreaction and that provoked a number of lawsuits against the agency. In addition, nearly twenty grant awardees, including Joseph Papp of the New York Shakespeare Festival, refused their grants as a protest and attracted extensive negative press coverage.[74]

Amid the protracted tumult, Congress called for a bipartisan Independent Commission headed by NEA "godfathers" John Brademas and Leonard Garment to help forge a political compromise and consensus that would allow the Endowment to be reauthorized in 1990. In the process, Congress—rather than the chairman—declared what the agency's policy priorities would be: arts education; an emphasis on programs for inner cities, rural areas, and other underserved communities; and larger block grants to the states. It also found much in need of reform in the agency's grant-making procedures, even while avoiding explicit content restrictions. Making a virtue of necessity, Frohnmayer adopted policy priorities that were consistent with these mandates. Frequent and significant staff personnel turnover as well as infighting with the White House personnel office resulted in long delays in filling key positions. The agency staff became demoralized and overloaded. The centralized administrative system Frohnmayer had inherited degenerated into a reactive management mode, ricocheting from one crisis to another. And relations between the National Council and the chairman devolved into mutual recrimination over inadequate leadership.

Between 1989 and 1992 this agency careened from one grant controversy to the next and was buffeted by annual budget cliff-hangers. In 1992 it became a campaign issue, first as conservative Republican Patrick Buchanan challenged President Bush in the primaries, calling the NEA the "upholstered playpen . . . [of] . . . the Eastern liberal establishment" and attacking the administration for "subsidizing both filthy and blasphemous art."[75] Legislative proponents of the agency also faced negative campaign tactics because of their support. Increasingly bereft of political allies or supporters either in the administration, in Congress, in the arts community, on the National Council, and within the agency, Frohnmayer himself had become a political liability and a hamstrung administrator. Having thought about resigning for months, he was forced to do so in February 1992 and left the agency a few months later.

If Hanks had been a case of the right person, with a range of skills, who took advantage of circumstances that presented opportunities, then John Frohnmayer was the wrong person, with few political or administrative skills, who tried to contend with a conflictual environment with few and uncertain allies. As chairman, Frohnmayer confronted extraordinary challenges that would have sorely tested even a bureaucratic virtuoso. In quiet times, he might have been an adequate chairman; in such turbulent times, he presided over the virtual disintegration of the political support system that had been built up over nearly three decades. Frohnmayer's tenure was characterized by "unprecedented public scrutiny and Congressional oversight" and left a legacy of vacillation "between attempts to appease Congressional critics and to appeal to the amorphous 'arts community.' "[76]

Following Frohnmayer's departure, the NEA was headed by two acting chairmen for a period of nearly two years until Jane Alexander was appointed by President Clinton in the autumn of 1993.

JANE ALEXANDER: THE PERILS OF A CELEBRITY ENDORSEMENT STYLE

The arts community had welcomed the election of Bill Clinton as president, anticipating support from a Democratic White House to complement and bolster Democratic congressional proponents of the arts. There was hope that electoral change might even prompt a resumption of budget growth for the NEA. After a long delay, President Clinton announced that his choice to head the Arts Endowment was Jane Alexander, a Tony and Emmy award winning actress. With Alexander coming to the helm, the arts community felt that one of its own would inspire a demoralized agency and personify its interests. Indeed a *Washington Post* editorial described her as someone who had "lived through and can describe with conviction, the extraordinary explosion in regional and nonprofit arts. . . . She has spent many years in the kind of regional, repertory, and arts education functions that are the NEA's strongest reason for existing. Her selection gives the endowment a nominee who can respond credibly to congressional criticism of what the NEA does and is supposed to do."[77]

Public expectations and the new chairperson's own statements provided early indicators of the leadership style Alexander would display: she was to become a celebrity spokeswoman for the agency. Key congressional supporter, Representative Sidney Yates (D–Ill.) observed that her task was to "restore confidence in the agency."[78] Planning to spend her first month learning how the agency worked, Alexander then launched a 50-state public relations tour, featuring town meetings where artists could speak about their experiences and where the agency could spotlight local arts organizations that enjoyed NEA support.[79] At her confirmation hearing she offered "inspirational anecdotes of how the arts had transformed her life" and said that her "vision for the arts in this country . . . [was] that every man, woman and child find the song in his or her heart."[80]

Politically, it was clear that as NEA chair, Alexander had been cast into a leading lady role. She noted that her confirmation marked the first time she had had to "audition in an awfully long time."[81] Senators Howard Metzenbaum, Daniel Patrick Moynihan, and Claiborne Pell joked that her hearing resembled a "deification" or a "coronation" rather than a confirmation.[82] She had had no prior government experience to draw upon; her political credentials were limited to involvement as a liberal activist on nuclear disarmament and wildlife conservation. Instead, she argued that her theatrical background in playing roles such as Eleanor Roosevelt or the first female justice of the Supreme Court (in "The First Monday in October") gave her a knowledge of politics and "a certain kind of authority."[83] Although she did not have administrative experience, she pointed out that her experience in producing films gave her some knowledge of "what it is to run something."[84]

Spending little time at the agency, she was constantly on the road, carrying the basic message that the "arts are part of the life of every single American"[85] and that her goal for the agency was to see that "the best reaches the most."[86] Although Alexander noted that the president sees "the arts as part of building community," the NEA did not see proposed increases in its budget. Instead it looked to other agencies for "creative partnerships" and "future collaborations" to augment arts funding.[87] Continuing Chairman Hodsoll's earlier initiative, Alexander endorsed the work of a revitalized President's Committee on the Arts and Humanities to increase private support. Simultaneously, she emphasized the economic impact of NEA money and the arts within local communities. She invited key congressional and administration officials—such as Representative Sidney Yates, Senators Simpson, Kennedy, and Metzenbaum, and OMB Director Leon Panetta—to make cameo appearances before the National Council for the Arts. Alexander herself appeared to be interpreting her role as the leading lady in the second act of a Biddle-like chairmanship. Her message echoes Biddle's drive for "access to the best," as did her interagency approaches for collaboration and emphasis on the economic impact of the arts. However, while Biddle had been proselytizing receptive Washington and arts communities, Alexander was pitching similar messages to a more constrained set of potential interagency allies, to more skeptical legislators, and to an ambivalent general public. Indeed, she seemed to invert the advice of Andrew Heiskell to "make systematic contact with the public" and bring their sense of "what culture means to them, their communities and the nation back to the NEA and the arts community."[88] Instead of listening to the public and bringing their perceptions back to the agency, she sought to explain what the Endowment does to people outside the arts community.

While producing appealing photo opportunities and good press, such tactics did not quite add up to a political strategy. As an early *Washington Post* editorial noted: "Ms. Alexander shouldn't believe that straightforward good spokesmanship is all the endowment needs to get out of its current jam . . . [rather] . . . she will need not only poise but also a clear political strategy."[89] Yet there was little evidence of an activist political strategy. Instead Alexander pursued an endorsement strategy[90] whereby she endorsed the agency as it existed, sought to boost positive public awareness of the NEA's record, and aimed to restore its credibility among artists. Although this approach was consistent with her skills and perhaps sufficient in a friendly political atmosphere, the weaknesses of Alexander's strategic vision became increasingly clear as the political environment changed.

In the spring of 1994 criticism arose over a grant to the Walker Art Center in Minnesota which supported, in part, a performance by Ron Athey, an HIV positive artist who carved ritual patterns on the back of a colleague, blotted the blood with paper towels, and hung these out over the audience on a clothesline. This episode ended Alexander's honeymoon with Congress. Bipartisan complaints led by Senate

Finance Committee leaders Robert Byrd (D–W.Va.) and Don Nickles (R–Okla.) put the agency's funding "in serious jeopardy."[91] Indeed, the Senate called for a 5 percent budget cut and took the unusual step of directing it at specific NEA programs, including theater and visual arts, which had been at the center of recent controversies.[92] Hoping to defuse the potential for even greater criticism, in August the National Council rejected a fellowship application from Andres Serrano, who had been a focus of an earlier furor over his photograph "Piss Christ."[93] However, this, as well as an earlier agency decision to eliminate certain dance, theater, and regranting programs following a FY 1994 budget reduction, raised complaints from members of the arts community. Indeed David Mendoza, head of the National Campaign for Freedom of Expression argued that "Alexander's massive PR show isn't working. . . . the endowment is alienating individual artists . . . it's alienating the foundation community" and that "The NEA under the Clinton administration is not any better than it was under Bush."[94] Thus the simmering problems of what the agency funded continued to provoke criticism both from opponents and from members of the arts community, highlighting the difficulty of retaining the support of the NEA's clientele while also avoiding renewed antagonization of its opponents.

Within the context of such recurring friction, the NEA came to confront a seminal challenge in the new political atmosphere that followed the 1994 congressional elections. As Democrats lost control of both Houses of Congress for the first time in 40 years, the NEA saw most of its key legislative allies demoted to minority status. As an agenda of budget cutting, government limitation, decentralization, and privatization drove the policy process, the NEA found its very existence challenged, many of its standard arguments turned against it, and the position of its opponents strengthened.[95] In the process, the debate shifted from a concern with the product and processes of federal cultural subsidies to more fundamental questions of the legitimacy and affordability of any federal role in support of cultural activities. The NEA, as well as the NEH and the Corporation for Public Broadcasting and even the Smithsonian Institution, became political and fiscal targets for the 104th Congress.[96]

The NEA was doubly vulnerable because it not only faced an appropriations debate but was in need of reauthorization, and indeed, had been operating since 1993 without a formal statutory commission. Chairperson Alexander found her agency caught in a procedural bind under the new rules of the 104th Congress, which declared that unauthorized agencies could not receive appropriations. Reauthorizing the NEA would be more difficult than ever. Yet as other federal agencies scrambled to design reorganization plans, consolidate programs, and devise alternative funding options, the NEA chose to hew to the status quo. Reluctantly, some in the arts community and among its political allies came to believe that saving the NEA might not be feasible and that preserving even some form of federal cultural support would require significant policy redefinition and bureaucratic restructuring as well as inevitable downsizing. This view marks a virtual reversal of the Biddle approach. The agency abandoned advocacy leadership and instead became a bargaining chip between the arts community and its critics.

As we have seen, in the changed political circumstances of 1995, Chairperson

Alexander's leadership approach has obviously had its problems. Tactics of celebrity endorsement and bureaucratic image enhancement undertaken by an artistic spokesperson were simply inadequate.

Perhaps the last years of the twentieth century call for a relatively thankless and unglamorous leadership style committed to transforming the NEA's policy rationale while preserving its institutional core. While the activities of the five chairmen of the NEA that have been discussed here provide certain lessons as to what has and has not been effective in the past, they also provide clues as to what might be needed in future leaders of federal cultural policy.

NOTES

1. For an overview of information on the populations, earnings, and employment of American artists, see National Endowment for the Arts, *Five-Year Planning Document, 1986–1990* (Washington, D.C., 1984), pp. 83–89 (hereafter cited as NEA, *1986–1990 Plan*).

2. According to figures in the *New York Times,* May 26, 1985, Sec. 2, there were 42 professional orchestras in the United States in 1960 and 166 by 1984. Thus orchestras increased by 400 percent. According to Opera America, *Profile 1984* (Washington, D.C., n.d.), p. 6, there were 17 opera companies in 1970 and 81 in 1984. And according to testimony by *Dance/USA* to the Appropriations Subcommittee on Interior and Related Agencies of the House of Representatives of the 99th Congress, 1st session on April 28, 1983 (p. 3), there were only 35 dance companies in 1965 (most located in the New York City area) and in 1983 there were 400 dance groups located in over a hundred communities nationwide.

3. Waldemar Nielsen, *The Endangered Sector* (New York: Columbia University Press, 1979), p. 39.

4. Comparisons are based on early figures found in Rockefeller Brothers Fund, "The State of the Arts: A Special Studies Project" (New York, October 13, 1969, mimeographed); more recent figures are drawn from the NEA, *1986–1990 Plan,* p. 116.

5. Kenneth Goody, "Art Funding: Growth and Change between 1963 and 1983," *Annals,* No. 471 (January 1984), pp. 144–157.

6. American Council for the Arts, *Americans and the Arts, 1980* (New York: ACA Publications, 1980).

7. Michael Straight, "A New Artistic Era [If the Money Lasts]," *New York Times,* October 20, 1974, Sec. 2; Malcolm N. Carter, "The National Endowment for the Arts: Will Success Spoil Our Biggest Patron?" *ARTnews,* May 1977, p. 47.

8. *New York Times,* September 4, 1977, p. 18.

9. In March 1969 the Ford Foundation released a report on "The Economic Crisis in the Arts"(See the *New York Times,* March 2, 1969). Similarly at its 1969 annual meeting the American Council for the Arts declared that it would focus its attention on the economic crisis in the arts (see the *New York Times,* February 3, 1969).

10. See Milton C. Cummings, Jr., "To Change a Nation's Cultural Policy: The Kennedy Administration and the Arts in the United States, 1961–1963," in Kevin Mulcahy and Margaret Jane Wyszomirski, *America's Commitment to Culture, Government and the Arts* (Boulder, Colo.: Westview Press, 1995), pp. 95–120.

11. In addition to the chairmen of the NEA and the NEH, the other federal members were to be the U.S. commissioner of education, the secretary of the Smithsonian Institution, the director of the National Science Foundation, the librarian of Congress, the director of the National Gallery of Art, the chairman of the Commission on Fine Arts, and a member designated by the secretary of state.

12. Fannie Taylor and Anthony L. Barresi, *The Arts at a New Frontier: The National Endowment for the Arts* (New York: Plenum Press, 1984), pp. 55–59.

13. Ibid., p.77; Michael Straight, *Twigs for an Eagle's Nest* (New York: Devon Press, 1979), pp. 14–16; NEA, *Annual Reports, 1965 through 1969* (Washington, D.C.: GPO, 1965–69).

14. *New York Herald Tribune,* February 13, 1966.

15. Rockefeller Brothers Report, "The State of the Arts," p. 7.

16. The House oversight committee (Education and Labor) originally suggested a two-year authorization total of $135 million for the NEA and NEH combined. The House eventually approved a one-year authorization of only $11.2 million. The Senate supported a two-year appropriation at a figure between the high and low variously suggested by the House. The final figure approved after conference called for a combined two-year total of $57.4 million for the two endowments. See Taylor and Barresi, *The Arts at a New Frontier,* pp. 116–117.

17. R. L. Coe, "The Politics of Art on Capitol Hill," *Washington Post,* July 17, 1969, as quoted in Taylor and Barresi, *The Arts at a New Frontier,* p. 122.

18. *Chicago Daily News,* November 15–16, 1969, p. 6.

19. Ana Steele, interview with the author, Washington, D.C., November 30, 1984.

20. Quoted by Sophy Burnham in "Nancy Hanks, Santa Claus to the Arts," *Town and Country,* December 1975, p. 125.

21. *New York Times,* September 6, 1969; also Lincoln Kirstein of the New York City Ballet, as quoted in Joan Simpson Burns, *The Awkward Embrace* (New York: Alfred A. Knopf, 1975), pp. 383–384.

22. *New York Times,* September 6, 1969; Lincoln Kirstein of the New York City Ballet, as quoted in Burns, *The Awkward Embrace,* p. 383; ibid., p. 384.

23. Janet Gracey, interview with the author, New York, December 18, 1984.

24. Excerpt from an interview with Nancy Hanks by Rodney Campbell as quoted in chap. 16, p. 7, of "Ten Years for Tomorrow" (NEA Library, unpublished manuscript).

25. Quoted from interview with Lawrence Reger by Rodney Campbell in "Ten Years for Tomorrow," chap. 16, p. 44; Gracey interview, December 18, 1984.

26. Press release, "Statement by the President on the Appointment of Nancy Hanks as Chairman of the National Endowment for the Arts," September 3, 1969 (Nancy Hanks Papers, the National Archives, Washington, D.C.).

27. Frank Getlein, "The Man Who's Made the Most Solid Contribution to the Arts of Any President since F.D.R.," *New York Times Magazine,* February 14, 1971; *Washington Post* critic Wolf Von Eckardt comments on May 3, 1972, and September 16, 1972, as quoted in an advertisement supporting President Nixon's reelection (see the *New York Times,* October 29, 1972).

28. Gracey interview, December 18, 1984.

29. See Straight, *Twigs for an Eagle's Nest,* pp. 31–33.

30. Ibid., p. 22.

31. Nancy Hanks, "Memorandum for the President," October 17, 1969 (draft 3), in Hanks Papers.

32. For an account of her appointment as chair and of the consultations with President Nixon and presidential assistant Leonard Garment on the administration's intended arts policy goals see Hanks interview in Campbell, "Ten Years to Tomorrow," chap. 16, pp. 2–8.

33. Hanks, "Memorandum for the President."

34. See the Hanks memorandum to President Nixon of October 17, 1969. Leonard Garment summarized her memo and forwarded it with his own cover letter to the president on October 23, 1969. He followed this with a detailed assessment of the proposed arts policy initiative; see his "Memorandum for the President" on "The Quality of Life in America: Presidential Leadership for the Arts and Humanities," November 26, 1969 (Garment Papers, the National Archives).

35. Richard M. Nixon, "Special Message to the Congress About Funding and Authorization of the National Foundation on the Arts and the Humanities," December 10, 1969, in *Public Papers of the Presidents: Richard M. Nixon, 1969* (Washington, D.C.: GPO, 1970), pp. 1018–1020.

36. In a December 28, 1969, note from Hanks to Richard Wangerin, president of the American Symphony Orchestra League, she reported that "responses are pouring in and the President couldn't be more pleased with wires, not to mention editorials, and the letters are starting. This will give us a lot of good sales talk when we approach Congress" (NEA storage files; Chairman's Office, 1969.)

37. See the *New York Times,* March 10, 1970.

38. *New York Times,* March 11, 1970. These grants could assist less than half of the existing major symphony orchestras in the country in 1970 and could not begin to address the much larger number of smaller professional orchestras.

39. *New York Times,* July 8, 1970.

40. On August 6, 1970, the *New York Times* reported that the NEA had just awarded $1.68 million to thirty-four orchestras. This was a marked increase from the previous year's grants of $706,000 to twelve orchestras. For a list of awardees see the *New York Times,* August 25, 1970.

41. On the history of the GSA's Art-in-Architecture Program, see Don W. Thalacker, *The Place of Art in the World of Architecture* (New York: Chelsea House, 1980).

42. The phenomenon of federal sponsorship of interest group formation is discussed by Jack L. Walker in his "The Origins and Maintenance of Interest Groups in America," *American Political Science Review,* 77, no. 2 (June 1983), 390–405. For a discussion of NEA policy toward arts service organizations, see Margaret Jane Wyszomirski, "The Politics of Arts Policy: Subgovernment to Issue Network," in Mulcahy and Wyszomirski, *America's Commitment to Culture, Government and the Arts,* pp. 47–76.

43. National Endowment for the Arts, "National Council on the Arts: Policy and Planning Committee Report on Service Organization Support" (Washington, D.C., 1980, mimeographed).

44. Gracey interview, December 18, 1984.

45. For examples and detail, see Margaret Jane Wyszomirski, "The Politics of Art: Nancy Hanks and the National Endowment for the Arts," in *Leadership and Innovation: Entrepreneurs in Government,* ed. Jameson W. Doig and Erwin C. Hargrove (Baltimore: Johns Hopkins University Press, 1990, abridged ed.), pp. 195–196.

46. As quoted in the *New York Times,* November 3, 1977.

47. Ibid.

48. For a discussion of the changed politics of the arts policy subgovernment from Hanks to Biddle, see Wyszomirski, "The Politics of Arts Policy, esp., pp. 53–60.

49. See Livingston Biddle, *Our Government and the Arts: A Perspective from the Inside* (New York: ACA Books, 1988), pp. 427–439. However, it should be noted that during her last years in office, even Hanks had seen erosion in her basic political strategy as she faced the necessity of building new executive support during the Ford interregnum and as congressional supporters called for a more populist emphasis and voiced some criticism that she had created a virtually independent fiefdom.

50. As stated by Norman Fagan, director of the Performing Arts and Public Media program. Quoted in Lawrence D. Mankin, " The National Endowment for the Arts: The Biddle Years and After," *Journal of Arts Management and Law,* 14, no. 2 (Summer 1984), 60.

51. See Margaret Jane Wyszomirski, "Controversies in Arts Policymaking," in *Public Policy and the Arts,* eds. Kevin V. Mulcahy and C. Richard Swaim (Boulder, Colo.: Westview Press, 1982), pp. 12–21.

52. Biddle, *Our Government and the Arts,* p. 412.

53. David B. Pankratz and Carla Hanzal, "Leadership and the National Council on the Arts," in Mulcahy and Wyszomirski, *America's Commitment to Culture,* p. 157.

54. Biddle, *Our Government and the Arts,* pp. 427–434.

55. See Biddle, *Our Government and the Arts,* p. 439, and the *New York Times,* January 24, 1980, which reports on the first of the three meetings held in New York City.

56. Biddle, *Our Government and the Arts,* pp. 440–444.

57. Ibid., p. 387.

58. The report alleged that the agency was advised by a closed circle of individuals, failed to adopt a national policy for the arts, lacked evaluation and audit procedures, had inexperienced staff, and had deficient contract procedures. Biddle repudiated the report as being "so flawed both conceptually and technically to be almost without merit" and succeeded in persuading Subcommittee Chairman Yates to set aside the report. See Biddle, *Our Government and the Arts,* pp. 397–402, and Mankin, "NEA: The Biddle Years," pp. 65–66.

59. Mankin, "NEA: The Biddle Years," pp. 68–69.

60. Mankin reports that the proportion of female panelists increased from 25.5 to 39 percent under Biddle's chairmanship and that the percentage of minorities doubled from 14 percent. Also the number of grants and the percentage of grant money going to minorities increased substantially. See Ibid., p. 67.

61. Indeed, the appointment of a deputy chairman for public partnership, rather than simply a program director, was a recognition of this new stature. Also Biddle worked with the newly formed National Assembly of State Arts Agencies and the National Assembly of Community (Local) Arts Agencies to

plan and hold a three-day national partnership meeting in 1980. See the *New York Times,* June 25, 1980.

62. See Joseph Wesley Zeigler, "Passionate Citizenship," *American Arts,* May 1983, pp. 22–26.

63. Pankratz and Hanzal, "Leadership and the National Council," p. 156.

64. For more detail see Mankin, "NEA: The Biddle Years," pp. 69–75, and Wyszomirski, "The Politics of Arts Policy," pp. 60–61.

65. During his presidential campaign of 1980, Ronald Reagan had promised to "end as soon as possible the politicization of the National Council on the Arts so conspicuous during the Carter-Mondale administration." Quoted in Joseph Wesley Zeigler, *Arts in Crisis* (Chicago: A Cappella Books, 1994), p. 45.

66. For a discussion, see Pankratz and Hanzal, "Leadership and the National Council," p. 159; Frank Hodsoll, written testimony submitted to the Independent Commission on the National Endowment for the Arts, Washington, D.C., July 25, 1990, p. 3.

67. Zeigler, *Arts in Crisis,* pp. 52–57, 60.

68. On the trend toward a philosophy of entitlement see Zeigler, *Arts in Crisis,* p. 66.

69. John Frohnmayer, *Leaving Town Alive: Confessions of an Arts Warrior* (Boston: Houghton Mifflin, 1993), p. 23.

70. Ibid., p. 80.

71. For a detailed account of the unfolding controversy during 1989 through 1993, see Margaret Jane Wyszomirski, "From Accord to Discord: Arts Policy During and After the Culture Wars," in Mulcahy and Wyszomirski, *America's Commitment to Culture,* pp. 1–19.

72. Ibid., p. 99.

73. Pankratz and Hanzal, "Leadership and the National Council," p. 162.

74. Zeigler, *Arts in Crisis,* pp. 105–122.

75. See Wyszomirski, "From Accord to Discord," p. 13.

76. Pankratz and Hanzal, "Leadership and the National Council," p. 164.

77. *Washington Post,* editorial, August 15, 1995.

78. As quoted in the *Washington Post,* July 30, 1993.

79. Eliza Newlin Carney, "How's This for an Acting Chairwoman?" *National Journal,* January 8, 1994, p. 83.

80. *Washington Post,* September 23, 1993.

81. *New York Times,* July 31, 1993.

82. *Washington Post,* September 23, 1993.

83. See the *New York Times,* October 16, 1993, and the *Washington Post,* October 14, 1993.

84. *New York Times,* October 16, 1993.

85. Ibid.

86. *Washington Post,* September 23, 1993.

87. *Washington Post,* February 5 and April 21, 1994.

88. Andrew Heiskell, "Art Lovers Can Seize the Offensive," *New York Times,* September 15, 1993.

89. *Washington Post* editorial, August 15, 1993.

90. The standard purpose of celebrity endorsers in marketing is to amplify a desired communication effect such as awareness or attitude by helping to draw attention to a "product." Sometimes they provide a measure of expert recommendation and credibility to the task, particularly if the members of a target market identify with the endorser. For a general discussion of the use of celebrity endorsers in advertising, see John R. Rossiter and Larry Percy, *Advertising and Promotion Management* (New York: McGraw Hill, 1987), pp. 289–305.

91. The phrase comes from a letter from Senators Byrd and Nickles sent to Chairperson Alexander and quoted in the *Washington Post,* June 22, 1994. Senator Jesse Helms commented that as a result of this grant, while he had "personal affection for her as an individual, she is a flop as of now."

92. See the *Washington Post,* July 20, 1994.

93. *Washington Post,* August 6, 1994.

94. As quoted in the *Boston Globe,* December 11, 1994.

95. The ascendance of Newt Gingrich as speaker of the House and Richard Armey as House majority leader put persistent critics of the NEA into key legislative positions, while the shift of crucial committee chairmanships and members meant a decline in the influence of other House members such as Sidney Yates and Pat Williams.

    Following the election, long-time NEA critic the Christian Action Network observed that "eliminating the NEA is finally within our reach"; see the *Boston Globe,* December 11, 1994. In May of 1995, when the CAN issued its "Pro-Family Contract with America," elimination of the NEA and NEH was high on its agenda of ten priority items; see the *Washington Post,* May 13, 1995.

    While the arts community had long argued that the NEA should be free of politicization in the name of freedom of expression and the first amendment, now Speaker Gingrich urged privatization and argued that "the arts are freer and more able to pursue their own end when they are in fact private rather than bureaucratic and government-controlled." *New York Times,* January 9, 1995. Meanwhile Senator Dan Coates would turn the NEA's claim to catalytic effect on its ear and observe that "the match is an indication of private interest and commitment"—thereby suggesting that the arts didn't need federal assistance. Similarly, the newly elected Senator Dewine (R–Ohio) referred to claims of the economic impact of the arts as "dubious economics." *Los Angeles Times,* January 27, 1995.

96. Jon Healey, "Opposing Interests Brace for a Culture Clash," *Congressional Quarterly Weekly,* February 28, 1995, pp. 272–275.

CHAPTER 11

Jack Kemp: How Jack Kemp Lost the War on Poverty

*JASON DEPARLE**

On the afternoon of July 2, 1991, Jack Kemp received a surprise visit from the man he variously called "pencil neck" or "the Prince of Darkness": the White House budget director, Richard Darman. It had been a year since Kemp was named chairman of the Economic Empowerment Task Force, a cabinet subgroup formed to develop antipoverty policy. During that time, he and Darman had repeatedly clashed over the substance and tone of domestic policy, where little could happen without the budget director's approval.

To Darman, Kemp had long established himself as a windy orator who clung to his eccentric ideas with a fervor bordering on the religious. Inside the White House, Darman would ridicule Kemp's showcase program HOPE (Homeownership and Opportunity for People Everywhere), which was intended to sell public housing units to their tenants. Estimates of renovation and finance costs were reaching $100,000 per unit and Darman would, derisively though not implausibly, argue that it would be cheaper to buy poor people new condominiums.

To Kemp, Darman was the chief bureaucratic roadblock between himself and his vision of an activist conservatism that aligns itself with the poor. Like most Bush Administration officials, he respected Darman's superior understanding of policy. But also like many others, he complained that Darman believed in little beyond his

*Copyright © 1993 by the New York Times Company. Reprinted by permission, from the *New York Times Magazine,* February 28, 1993.

own power. He would frequently say Darman used his position not to improve new ideas but to kill them.

Kemp was now seated at a conference table in the Old Executive Office Building, surrounded by assistant Cabinet secretaries from across the Government. He was midway through a lecture on the welfare system, saying how unconscionable it was that the Government takes away a dollar of welfare benefits for virtually every dollar a recipient earns. In some cases, Kemp pointed out, women who try to leave welfare for the world of work actually see their incomes fall.

Darman then appeared at the door. Declining Kemp's offer of a seat, the budget director absorbed a few minutes of the familiar oratory. As a top planner in the former Department of Health, Education and Welfare, he probably knew more about welfare than any of the dozens of officials in the room. And he was not one to disguise it.

Work disincentives were a concern, he agreed. But Darman pounced when Kemp suggested that welfare recipients should be allowed to keep 85 cents of every new dollar they earn without having their benefits reduced. Doing some quick arithmetic in his head, Darman concluded that such an approach would allow people to collect welfare when they were earning as much as $70,000 a year.

Darman also noted that the group had talked of cutting off welfare benefits after two years. What, Darman asked, then happens to the family's children? Do they simply starve? The budget director talked on for 15 or 20 minutes, before ending his lecture with a curt suggestion. There is a large technical literature on welfare, he said. Perhaps, before your next meeting, you should read it.

For Kemp and a small group of loyalists, the skirmish was one in a line of setbacks that ultimately destroyed their hopes for a conservative War on Poverty. From the earliest moments of the Bush Administration, Kemp had urged the White House to spend more money, create more programs and lend the fight more Presidential commitment.

But he did so with an odd set of outsized talents and peculiarities. Kemp brought unusual devotion and eloquence to his crusade. But he also brought a grab bag of marginal ideas and a personal style that alienated some of the allies he most needed. Chief among them was George Bush.

Kemp's efforts drew him into constant clashes with Darman, who frequently derided his ideas as costly and unlikely to achieve their goals. Darman, the superior bureaucrat, almost always won.

The story of their fight—pieced together through hundreds of pages of internal Government documents and interviews with scores of officials—offers an unusually candid view of the policy-making process.

In Kemp's telling, the narrative is reduced to a demonic tale of the man activist conservatives have come to hate.

"Darman not only cost those of us who believe in the War on Poverty; I believe that in no small way he is responsible for the President losing the election," the 57-year-old Kemp said in one of several interviews during his last weeks in office.

He said Darman "dropped poison" on new ideas to maintain his power and brought "a really sick attitude" to the poverty debate. "He didn't care about poverty; he cared about what the budget looked like," Kemp said. "There's not a single inner city of the United States who even knows who Dick Darman is, other than the Prince of Darkness who opposed everything I tried to do." (Darman has declined to comment on any of Kemp's assertions.)

But if Darman was one of Kemp's enemies, Kemp himself was another. To his credit, he may have brought more zeal to America's poverty problems than any national politician since Robert Kennedy. Kemp may be the only official to have won standing ovations in black ghettos by calling for a capital gains tax cut.

And yet Kemp sold his solutions with a recklessness that ignored their limitations, exhibiting a fervor that reminded one ally of an adolescent who had just read *The Fountainhead.* In advocating tenant management, for instance, Kemp would constantly cite the achievements of a St. Louis housing development called Cochran Gardens, where tenants had succeeded in reducing crime and vandalism. What Kemp declined to say, however, was that the celebrated development had done virtually nothing to reduce poverty: average household income remained stuck at less than $5,000 a year.

Kemp did his cause further damage with a personal manner that alienated many of his Cabinet colleagues. Always impatient, he would flop in his Cabinet seat like a beached fish, sink his head into his hands, roll his eyes and scribble exasperated notes. Talking once about how he planned to seek better relations with Senator Barbara Mikulski, head of his appropriations subcommittee, Kemp leaned back and stuck a finger down his throat, as if gagging on the very thought. "I mean my body language is worse than anybody else's, you know," Kemp said. "I can't hide my feelings." Speaking of his bureaucratic enemies, Kemp said, "They're wee-weeing on me."

Beyond their unusual egos and flaws, both Kemp and Darman brought formidable talents to the table, Kemp as a public spokesman and Darman as a deal maker and analyst. But missing almost entirely from the equation was the interest of the President. In four years George Bush never paid more than casual attention to the bitter disputes that simmered beneath him, or to their impact on the lives of America's 36 million poor people.

Bush made a rare but revealing appearance in the story on Feb. 27, 1991, after Kemp finally persuaded him to give a speech advocating many of his ideas. Rebuffing Kemp's pleas to deliver the address to an audience of poor people, Bush gave it instead to a group of well-paid lobbyists in a Washington hotel ballroom. The lobbyists responded with stony silence.

Bush never really stopped complaining about the speech, aides say. In subsequent months, he had a running joke with his speech-writing staff, warning them against another antipoverty speech. When James Pinkerton, a campaign aide, visited the President in the Oval Office more than a year later, the wound was still fresh. "Boy," Pinkerton recalls the President saying. "I never want to do that again."

The war over the War on Poverty was under way from the time that Bush invited Kemp to discuss taking the job of Secretary of Housing and Urban Development. Kemp, a Bush rival in the 1988 Presidential primaries, had long held what most Republicans regarded as an eccentric interest in poverty. Meeting now with Bush and his inner circle, Kemp told them he wanted to "wage war on poverty."

Bush recoiled at the term, saying it conjured up the Great Society and Big Government. Kemp recalls arguing back that he had something different in mind, an activist agenda driven by markets, not bureaucracies. He said he wanted tenant ownership of public housing, "enterprise zones" that lured businesses to distressed areas through tax cuts, and unspecified "radical welfare reform" that wouldn't punish the poor when they got a job.

The President had one caveat. "He didn't want me to call it a 'War on Poverty,'" Kemp said. Still, Kemp talked continually of the need to "wage war on poverty" from the moment he stood beside Bush to accept the Cabinet appointment.

Kemp suffered his first bureaucratic rout on June 23, 1989, when he visited the office of John Sununu, the White House chief of staff. He arrived with an inch-thick folder outlining his proposals—not just enterprise zones but expanded subsidies for low-income renters, social services for the homeless and elderly, and tax changes to help first-time home buyers. His signature program was HOPE, the plan to sell public housing to tenants. Kemp wanted $1 billion for the program's first year.

There was reason to be skeptical. Enterprise zones had been tried on a state level, with only modest impact. Kemp argued that adding Federal tax breaks would give businesses a greater incentive to move to blighted areas, but there was little proof. Tenant ownership was an untested idea that threatened to consume Federal money without creating cheap housing.

Darman arrived at the meeting with what proved to be a more persuasive handout, a single page tallying up the costs of all Kemp wanted to do. According to Thomas Humbert, a Kemp aide who was there, Darman's estimates came in three to five times higher than Kemp's. "It just blew apart Kemp's ideas, before they ever got started," Humbert says.

When Sununu suggested there might be no money for HOPE at all, Kemp leaped from his seat, resorting to what would become a familiar tactic: threatening to resign. "Sununu got up and said: 'Jack, you're getting overheated. Sit down,'" Humbert recalls. Kemp left the meeting with a $250 million pledge for HOPE and a painful message to scale back his ambitions.

Kemp argues that Darman and his aides brought a "penny wise, pound foolish" attitude to programs for the poor. By refusing to invest more in poverty prevention, he says, the "budgetmeisters" courted more expenses later—in welfare, crime and misery.

But Kemp's detractors also have a point when they say his constant desire to raise spending while cutting taxes showed a dangerous irresponsibility toward the Federal deficit problem. "The death question was always, 'How are you going to pay for it?'" said one Administration official. "And these people had no clue."

For much of his first year, Kemp was consumed with the influence-peddling and mismanagement scandals he inherited at H.U.D. In the meantime, the White

House had reconstituted an obscure planning group known as the Low Income Opportunity Board, which brought several antipoverty proposals to the Cabinet. More than once, Cabinet members told the planners they were enthusiastic about fighting poverty. But each time the planners suggested a specific program, the Cabinet found the cost too high, the politics wrong or the promise of success too thin.

In November 1989, when the planners suggested a series of "opportunity zones" that would allow local governments to experiment with antipoverty money, Kemp and Darman both instructed them to come back with something more ambitious. "And whatever you do, don't call it opportunity zones," Darman said, according to notes taken at the meeting. Two steps ahead as usual, Darman had spotted the acronym and the public relations disaster of consigning the poor to a Land of OZ.

The following spring, the process was still stalled. In May, Clayton Yeutter, the Agriculture Secretary, weighed in with a letter that in retrospect appears to have captured perfectly the Administration's antipoverty philosophy. "The Federal deficit is already much too large!" he wrote in a four-page letter to White House planners. Then Yeutter came down on the side of what might be called daring inaction. Fighting poverty "calls for boldness and leadership," he said. "But it also calls for prudence and circumspection." Notably eager for prudence himself, Bush may have recognized a soulmate; he later named Yeutter White House domestic policy czar.

When the Cabinet decided in late June simply to recommend more studies, Kemp exploded. "Meanwhile, what's going on in our neighborhoods and on the streets?" he wrote in a July 12 letter to Attorney General Dick Thornburgh.

Kemp had just the solution to the stalled antipoverty plans. "Perhaps a Cabinet secretary ought to head the effort," he wrote.

The idea of putting Jack Kemp in charge of the Government's antipoverty planning did not sit well with his Cabinet colleagues. He was already acting as if he had his own monetary and foreign policy, only half-joking in March when he held a private ceremony at H.U.D. recognizing the new Government of Lithuania, 18 months before the State Department did.

Darman joined the majority of Cabinet officers who voted against the idea. But Kemp's cause was then resuscitated by an unlikely ally, John Sununu. A White House domestic policy aide, John Schall, recalls Thornburgh asking Sununu to "give Jack the ball and see if he can run with it" in a spirit that was half acquiescent and half calling Kemp's bluff. Sununu went along, Schall said, and weighed in with Bush, who approved a memo on August 6, 1990, putting Kemp in charge.

Expectations were low, however. The White House waited a month and then released a memo, quietly acknowledging the new Economic Empowerment Task Force, with Kemp as its head.

From the start, Kemp's fledgling cause was overshadowed by the two major developments of 1990: the budget deal and the buildup to the Persian Gulf war. On June 26, Bush had sent conservatism into a tailspin by saying he might approve "tax revenue increases" to cut the deficit—in effect renouncing his famous campaign pledge.

Kemp had built his political reputation as a tax cutter, and he spent months fighting the deal, to which Darman and Sununu were attaching their professional reputations. While making no headway with Darman or Bush, Kemp was emerging as a hero to a clique of young White House conservatives who shared Kemp's dislike of the budget director and his deal. Chief among them was James Pinkerton, a protégé of Lee Atwater. In Bush's slash-and-burn 1988 campaign, it was Pinkerton who had unearthed Willie Horton.

In the winter of 1990, Pinkerton began a series of speeches advocating what he called a "new paradigm" for Government action that emphasized market forces over bureaucracies. Like Kemp, Pinkerton often talked of using the approach to "empower" the poor.

Debating the meaning of "empowerment" was one of the more consuming activities of the Bush domestic planners. When pressed, Kemp and Pinkerton would fall back on a familiar roll call of policies: enterprise zones; vouchers that let parents choose their children's schools; tax credits for the poor; and the HOPE program. They had a hard time coming up with other examples, but championing the phrase was a way of sounding activist and conservative at once.

Darman derided the phrase, which had originated with 60's radicals, saying it had changed definition so often it had become meaningless. And though Kemp was talking about empowering the poor, Darman could argue he himself was actually doing it, but without the rhetoric. After all, the reviled budget deal happened to contain $18 billion in new tax credits for low-income families. The appropriations for Kemp's HOPE program were minuscule by comparison, peaking at $256 million a year.

Angered at Pinkerton's attacks on the budget deal, Darman struck back with a November 16 speech on what he called "Neo-Neo-Ism." In it, he attacked the "incipient faddism" of those unnamed Washingtonians bandying about terms like "empowerment" and "new paradigm."

"Hey brother, can you paradigm?" Darman mocked.

Washington exploded into an intra-conservative brawl. Conservative congressmen like Newt Gingrich and Vin Weber rallied to Pinkerton's defense, and Kemp retaliated with talk of what he called "Social Darmanism." The war on poverty was becoming the battle of the sound bite.

Kemp took charge of his task force with characteristic bluster and zeal. When a group of young White House aides visited his office early on, they found him ranting that this was a fight for the "soul of America."

Then suddenly Kemp fixated on the attire of Richard Porter, a 30-year-old lawyer in the empowerment camp. "Purple suspenders!" Kemp exclaimed. How did Porter expect to have any credibility with poor people if he dressed like that? Porter smiled nervously, but Kemp wouldn't let it go, carrying on about proper antipoverty dress. "You have to go through an initiation ceremony with Kemp," recalls Porter, who has remained an important ally. "You had to prove you were on his side."

Suspenderless, Kemp and his helpers began to beat the bushes of the Federal bureaucracy, looking for what they called "ambitious, far-reaching ideas" to empower the poor. What they got back was mostly oatmeal. The Education Department touted an "800" number. The planners themselves suggested changing the name of the Small Business Administration to the "Agency for Entrepreneurship."

Exasperated, Kemp convened a November 15 meeting with emissaries from each of the domestic agencies. "If you don't come up with good ideas your department can implement, I will think them up for you," he said, according to meeting notes.

When the Cabinet reconvened on November 28, Kemp brought 13 proposals, mostly familiar. He also tacked on a suggestion to raise the personal tax exemption to $6,000, the equivalent of a $50 billion tax cut. It had about as much chance of passing as a White House salute to Saddam.

It was nearly two weeks after the "neo-neo" speech, and Kemp's cover letter was filled with barbs at Darman. "Solving poverty does not mean green eyeshade thinking about 'resource allocation' and 'better administration,' " Kemp wrote.

While Kemp's allies awaited fireworks, Darman delivered this surprising pronouncement: "I have already decided to put some of these items in the FY92 budget."

Among the messages communicated by these words, of course, was the central fact of the Bush Administration's domestic policy: Darman's own power. *I have already decided. . . .* Darman ditched the $50 billion tax cut, but included in the budget a special section calling for enterprise zones, the HOPE program and other Kemp causes.

The concession was small—most of the items already had the Administration's backing—and Darman may also have been beating a strategic retreat, hoping to stem the conservative anger toward him over the budget deal. Darman offered one other concession by including Kemp's favorite word in the budget, adding a section that said "the goal is to empower low-income individuals." Now Darman and his aides could say they had given Kemp what he wanted, and ask, in feigned or real exasperation: what more does the guy want?

The answer was Presidential backing. Kemp began to push for a meeting with Bush. White House aides say Darman helped forestall it, calling it a waste of a busy President's time. The power struggle then shifted back to the word "empowerment," which again became a proxy for the entire dispute over domestic policy.

Porter recalls Darman calling him from a car phone early that winter. "He says, 'Richard, let me do you a favor—don't use the word empowerment in any memo you send,' " Porter says. "He said, 'You people don't understand the connotations of the word from the 60's.' Of course we did. I was going to say that's what's fun about it— stealing one of the Left's words. But I didn't get that far. I just got a couple of words out. He said, 'Look, don't do it.' So I didn't."

Kemp's reaction, after he was told about the phone call, crossed the usual boundaries of Washington disputes. "I mean he's not a sick man," Kemp said of Darman, "but I mean, that's a sick thought."

The linguistic ban took hold, and Kemp's cause was dying. Bush's February antipoverty speech to the lobbyists flopped. A week later, he went before a joint session of Congress to describe what he called the postwar "mission here at home." He talked about crime and transportation.

Shortly thereafter, Anna Kondratas, Kemp's chief aide on poverty policy, went before Congress to testify on the work of the empowerment task force. She wrote Kemp a memo in May complaining that the budget office had cut her testimony in half and barred her from speaking about agencies other than Housing. "I was embarrassed to be so unspecific," she wrote.

That month Kemp did get Bush to visit Cochran Gardens, the St. Louis public housing development run by its tenants. But the Presidential tour did nothing to bolster Kemp's bureaucratic position. During the June battles over a Congressional appropriations bill, Kemp was left to fight for his HOPE program on his own. He won a slight increase, only after standing in a Capitol hallway and accosting his former House colleagues as they filed in to vote.

When Kemp arrived at a June 20 Cabinet meeting with the President, White House aides stopped him from distributing a printed report from the task force. Cabinet rules required prior clearance. Notes from the meeting show that when Kemp launched into a stemwinder, Sununu warned him to "keep the speech making to the campaign trail."

The meeting disintegrated into a technical discussion of welfare experiments. As its end drew near, Bush, who had been chewing absentmindedly on the stems of his glasses, left to take an overseas phone call. He did not return.

In January, Bush named Yeutter to the top White House domestic policy job. On April 3, the White House abolished the Economic Empowerment Task Force.

A few weeks later, the Los Angeles riots gave Jack Kemp a last hurrah. At a meeting the day after the riots, Darman warned that Kemp, left unmonitored, would use the occasion to upstage Bush. The President's other advisers shared the worry, but also recognized that Kemp was the only political asset they had. "We were happy that, whatever he'd done in the past, we had him around," one aide said.

Kemp peppered the White House with memos and suggestions. But he did not actually speak to Bush until the Cabinet convened the following week. Kemp arrived distributing copies of an urban policy brochure he had written months earlier. "I'm sitting kind of to the left for the photo op," Kemp recalled, "the only time I was near the president for four years."

As Kemp recalls it, the meeting was filled with high drama, though others say the emotion was mostly his own. In the middle of a patented Kemp discourse, another Cabinet official, unnamed by Kemp, "just literally slammed his fist down" and shouted, "What's our policy? We don't have a policy."

Kemp remembers flinging his brochure across the Cabinet table. The official, said by others to be Nicholas Brady, the Treasury Secretary, flung it back, as if to say, "Here's what I think of you and your brochures, loudmouth."

"I said, 'Mr. President, now you know what the problem is in our Administration,'" Kemp recalls. "Your senior Cabinet leaders, officials, don't even understand what it is that you and I want to do."

When Kemp joined the White House entourage in Los Angeles a few days later, his passions and peculiarities were on full display. White House aides watched in wonder as a group of black Democratic mayors, awaiting a meeting with the President, swarmed around Kemp. "Jack Kemp is a beacon of light," one of them, Mayor Edward Vincent of Inglewood, said recently.

But Kemp had a talent for courting Presidential disapproval. When the entourage arrived at a Los Angeles boys' club the next day, Kemp acknowledged the applause by taking off his coat, then stood at the President's side and stole the crowd's attention with several exaggerated shoulder rolls. The pantomimed gesture seemed to say to Bush: *Take off your coat. Be more like me.*

"It was a little bit of a goofy thing to do," says a Kemp ally who was there.

When Kemp arrived at a reporters' breakfast a week later, the future of an urban aid bill was already in doubt; Republicans fretted that it rewarded rioters and Democrats deemed it paltry.

Kemp was at his oratorical best. When a reporter asked where Kemp's passions came from, Kemp recalled the dozen years he spent as a professional quarterback and the lessons of racial equality he had picked up in locker rooms filled with black athletes.

"This is my way of redeeming my existence on this earth," Kemp said. "I wasn't there with Rosa Parks or Dr. King or John Lewis, but I am here now and I am going to yell from the rooftops about what we need to do."

Kemp said that during the civil rights movement the Republican Party had "missed the opportunity" to oppose racism. "And frankly," Kemp warned, "to miss this opportunity is to lose what history rarely grants—a second chance."

The White House, with Darman's help, worked hard to pass an aid bill in the House that would bring about, at long last, Kemp's cherished enterprise zones. But the effort soon fell apart in the Senate, which turned the bill into a more ambitious vehicle for higher taxes and more spending. On the day after losing the election, Bush vetoed the bill.

After four years of Kemp's crusade, Government figures offer this gauge of its accomplishments: 3.5 million more Americans now live in poverty than when the effort began.

CHAPTER 12

Colin Powell: How Colin Powell Plays the Game

JON MEACHAM*

On one of the first days of 1991, as U.S. troops massed near the Saudi/Kuwaiti border, Stephen Solarz's telephone rang in his Capitol Hill office: General Colin Powell was on the line. Solarz, then a New York congressman, had just written a long article for *The New Republic* making the case for war in the Persian Gulf. At the time, President Bush was trying to build support for the use of force against Saddam Hussein; congressional hearings were underway, and with Senator Sam Nunn and two former chairmen of the Joint Chiefs of Staff (JCS)—Admiral William Crowe and General David Jones—publicly arguing to give economic sanctions more time, Solarz was a key Democratic hawk. The Powell call was brief but kind, a valentine about the magazine piece. "He was very generous and congratulated me on it," Solarz recalled recently. "But then I read in subsequent books that he was actually opposed to the points I was arguing, so I'm not sure what to make of that."

Solarz's mystification makes sense. According to Bob Woodward's book *The Commanders,* for which Powell was a major source, the general had reservations about going to war, favoring a containment strategy. Yet, once Bush decided to fight, it was Powell's job as chairman (the principal military advisor to the president) to carry out the wishes of his civilian boss. That Powell, an officer with a high sense of duty, did this is not at all surprising. What *is* striking about Powell around this time

---

*Reprinted with permission from *The Washington Monthly,* December 1994. Copyright by the Washington Monthly Company, 1611 Connecticut Ave., N.W., Washington, D.C. 20009, (202) 462-0128.

is how adroitly he cast himself as a member of the winning war party within the administration.

Hence the stroke call to Solarz; blind accounts in magazines and newspapers about Powell's eagerness and toughness; and his appearance with Secretary of Defense Dick Cheney before the Senate Armed Services Committee on December 4, 1990. There, he took on those such as Nunn, Crowe, and Jones, who believed that sanctions or limited air strikes could force Iraq out of Kuwait. "Many experts, amateurs and others in this town believe that this can be accomplished by such things as surgical air strikes, or perhaps a sustained air strike. And there are a variety of other nice, tidy, alleged lowcost, incremental, may-work options that are floated around with great regularity all over this town," Powell said. "Those strategies may work, but they also may not. Such strategies are designed to *hope* to win. They are not designed to win."

For Powell to be this dismissive of a position for which he had had such sympathy indicates that the general had decided not only to carry out his duty but also to carry political water for Bush. This was a tough Washington hand to play, but Powell did it beautifully. By the end of the war, he had, in the words of *U.S. News & World Report,* restored "the public's faith in its fighting force." People like Crowe and Jones were discredited, and Powell, who had privately told them—but never Bush—that he was on their side, came up a national hero, "America's Black Eisenhower" (as *National Review* dubbed him).

Now the Powell-for-President drumbeat is sounding throughout the land. In an October *Newsweek* cover story, Joe Klein wrote this of the general: "He stands, at 57, as the most respected figure in American public life. He is an African-American who transcends race; a public man who transcends politics. He seems a distinctly American character, with an easy confidence that inspires trust even among the most skeptical." R. W. Apple, Jr., in *The New York Times,* called Powell "a coveted general" in a page-one story about competing GOP and Democratic hopes to claim him as one of their own; in the *Los Angeles Times,* James Pinkerton published a column headlined "Colin Powell: A President for All Seasons."

Implicit in speculation about Powell's potential as a dream candidate is that he is somehow not of Washington, a figure (as Klein put it) who "transcends politics." His poll numbers reflect his popularity: 58 percent of Americans view him favorably and a phenomenally low 6 percent unfavorably (compare that to Bill Clinton's 41 percent negative rating in the same recent NBC News/*Wall Street Journal* survey). And a *Newsweek* poll found that 54 percent believe it's a plus that Powell "has no ties to politics as usual."

Powell, however, operates in Washington as shrewdly and capably as anyone in modern memory. He has held a string of some of the most prestigious and important posts in the capital—White House Fellow, military assistant to Secretary of Defense Caspar Weinberger, national security advisor to President Reagan, JCS chairman under Bush. "It was very clear early on that the advice and counsel he brought were more political than you might have expected from a man who's been in the military," recalls Tom Griscom, Reagan's director of communications from 1987 to 1988, when Powell was at the National Security Council. Margaret Tutwiler, James Baker's longtime aide, says Powell "knows how to work the departmental and interagency process." And the general was very helpful to prominent reporters, from Woodward on down. "He was clearly the guy to go to at the Pentagon, of all the civilians and all the officers, if you wanted direction on a story," says NBC News' Fred Francis, who covered the Pentagon from 1984 to 1993. "He was not a leaker in the traditional sense, but he wouldn't let you broadcast a bad story and if you already had information, he would generally confirm it. He always made himself available."

People who know Powell universally salute his efficiency, sense of humor, and ability—rare in a city seemingly dedicated to spinning its wheels—to get things done. "Weinberger was sometimes a difficult man to deal with, so I used to go to Colin," recalls Lawrence Korb, a former assistant secretary of Defense, of Powell's days as military assistant. "He's got a photographic memory, handles pressure very well, and is able to make things happen. It's a very rare combination."

At the moment, Powell has not only not announced whether he will run for president but also has yet to say officially whether he is a Republican, a Democrat, or something in between. "Nobody knows," claims Weinberger. For three decades, however, Powell's political patrons have been Republicans (Weinberger, Frank Carlucci, Reagan, and Bush); his best friends are former Assistant Secretary of Defense Richard Armitage (to whom Powell spoke by telephone every morning at 5:30 or 6:00 A.M. during the Reagan and Bush administrations) and Kenneth Duberstein, Reagan's last chief of staff; and his outlook seems generally conservative. During the 1988–89 presidential transition, for example, Powell wrote a *New York Times* op-ed titled "Why History Will Honor Mr. Reagan." For Republicans, fresh from their historic mid-term thrashing of Clinton and the Democrats, the partisanship of Gingrich and Dole may wear thin by 1996—which could mean that the GOP will move not to a presidential nominee such as Dole or Phil Gramm but will instead try to recruit a figure of national unity to head the ticket, leaving congressional Republicans to play hardball on the Hill. And about the only figure of national unity with Republican leanings is Colin Powell. Alternatively, from Powell's point of view, the GOP's gains in November may prompt him to embrace the Republicans and run as a moderate who can bridge the gaps in the party. Or there is yet another scenario: Powell could bypass traditional politics altogether and run as an independent.

Who is Powell? is the question animating Washington political chat these days. In a way, there seem to be two: Powell the rhetorical critic of domestic culture and Powell the military man. Oddly, the better of these seems to be the domestic thinker, the one we supposedly know the least about. Powell's vision of the country—formulated during his meritocratic rise in the military—is affecting. "I am where I am today because the Army takes care of its own," Powell said in his farewell address as JCS chairman. "I was allowed to rise based on performance." In a remarkable 1989 piece for *The Washington Times* on Martin Luther King, Jr.'s birthday, Powell movingly endorsed the civil rights movement that had taken shape in the summer of 1963 while he was overseas and his young family was living in Birmingham, his wife's hometown. Powell had returned home at Christmas from duty as a military advisor to the South Vietnamese army. "I was stunned, disheartened, and angry. While I had been fighting in Vietnam alongside brave soldiers trying to preserve their freedom, in my own land a long-simmering conflict had turned into an open fight in our streets and cities—a fight that had to be won."

He went on to articulate what could be the thematic outlines of a Powell presidency, one that rightly challenges both conservative and liberal assumptions. (It is a sensibility, ironically, very much like Clinton's, against whom Powell might run in 1996.) "Martin's vision was that the day would come when all Americans would someday sit together at the table of brotherhood. . . . We are not there yet. Martin would see that institutional racism is still a part of our society. He knew that character and ability are formed in the home and in the school. If he were alive today, he would be working hard to strengthen the black family. He would not be satisfied with education systems that still do not prepare our young people to take advantage of the opportunities available to them. I am sure he would have as a major goal a quality education for all Americans. He would also be determined to provide a good job for every American as a solution to underlying causes of second-class citizenship."

Powell could well be a candidate, like Clinton in 1992 and Robert Kennedy in 1968, able to unite whites and blacks, affluent and poor, with an explicit call for mutual responsibility. He could successfully argue that the country owes the little guy a hand up, and the little guy in turn owes the country discipline and hard work. These issues are inevitably charged with race, and Powell could, on the only-Nixon-could-go-to-China principle, be the leader who finally talks straight to minorities about work, crime, and self-pity. In fact, he already has. At the time of the Los Angeles riots in 1992, during a commencement address at the predominantly black Fisk University in Nashville, Powell said, "Let the fact that you are black or yellow or white be a source of pride and inspiration to you. Draw strength from it. Let it be someone else's problem, but never yours. Never hide behind it or use it as an excuse for not doing your best."

Like Eisenhower, who understood the American people's need for a dignified leader, Powell knows how to conduct himself; he was a powerful, quiet presence briefing the country on the Gulf War and the Carter mission to Haiti. Remember, too, how self-assured and, well, presidential he seemed the Saturday evening in June 1993 when he and then-Secretary of Defense Les Aspin publicly explained the bombing of Iraq in retribution for the alleged assassination plot against George Bush? The merits of the operation aside, Powell, in his Army green and bright decorations, was the grown-up; Aspin looked rumpled and out of his league in a khaki poplin suit.

Of course, the presidency is also about solving problems, and one rationale for a Powell candidacy would be that here's the man who ran the Gulf War; why not give him a shot at health care, inner city schools, the deficit? Surely, this line of thinking goes, the general can't do any worse than those who have gone before. This argument will be familiar to anyone who remembers presidential boomlets for figures such as Douglas MacArthur, Ross Perot, and Lee Iacocca.

The problem with thinking of Powell as a savior who will throw the money changers out of the Washington temple is that for a long time he has been one of the money changers. This is the second Powell, and the lesson of his public life is that he is a consensus seeker, a man who wants everyone on board before he moves. The general's common denominator, from giving each service roughly the same budget to defending troubled weapons systems on behalf of the Pentagon, is the search for the thing surest not to upset the status quo. The most famous example of this character-istic is the Powell Doctrine, which holds that the U.S. should only deploy military force in overwhelming numbers and in favorable climes so that our side is virtually guaranteed victory. Applications of the doctrine mean that going into desert combat, with heavy armor and air superiority, is good; fighting in jungles (as in Vietnam) or mountains (as in Bosnia) is more difficult, because determined guerrillas could wear U.S. troops down and should therefore be avoided.

While caution in deploying troops can save lives, Powell's parallel characteris-tic—the urge for political consensus—is demonstrably less desirable when it comes to brokering the claims of competing special interests (in his case, among the Army, Navy, Air Force, and Marine Corps). Making tough calls is what sensible Americans should want a president to do, and Powell already has a substantial record, one that is less about knocking heads together than it is about log-rolling. If he runs for na-tional office, this record should be on the table. Should he not run, we can still learn from his career how even the ablest, most extraordinary men—the general is surely one of these—have trouble overcoming those forces in Washington that encourage inertia.

A SOLDIER'S STORY

To understand Powell, you first have to understand where he comes from. The son of Jamaican immigrants, Powell grew up in the South Bronx in the forties and fifties, years when the neighborhood was middle class and racially and economically mixed. Powell got ahead in life by dint of two institutions: City College of New York and the Army's ROTC. Graduating from CCNY in 1958, Powell began his career as a second lieutenant and served two tours in Vietnam. There, he rescued his commanding offi-cer from a burning helicopter; in 1969, he graduated second in his class at the Com-mand and General Staff College at Fort Leavenworth. Back in the U.S., in 1972, he was stationed in Washington, getting a master's degree in business administration at George Washington University when he was selected as a White House Fellow—and his career took off.

White House Fellows are young lawyers, military officers, business executives, and aspiring politicos selected to spend a year working in the executive branch. Alumni include Henry Cisneros, Robert McFarlane, Tim Wirth, Doris Kearns Good-win, and CNN president Tom Johnson. Powell won one of the precious slots and was quickly picked up by Weinberger and Carlucci, who were then at Nixon's Office of

Management and Budget. In 1991, Powell told the *Los Angeles Times* that the fellowship was "a defining experience," and the year in the White House taught him that, in Washington, "the whole thing is greased by compromise and consensus."

So the life experiences in the military and the government that created the good about Powell—his appreciation of equal access to good schools, of the importance of work, and of the ability to make government a force for good—have also produced the bad about him. Which is this: While Powell is regarded by those who have worked with him as a straightshooting broker, his Washington years taught him not to ruffle feathers, even if the feathers in question desperately deserved to be ruffled.

"I've always thought of General Powell as sort of on the leading edge of the conventional wisdom," says David Evans, a former military reporter for the *Chicago Tribune* who is now director of national defense programs for Business Executives for National Security. For a man who was at the Pentagon with Weinberger, at the National Security Council with Reagan, and head of the JCS, the conventional wisdom was to preserve as much as possible of the federal pie for defense, even in a time of dwindling threats and rising deficits.

On becoming chairman, Powell set up a small working group in the Joint Chiefs' office, with lines to the comptroller's office and to Cheney's shop, to produce the first major military downsizing plan. "He thought he had to take the lead and get out in front of Congress and the administration," says Tom Christie, a former member of Cheney's staff. "Powell wanted to do it on his terms." The result was perhaps Powell's finest bureaucratic hour when, in 1990, he convinced Bush and Cheney to maintain what Powell dubbed a "base force" of 1.6 million with overall defense spending set at about $290 billion by 1993. In a pre-emptive interview with *The Washington Post* before the administration had officially announced its position, Powell said a "a fundamental break point" would occur "somewhere in the neighborhood of maybe a 20 to 25 percent reduction from where we are now" in both force size and military expenditures.

But when you look at the big picture, Powell helped preserve an essentially Cold War budget with no Cold War foe to fight. To be sure, there were cuts from previously planned levels and the real costs of the base force by 1995 would have been roughly 20 percent lower than they were in 1989, but the containment of the Soviet Union accounted for more than 50 percent of that 1989 defense budget. Evidence that more could have been done came when the Clinton administration both cut planned spending by $60 billion more and the force to 1.45 million troops with—this is essential—*no obvious effect on readiness,* according to the Congressional Budget Office and a Pentagon commission on readiness comprised of flag officers and chaired by retired General Edward Meyer. The savings came from killing some weapons systems and much of the SDI program. To be sure, there have been reports this fall questioning the readiness of a few Army divisions, but these shortfalls are not the result of too little money being spent on defense but of too much money being spent on the wrong things. Instead of earmarking enough dollars, for example, to keep important troops well armed, billions go to weapons systems such as the F-22 that are of dubious necessity and quality and to funding overlapping projects such as separate service air fleets—two areas, by the way, Powell did little to reform. Obviously, as a soldier, Powell's inclination was to protect the military's turf as far as he could, and this meant preserving the largest base force he could get away with to satisfy, on the one hand, calls in Congress for a peace dividend and, on the other, the chiefs' reluctance to cut *anything.*

Part of the reason for Powell's protectiveness of the basic military structure is cultural: A chairman meets twice a week in The Tank, a secure, top-secret Pentagon conference room, with the service chiefs; he knows them, came up through the ranks with them, wants to make them happy. Powell fell victim to this tendency even though he was the chief implementer of the landmark Goldwater-Nichols Act of 1986, which bolstered the JCS chairman's power. Before the act, a chairman could not make official recommendations to the Secretary of Defense or the president without unanimous support from all the chiefs—a situation that reduced most chairmen to irrelevance, since such consensus was virtually impossible to achieve. After the act, however, the chairman alone was made "principal military advisor" to the president, was given a deputy, and now controlled the Joint Staff.

In spite of Powell's newfound statutory power, his experience as chairman suggests that the basic urge for consensus remains ingrained in the military (and political) world. The chiefs are, after all, still the chairman's constituency, even though the chairman is officially a presidential appointee. It is much easier to take a few hits on the Hill than to irritate your people, the guys who, after all, are in *your* business. "Powell's formula was the same old force reduced by whatever it took to meet congressional demands that could not be resisted for a smaller budget," says Edward N. Luttwak, a defense expert and author of *The Logic of War and Peace,* "and this assurance of continuity cemented his ties to the service chiefs, who gave him their loyalty and respect in return."

By the early nineties, however, with the Soviet Union dead, the bills for the Reagan spendup coming due, and the deficit continuing to rise, even conservatives such as Sam Nunn were eager to make the Pentagon spend its money wisely. So on July 2, 1992, Nunn took to the Senate floor and attacked the military's expensive redundancies, arguing that billions could be saved and military capability preserved by commonsensically cutting huge areas of overlap.

Powell's answer to Nunn came in the form of a February 1993 report to Congress on the military's warfighting roles and missions (which branch gets which weapons, helicopters, missiles, etc.). Like all bureaucracies, public or private, the military never exactly jumps at the chance to make major changes; the existing structure was originally hashed out at Key West between Secretary of Defense James Forrestal and the service chiefs in 1948. Since then, the different services have been geniuses at securing and clinging to pieces of technological and budgetary action for themselves—the Navy and the Air Force both build and operate satellites, for instance, and both design, build, test, and field cruise missiles. The branches' love of their own fleets of aircraft prompted Barry Goldwater to say frequently we are the only military in the world with four air forces.

After Nunn's speech, Powell and his staff circulated three drafts of the chairman's recommendations; each got progressively less ambitious as it made its way around the Pentagon. Insiders say Powell wanted to be bolder but, with no political backup from the executive branch or the Hill, was afraid of infuriating the services. As Bush fought for re-election, he and Cheney were uninterested in sweeping change; neither Clinton nor Aspin seriously pursued restructuring after they came to power. "Inside the building, Powell was taking a lot of heat, and he saw himself fighting this battle all alone," says a former top Pentagon official. "So he decided the hell with it and sent up a modest report."

With the report, the general managed to disappoint everybody outside the services, from Nunn on the right to House Armed Services Committee Chairman Ron Dellums on the left. Reviewing Powell's product, the nonpartisan General Accounting Office found "it did not recommend significant reductions in overlapping functions," and the GAO cited 15 areas of possible major change that Powell did not address.

Take two cases. The first: Both the Army and the Marines have expeditionary troops to respond quickly to a crisis anywhere in the world. Each of the Marines' three 10,000-man divisions and four of the Army's 12 divisions (the 82nd Airborne, which is for paratrooping; the 101st air assault, which is for helicopter attacks; and two light infantry divisions, which put soldiers on the ground) are designed for rapid deployment. There is no historical evidence, however, that we need more light infantry capability than the three Marine divisions and elements of the 82nd and 101st can provide.

Between 1945 and 1978, for example, the Congressional Budget Office found that of the 215 incidents that resulted in some sort of U.S. military action, only 5 percent required a force of division size or more of these contingency forces. Since 1978, only one operation—the Gulf—required more than a full expeditionary division. This includes Grenada, Beirut, Panama, Somalia, Rwanda, and Haiti. And even in the Gulf, the largest American clash of arms since Vietnam, neither of the two ground Army light infantry divisions—which since 1983 have, unlike their predecessors, included no tanks—were deployed, because what was needed were heavily armored troops, not light infantry soldiers. (Heavy Army divisions, by the way, are what the military *has* agreed to cut, even though experience suggests precisely the opposite course would be best.)

Another division in the light infantry force structure Powell left untouched is the 82nd, designed to drop troops into hostile territory from the air by parachute. But the last time the U.S. conducted a full-scale parachute operation with an entire division was World War II. In three major operations since—Korea, Vietnam, and Panama—the 82nd dropped at most a third of a division; in the Gulf the 82nd was involved in no major battles.

The GAO estimates that if the U.S. had another Desert Storm deployment, we would still have enough light infantry troops in our current force structure to maintain a presence in all parts of the world and conduct two—not one, but two—operations equivalent in size to the 1989 invasion of Panama. So the wise thing to do would be to eliminate the two Army ground light infantry divisions and combine the airborne and air assault divisions (with a third of the resulting force designated for parachute drops). The CBO says the savings from this step would be about $16 billion. If, to get the Army to go along, you wanted to preserve one of its ground light infantry divisions—which could be useful if the Marine divisions were all somehow tied up in one place, however unlikely that is—it would be essential to equip them with some kind of tank component for protection. During the Somalia operation, remember, ground commanders of light infantry troops thought they needed more tanks than they had prior to the 1993 firefight that killed 18 American servicemen. Keeping one division would still save $14.5 billion.

This is not liberal whining about spending money on defense. Nunn and private-sector groups such as Business Executives for National Security argue for such efficient, cost-saving steps in order to make sure existing troops are well trained and well equipped. If you fear—as anyone sane should—a "hollow force" of ill-trained and ill-equipped soldiers, you should be especially interested in making sure that money spent on defense is spent wisely; conversely, this means that money wasted on whole divisions we don't need can't be used to arm the divisions we do need.

But did Powell acknowledge that the Army's light divisions are at worst redundant and at best ill equipped? No. He said the Army and the Marines should maintain separate expeditionary forces. ("The capabilities of the contingency and expeditionary forces in the Army and Marine Corps provide decision makers with valuable alternatives and should be retained.") Then Powell took the time-honored Washington step of suggesting that the issue be studied further. A commission on roles and missions was formed and is expected to report next summer, but the Secretary of Defense is under no obligation to do anything the commission recommends.

PLANE TRUTHS

Powell did not limit his log-rolling to the Army and the Marines. He took care of the Navy and the Air Force, too. Right now, the U.S. can use either or both of these services for air strikes. The Air Force operates long-range and medium-range bombers from air bases; the Navy flies attack aircraft off carriers at sea. With the end of the Cold War, though, the need to hold in check the Air Force's long-range bombers (B-1s, B-2s, and B-52s) for possible nuclear missions disappeared, leaving more of its aircraft available for conventional strikes. Meanwhile, the Navy is building toward a 12-carrier fleet (carriers are famously expensive and cumbersome to operate). In the old days, the admirals defended building carriers because, as World War II demonstrated, carriers are ideal for fighting other large navies. Then the Soviets collapsed, and there were no other navies. No problem, said the Navy; now we need carriers because they can defend U.S. interests in regional conflicts.

While it is true that there are some missions that carriers can more effectively execute, in many cases the U.S. already has bases around the world and Air Force aircraft to handle tasks the Navy likes to claim only carriers can complete. There is, for example, a U.S. base in Turkey from which we could launch aircraft to fight in the Persian Gulf. The other potential hotspot Pentagon planners worry about these days is Korea, and we could use our bases in Japan to fend off a North Korean invasion of the South. And of course any crisis in our hemisphere could be handled by the numerous U.S. bases here.

Even with carriers available, it often makes more sense to use the Air Force's land-based fleet of roughly 200 long-range and 300 medium-range craft (the F-117, the F-111, and the F15E). In the Gulf War, for instance, although there were six carriers in the region, land-based Air Force and Marine planes flew 76 percent of the missions; the Navy flew just 24 percent. Moreover, the Navy planes had to use land bases to be able to carry their maximum bomb loads. In fact, the greatest naval success story of the Gulf War was not its carrier air attacks but its Tomahawk missile launches. Problem is, the Tomahawk example is not an argument for more *carriers,* because the missiles can be fired from smaller vessels, including Aegis cruisers, Arleigh Burke destroyers, and attack submarines.

Moreover, in the future, sea-based aircraft may be even less effective than they already are. The Navy is retiring its A-6 and has firm plans for only an interim replacement—the E/F model of the F/A-18. And because the F/A-18 has a shorter range and smaller payload than the A-6, the floating cities we are paying for now may not have effective planes to carry. And a final point: Carriers bring legions of ships with them, severely limiting a carrier group's offensive capability, because you also have to defend the cruisers, destroyers, and supply ships that come along. Roughly, $10 billion spent on a carrier group can buy you 30 offensive aircraft; $10 billion spent by the Air Force can buy you about 300. Nevertheless, in 1993, under Powell's chairmanship, the Navy asked for an $800 million down payment on a new $4.8 billion carrier. Nunn—hardly a flowers-in-his-hair peacenik—asked Powell to consider the proper balance between the two kinds of air power. The JCS chairman responded that there was no need for change. He thereby preserved the Navy's favorite boondoggle.

Eliminating five carriers would net $17 billion and this year would have enabled the country to have met each military crisis that arose in which carriers were deployed, including the flare-ups in the Persian Gulf and in Haiti. Just cutting back two carriers would have saved $7 billion. But Powell ducked the issue altogether, content to let the Navy keep its toys. "Roles and missions ends up in every chairman's 'too-hard-to-handle' box," says General David Jones, a former JCS chairman. "It's just very difficult."

One of the most enduring images of Powell is as the victorious master of the Gulf War; any future political campaign will inevitably include stirring pictures of the troops in the desert. What the ads won't mention is that one of the central goals of the war—destroying Saddam's army, especially his elite Republican Guard—did not happen. "First we are going to cut it off," Powell declared of the Iraqi army as the war began, "then we are going to kill it."

Instead, most of the Guard escaped from Kuwait with much of their equipment, assets that enable Saddam to remain in power. General Norman Schwarzkopf had planned a two-pronged attack. As James G. Burton, a retired Air Force colonel and author of the book *The Pentagon Wars,* points out, there were two escape routes for the Iraqis out of the Kuwaiti theater, one westward through the Euphrates River corridor and one north out of Basra. To cut off both routes, Schwarzkopf planned to "close the back door" to Iraq by having the Army's XVIII Corps and VII Corps form a hook that blocked both. On the ground, however, the VII Corps moved too slowly across the desert, leaving the northern hatch open. Meanwhile, the Iraqis, sensing major defeat, began fleeing to the north.

About this time back in Washington, television reporters were beaming back images of the so-called "Highway of Death," a ragtag collection of fleeing Iraqis— not the Republican Guard. The White House, sensitive to the appearance that we were bombing a retreating force, pressured Powell to wrap things up quickly, according to Schwarzkopf's memoirs and the forthcoming *The Generals' War* by Michael R. Gordon and General Bernard E. Trainor. "In recommending an end to the war," Gordon and Trainor write, "Powell was motivated by considerations that went beyond military concerns. Determined that the military would erase the stain of Vietnam and come out of the Gulf War victorious with its honor intact, the JCS chairman wanted to avoid the impression that the United States was piling on and killing Iraqis for the sake of killing them. If that meant erring on the side of caution, Powell was prepared to live with that."

At the time, Schwarzkopf thought the Guard was trapped. So he held his famous February 27 press conference, declaring, "The gates are closed. There is no way out." A few hours after Schwarzkopf's press conference, Powell called him to ask if he would agree to an end to offensive operations the next morning. Schwarzkopf initially told Powell he wanted another day to mop up. When Powell called back and pushed again, Schwarzkopf said OK, agreeing to a cease-fire roughly 100 hours after the ground war had begun. A few hours after that, Schwarzkopf found out that the back door was not in fact closed; he had received bad information from the field, but the cease-fire had already been announced.

As it developed, no field commanders thought the Guard had yet been destroyed or that closing the circle would have cost many U.S. lives. But the Washington political pressure, combined with confusion, had ended the war. Powell's instincts in this case—wrap it up and save lives—were of course the right ones, even though the inadvertent result was leaving a strong Saddam in power. What's interesting, however, about the general's performance is that his role was as much political as it was military; he was, in this case, a general in the tradition of an Alexander Haig, a man of policy and Washington rather than of the battlefield. Of dealing with Powell during the war, Schwarzkopf later told Gordon and Trainor he was never sure when Powell was offering a Powell view or was representing the views of others—a classic political tactic: "I never had the ability to sort out what was Powell, what was Scowcroft, what was Cheney, what was the president."

Job performance aside, for politics today the question is: Will Powell run? Already, a "Draft Powell" committee has been formed by Chuck Kelly, a Washington hand who also worked for the last general to become president: Eisenhower. This is a useful parallel, for in his military career Ike was also derisively described as a "political general" who never forced major change. Yet, in the White House, Eisenhower effectively kept defense spending under control in part because his impeccable military credentials prevented the Pentagon from attacking him. Like Eisenhower and like Franklin Roosevelt, who served eight years as assistant secretary of the Navy, Powell knows government intimately, which means he knows the tricks bureaucrats and agencies play to keep themselves afloat even after their usefulness has disappeared. There is much potential, then, for Powell to emulate some of our greatest presidents.

Yet, it seems probable that Powell, a proud man who has a military man's love of precision, won't put up with what it takes to run. NBC's Fred Francis, who considers Powell a professional friend and says that in 13 years of official and semi-official contact Powell never misled him, sometimes saw the results of the general's obsession with accuracy. "When I did something that he thought was wrong, I'd go on the air at 7 o'clock, and the phone would ring right after that," Francis recalls. "It would be Powell on the line saying 'Francis, you're full of shit.' " A presidential campaign, with its Alice-in-Wonderland quality and slap-dash reporting, is not designed for a man of Powell's temperament. He may decide, with his lucrative lecture fees and his already-mythic reputation, to lead a comfortable, quiet life as an undisputed hero.

If the general were to run and turn out to be a dragon-slayer, one with a vision of unity at home and the courage to take on competing special interests, then he could be a great president. But judging from the record, this would require a different Colin Powell—not the one the nation currently idolizes.

CHAPTER 13

Michael S. Dukakis: Blending Principle with Politics in Leading State Government from "Duke I" to "Duke II"

RICHARD A. LOVERD[1]

I sit here all day trying to persuade people to do the things they ought to have sense enough to do without my persuading them.[2]

—Harry S. Truman

My parents often told me when I was a boy that much had been given to me and much was expected of me. Those words apply with even more relevance to the Commonwealth of Massachusetts. . . . Our standards must be high. Our commitments must call for the best in us. And our goals must be lofty ones.[3]

—Michael S. Dukakis
First Inaugural Speech (1975)

Now the citizens of Massachusetts have *given* me something that is rare in public life—a second chance. They have a right to expect that in return I will strive over these next four years not only to do well, but to do *better*—and to lead this great state on their behalf.[4]

—Michael S. Dukakis
Second Inaugural Speech (1983)

In an interview some years ago, Michael Dukakis was asked whether the rantings of his critics bothered him. In reply, he noted that "[House Speaker] Sam Rayburn said any jackass could knock down a barn, but only a carpenter could build one. So you've got to decide in life whether you're a jackass or a carpenter."[5]

In a very real sense, as governor, Michael Dukakis was a carpenter, an active reformer who tried to improve the quality of Massachusetts government by providing the kind of leadership and forging the sorts of institutional mechanisms that would make it more open, efficient, rational, and moral in its proceedings. He sought to build more integrity and competence into that government through substantive reforms which would eliminate the cronyism, corruption, inefficiency, and irrational behavior of the past, behavior which, according to Theodore H. White, placed it among the "most squalid, corrupt and despicable" states in the union.[6] In his so doing, his expectation was that the public service would reflect the principles of a noble profession, one worthy of attracting the best of its citizens, who in turn would use government as an instrument of public good for all.[7]

In the pages that follow, a number of ways in which Governor Dukakis attempted to exercise his leadership in promoting his principles and reforming state government will be presented, with particular regard to his first (1975–1979) and second (1983–1987) terms in office, commonly referred to as "Duke I" and "Duke II." As we will see, much as one of his heroes, Harry Truman,[8] was faced with the challenge of "persuading people to do things they ought to have sense enough to do without his persuading them," so too was the governor himself similarly tested as he sought to raise expectations and move Massachusetts forward.

THE EARLY RECORD

By the time Michael Stanley Dukakis was inaugurated as governor in January of 1975, he had already attained considerable stature as a man of competence and integrity, traits well suited for a leader seeking to reform Massachusetts government and reverse its reputation as one of the nation's most corrupt and inept states. From his childhood in progressive suburban Brookline, through his college years at Swarthmore and Harvard Law School, and into his early political career in the State House of Representatives, such traits were present. For example, during his childhood his bright, Greek immigrant parents stressed the need for truthfulness, hard work, frugality, and a sense of obligation to those less fortunate;[9] and while he was in high school, his intellect and natural leadership abilities sent him to the top of his class. In addition, his *sense of pace* (as a steady, persistent person who could run any number of figurative and physical races well, including the Boston marathon) and his *sense of self* (as one noted for his self-confidence and his unwillingness to be peer-driven) only heightened his uniqueness among his peers.[10]

So too at Swarthmore College was he noted in its 1955 yearbook as a "natural leader" who was "self-confident" and a "man of ideals seeking to apply them." Interestingly, in one such application the yearbook further records his "unpopularity with the local barbers," a reference to his enterprising, and ethical, business of cutting hair for blacks, and for other boycotting white students, when the local barbers in the town of Swarthmore would not.[11] And in another formative instance, while still a freshman this future governor worked on the campaign of Philadelphia mayoral candidate Joe Clark, a principled Brahmin who, as city controller, had spent two years uncovering graft and corruption (with nine Republicans committing suicide in the process).[12] As Dukakis watched and participated firsthand, candidate Clark, with the symbol of a broom and the slogan "Sweep out corruption," made history by turning out the reigning Republicans for the first time in 67 years.[13]

Little wonder, then, that such socialization would produce a man with a strong desire for honest, productive governance that promotes competence and open access instead of the exchange of personal favors, intervention on behalf of special interests, and a form of "go-along-to-get-along" cronyism that is often suspect.

Little wonder also that Dukakis's first move as a state legislator in 1963 would be an attempt to depose John F. Thompson, the "ham-fisted, hard-drinking House Speaker [universally known as "The Iron Duke"] . . . who ruled the House with a combination of braggadocio, bullying and shrewdness"[14] and represented the very cronyism he despised. While this move proved ultimately unsuccessful, other more promising ones followed during his years as a legislator from 1963 to 1970. Among them were such efforts as curbing the powers of the Governor's Council and independent public authorities, exposing abuses in the awarding of architectural contracts and subsequently creating a Designer Selection Board to get the architectural selection process out of politics, reforming the civil service, creating a merit promotion system for the state police, strengthening conflict of interest and campaign finance laws, and providing executive reorganization authority for the office of the governor.[15]

In perhaps his most significant achievement as a legislator, Representative Dukakis was instrumental in the passage of the nation's first no-fault auto insurance bill. As Charles Kenney and Robert Turner note, this legislation showed much of the Dukakis substance and style in action:

> First, it was a reform, pitting consumer interests against those of politically powerful forces, namely, the doctors and lawyers who were pushing up insurance costs with expensive court cases.
>
> Second, it was a rational approach to the problem—a solution advanced, in fact, by two academics [former Dukakis torts teacher and Harvard Law School Professor Robert Keeton and his assistant, Jeff O'Connell].
>
> Third, stubborn persistence through six years of defeats was needed, and Dukakis had it.[16]

And as Kenney and Turner go on to say, even the climax was instructive:

> When the bill finally passed both branches of the legislature in 1970, Dukakis was appointed to a conference committee to iron out the differences, but after wrangling among the participants threatened the whole bill, a new conference committee was appointed, and Dukakis was not among those making the final changes. A few days later, however, he took the microphone in the House to address any final concerns before the bill was sent to become law. For two solid hours, Dukakis answered questions calmly and in detail, drawing from a deep well of knowledge to describe the bill's intricacies

and implications. When the last question had been answered, his colleagues rose in applause, an extraordinary tribute rarely seen in the chamber.[17]

Therefore, with this record of competence and integrity to support him, it should not be surprising that when, in 1974, a fiscal crisis and the ill winds of Watergate corruption were howling, a free-spending[18] Republican governor in the person of Francis Sargent would be swept aside in favor of the frugal, honest Democrat Dukakis.

DUKE I: BALANCING THE BOOKS AND HOLDING TO PRINCIPLE

Unfortunately for Dukakis, some of the forces that helped elect him to office in 1974 now threatened to push him out, particularly those related to the state's fiscal crisis. After having campaigned on a platform of efficient management and clean government, with a "lead pipe" promise of no new taxes, he soon discovered that the budget deficit and overall economic condition of the state was far worse than had been originally thought. Through a combination of "the 1973 oil embargo, a national recession, rampant inflation,"[19] and considerable spending during the Sargent years, less and less money was available for the state budget at a time when more and more was being demanded from it. In the process, a suspected preelection shortfall of $100 million soon ballooned into a multiple of that, making it far more difficult to balance the books and restore the public's, and the financial community's, faith in the government and the governor.

Much to Dukakis's chagrin, he noted that "We were rapidly getting a reputation as the New York City of state governments. The New York City situation started to affect our own ability to function [and] we came very close to defaulting on our obligations."[20] In fact, he further stated that "for the first 18 months at least, that was the most important single issue."[21]

In the end, the fiscal issue was resolved, but not without considerable pain, some of which was made worse by the actions of the governor himself. For example, rather than seek legislation to raise taxes during his early months when legislative leaders were urging him to act quickly (because they considered doing so inevitable and because blame could be placed on the preceding governor), Dukakis chose to ignore their advice and hold to his no-tax campaign promise, seeking budget cuts in the hope that they would solve the problem. However, by the spring of 1975, as the deficit deepened to over $500 million, it became woefully clear that cuts alone would not solve the problem. More taxes would have to be imposed. As a result of his cutting expenditures *and* raising taxes, a whole range of constituencies felt aggrieved and placed the blame on Dukakis: liberal Democrats and state employees were upset by his cuts in social programs and state spending, while conservatives were offended by his increased taxes. And by his holding to his principles of fiscal austerity and no new taxes for so long, people were left with the impression that the governor's leadership reflected an unwillingness to listen, a self-righteousness, and perhaps even a certain counterproductive stubbornness.[22]

This sort of principled leadership revealed itself in other ways as well. For example, in his quest for a more open, honest, and competent government divorced from the corrupting influences of politics, the governor abolished the patronage office. Obviously, for legislators used to the exchange of favors through gubernatorial patronage appointments, this sort of good government reform was not good news and could hardly be expected to win their support. But the governor felt differently. For while the absence of patronage "certainly didn't help legislative relationships . . . it [did make] it possible for cabinet secretaries and commissioners to do their jobs without getting calls every second day from the governor's office to put some other political worthy on the payroll." Furthermore, to accept the tradition of patronage meant "making room for some folks who are not very good, and for a limited number who are good," and Dukakis believed that was "not how government ought to run."[23] Instead, he sought "to go about the business of legislating in the public interest without jobs or favors, preferring to 'neither threaten nor cajole' the legislators, [and relying] on reason to win them to his side."[24] By taking such a stand, he realized there were problems; but as he saw it, "you give up something . . . on the political side, [while] you gain on the management and policy side,"[25] and it was a loss he was willing to bear.

The nonpolitical criteria provided by the governor in selecting top-level personnel are particularly instructive in pointing out his policy/management emphasis. In particular, his "marching orders" for those chosen required that they (1) have generalist rather than specialist qualifications, (2) need not have political experience, (3) be strong enough not to be co-opted by constituency groups, and (4) be good managers who can run bureaucracies. Through this approach, the governor expected that his appointees would demonstrate competence over politics and help to transform the governmental climate of the state from one for the advocates of special interests to one favoring a broader public interest.[26]

Of course, with these new selection procedures in place, the constituencies who lost access and influence were none too pleased; nor, for that matter, were the individuals with political savvy, including those who had worked on the Dukakis campaign who would most likely need to look elsewhere for a job. And for many of the governor's top nonpolitical appointees, with views more attuned to policy than to politics, a certain difficulty in working within that political system would most likely ensue. In this latter regard, the consumer-oriented, and impolitic, views of insurance commissioner James Stone and banking commissioner Carol Greenwald were particularly disturbing to insurance executives and bankers and did little to endear this administration to the business community. Indeed, in Greenwald's case, "Her determined pro-consumer efforts, combined with a style that could be abrasive and heavy-handed, made her, in her own words, 'almost a nationally hated symbol to bankers across America.'"[27]

Beyond personnel selection, the organization and management of the Dukakis administration had a decentralized thrust, and perhaps nowhere was this more evident than in the governor's preference for cabinet government. After having seen what he considered to be an excessive amount of influence by central staff over the chief executives and cabinet officers in both the Sargent and the Nixon administrations, Dukakis chose a purposefully lean staff for his office, an arrangement that allowed the ten cabinet secretaries to handle the policy and administration at their levels without "a lot of gubernatorial advisors who were second-guessing them."[28] Cabinet heads were allowed to select their own subcabinet members, conduct their own legislative relations, and do their own testifying before the legislature.[29] Furthermore, cabinet officials were also told that they and their agency heads could testify in favor of bills on which the governor's office had no position, as long as they made it clear that their testimony was personal and not meant to represent official positions.[30] In so doing, this sort of delegation encouraged a considerable amount of freedom of action which was not without its risks; for with only the thinnest of centralized gubernatorial supervision, the different department heads could shift attention to themselves and further their own individual policy prerogatives while ignoring the governor's needs and sending the administration in many different, sometimes unwanted, directions.

Indeed, with regard to the uncontrolled behavior of cabinet heads, an exasperated communications director, Michael Widmer, exclaimed, "It was ridiculous. . . . The cabinet announces the good news, and you get to announce the bad news."[31] For example, "Just before the start of the . . . re-election campaign of 1977, when the struggling administration had finally produced its first budget surplus, the best news of the term was announced by Jack Buckley, the secretary of administration and finance—to the fury of the senior staff, who had not even been told by Buckley that he had a surplus to announce."[32]

Interestingly, as another part of his effort to make his cabinet work in a cooperative, decentralized fashion, the use of open, public cabinet meetings proved to be less successful than Dukakis had hoped; for while they might have demonstrated his accessibility, they did little to further managerial aims. As the governor noted, "They tended to be more show-and-tell operations for the press and the public than they were serious and deliberative sessions,"[33] and this custom only made central, coordinated direction of the agencies and their heads that much more difficult.

With the preceding actions in mind, it is clear that the governor held to his principles and tried to economize, curb patronage, promote competence, and decentralize power in ways that reflected his desire for a more rational and less political government. However, it is also clear that, in so doing, he undercut his own ability to lead.

By his decentralizing power, less central policy direction as well as political counsel were available to him from his immediate staff. By his cutting the budget and raising taxes, a wide range of liberal and conservative interest groups turned against him. Eliminating patronage and acting dismissive toward the legislators made it more difficult to work with them. And selecting top personnel with nonpolitical criteria tended only to heighten their, and his, inability to deal with their surrounding political climate. As a result, there was less focus, less listening, less coordination, and in the final analysis, less politics than there should have been, factors that undoubtedly played key roles in his primary election loss to fellow Democrat and next governor, Edward King, in 1978.

Perhaps as a way of underscoring the point, soon after that loss, Dukakis's former appointments secretary, Andrew Sutcliffe, noted that the governor "definitely recognizes his shortcomings. He knows that being governor means being a governmental leader and a political leader. He knows that he was a disaster in the second."[34]

DUKE II: MAKING THE MOST OF A SECOND CHANCE

In January 1979, after having lived through what wife Kitty described as a "public death" and what transportation secretary Frederick Salvucci later called a "cold shower,"[35] Michael Dukakis characteristically moved on, trying to put the pain behind him and analyze his loss while teaching students and consulting key figures at Harvard's John F. Kennedy School of Government. In so doing, he learned a number of lessons, including the need to become a better listener by working to overcome his image of aloofness and rigidity and by reaching out to others. In addition, he came to recognize that "being 'political' was not necessarily bad, and rewarding friends and supporters who had been loyal and competent was an acceptable, perhaps even intelligent, way of behaving."[36] Also of particular importance during this time was the relationship he developed with one John Sasso, a seasoned Kennedy political operative who would come to serve as Dukakis's 1982 campaign manager, Duke II chief of staff,[37] and ongoing political alter ego in the years to come.

Meanwhile, as Dukakis continued to hone his leadership skills, the climate which once supported Governor Edward King began to erode as his talents came more and more into question. As King sought to promote conservative policies and not only cut but dismantle the state government, the liberals who had rejected Dukakis in 1978 began to look back toward his years in office with fondness, particularly after Ronald Reagan pointed to King as his "favorite Democratic governor." In addition, King's resistance to the provision of more state aid to localities in the face of property tax limits set by the passage of Proposition 2½ only served to anger those localities. And finally, during the 1982 campaign the Dukakis reputation for honesty and integrity was particularly showcased as several well-publicized scandals in the King administration involving bribery, larceny, and suicide challenged its governor's honesty and competence. Given these self-inflicted wounds, in a very real sense one might say that Governor King's reelection was his to lose rather than Dukakis's to win.

In any event, regardless of whether it was a change of heart on the part of Dukakis or a lack of sense on the part of King, on January 6, 1983, it was Michael Dukakis who once again strode back into the State House, given a second chance, and determined to do better this second time around.

For Dukakis, things would be different this time, and they were. After all, he was more seasoned.[38] This time he knew the ropes, and this time he'd know which ones to pull. As he himself observed; "I am a different person: more comfortable in the job, more experienced. And I knew what I had in front of me. You can't know what kinds of problems will confront you until you've actually been elected and have had the experience of trying to take over and manage. It makes all the difference in the world to have been there before."[39] Even the economy seemed to cooperate, with, for the most part, soaring revenues and low unemployment this time around.[40]

On the basis of his seasoning, the governor sought a different kind of government for Duke II, one that had executives with (1) *more experience and loyalty*, (2) *more central coordination and control,* (3) *more continuity,* (4) *more focus,* and (5) *more listening and consensus building.* For example, in the first instance, top personnel were chosen by the governor on the basis of their demonstrated governmental experience and political savvy, as well as any technical and managerial ability, so that they would not only know what to do but also be able to reach out and work with the different publics around them.[41] And in that selection process, loyalty would also matter, so that they could be trusted to work in the governor's interests instead of their own.[42] As a consequence, unlike Duke I, this governor selected many from the campaign organization, particularly seasoned managers that he knew and trusted who could work together for him.[43] In addition to John Sasso, who moved from being the campaign manager to the governor's chief of staff, these managers included Alden Raine (to director of economic development) , Frank Keefe (to secretary of administration and finance), Frederick Salvucci (to secretary of transportation), and Ira Jackson (to director of the Department of Revenue).

As a complement to the loyalty and competence in the selection process, much more coordination and control from a larger central staff was also in evidence, reflecting a change from earlier notions of decentralized cabinet government to closer centralized supervision of key executives. In the process, "to achieve gubernatorial control and initiatives reflecting his preferences—to balance innovation and accountability—[Dukakis] created a new governor's office with separate oversight staffs for human services, economic development and education."[44] This organizational change was not altogether unwelcome by those executives. In fact, one of the governor's most successful cabinet officers observed that "Entrepreneurs like me and the other aggressive program advocates around here might be dangerous without . . . someone like Michael to rein us in."[45] As a result, "Many were bold, but not wild as in Duke I, where there was no political manager to keep them in line."[46]

As was suggested earlier, John Sasso in particular was instrumental in providing such political management, moving from informal advisor to 1982 campaign manager to the governor's chief of staff, and always thinking about the political aspects for Dukakis. While it is an exaggeration to say, as did former governor Frank Sargent, that "Sasso *made* Dukakis,"[47] they clearly complemented each other. And perhaps Jack Corrigan, a close confidant of both men, said it best when he observed that "Mike Dukakis gets up in the morning and thinks about good government [while] John Sasso gets up in the morning and thinks about politics."[48] In the process, the two worked well together and, unlike in the time of Duke I (when the campaign manager, Joseph Grandmaison, was left behind), their teamwork continued from the campaign to the State House.

Along with that teamwork, the major policy themes addressed during the campaign were used to frame the governor's policy agenda once he was in office, providing much more continuity and a much sharper policy focus for Duke II than Duke I.[49] In fact, four of Dukakis's campaign themes, covering the areas of (1) job creation and economic growth, (2) law enforcement and crime prevention, (3) state aid to localities adversely affected by Proposition 2½, and (4) restoring integrity in state government, were included in his inaugural address.[50]

And in a major departure from his earlier term, the governor worked to be a better listener and consensus builder. He made a major effort to hear what individuals and groups around him had to say and tried to work with them. In this regard, perhaps no single group felt more aggrieved during Duke I than the members of the state legislature, and the governor was determined to make peace with them. For example, during his inaugural address he took pains to provide them with a "special message," stating:

> My administration will listen, we will be responsive to legislative initiative, and we will welcome the advice of legislators who bring a wealth of knowledge and experience to the formulation of public policy.
> We will work with you to achieve reasonable and sensible compromise. And we will spend as much time as is necessary to understand conflicting views and work to resolve them.[51]

And even before that inauguration Dukakis took pains to counteract the earlier legislative views of him as aloof, arrogant, and "above politics" by taking a number of steps, including:

1. Assigning a full-time political operative to work with the legislature the summer before the election,
2. Refraining from criticizing or even commenting on the creation of new jobs and pay increases for many continuing employees that were pushed through in the final frenzied days of the legislature's lame-duck session,
3. Involving legislators (including some who had not worked in the campaign or supported Dukakis) in the working groups set up to put flesh on the bones of the proposals for the four priority areas on which Dukakis wanted to suggest legislation,
4. Assigning a person to monitor legislation closely after the election,

5. Giving early, personal, and careful consideration to the requirements of the job of director of legislative relations on his staff, and appointing a well-liked former legislator to the job.[52]

And in the instance of business interests, much the same kind of care was exercised. For example, this time he told a top business regulator to "Be pro-consumer without being anti-business."[53]

Moreover, unlike in his first term (when he "typically staked out the position he believed was right and refused to budge"[54]), he sought to bring people together, compromise, and build consensus among interests in forming policies. In a very real sense, this form of consensual politics was the hallmark of the governor's new approach to his office. And, of course, it was not without its critics: "liberal activists consider him too timid, and many business leaders, though more positive than during his first term, still consider him too wedded to the notion that government can solve all problems."[55] Still others felt that "by compromising on so many issues, Dukakis has been a follower, not a leader."[56]

Nonetheless, as others pointed out, this new approach certainly helped the governor to resolve issues and move his agenda forward. As political analyst Ralph Whitehead observed, "You can't judge Dukakis's consensus style by saying, 'My God, the Duke has gone halfway. . . .' He has also brought his adversaries halfway. We have a far more enlightened corporate establishment than we did five years ago. And the legislature has basically moved the governor's program."[57]

NOTES

1. Funding for this research was provided by the Northeastern University Research and Scholarship Development Fund and the Gordon Fund.

2. Cited in Richard E. Neustadt, *Presidential Power: The Politics of Leadership from FDR to Carter* (New York: John Wiley and Sons, 1980), p. 9.

3. "Inaugural Address of His Excellency, Governor Michael S. Dukakis," in *Legislative Documents: Senate,* No. 1 (Boston: Commonwealth of Massachusetts, 1975), p. 5.

4. "Inaugural Address of the Honorable Michael S. Dukakis, Governor, Commonwealth of Massachusetts," in *Legislative Documents: Senate,* No. 1 (Boston: Commonwealth of Massachusetts, 1983), p. 3.

5. Jack Thomas, "The Ordinary Life of Mike Dukakis," *Boston Globe,* May 14, 1992, p. 85.

6. Theodore H. White, *The Making of the President: 1960.* In addition to Theodore H. White's quote, see also Edward R. F. Sheehan, "Massachusetts: Rogues and Reformers in a State on Trial," *Saturday Evening Post,* June 5, 1965, p. 27, where Massachusetts is described as "the nation's most corrupt state."

7. Ira Jackson, interview by author, September 17, 1992, Boston.

8. Michael Dukakis, interview by author, December 14, 1993, Boston.

9. Euterpe Dukakis, interview by author, May 21, 1993, Brookline, Mass.

10. Charles Kenney and Robert L. Turner, *Dukakis: An American Odyssey* (Boston: Houghton Mifflin, 1988), pp. 30–31.

11. *The Halcyon* (Swarthmore, Pa.: Swarthmore College, 1955), p. 128.

12. Richard Gaines and Michael Segal, *Dukakis and the Reform Impulse* (Boston: Quinlan Press, 1987), p. 20.

13. Ibid.

14. David Nyhan, *The Duke: The Inside Story of a Political Phenomenon* (New York: Warner Books, 1988), pp. 38–39.

15. Letter from Michael S. Dukakis to the author, June 8, 1993, Boston.

16. Kenney and Turner, *Dukakis,* p. 62.

17. Ibid., p. 63

18. For example, according to David Osborne, "Between 1975 and 1979, overall state spending grew only 5.5 percent in inflation-adjusted dollars; between 1970 and 1975, under Sargent, it had grown 23.5 percent." See David Osborne, "The Education of Michael Dukakis," *Across the Board,* October 1988, p. 15.

19. Marshall Kaplan and Sue O'Brien, *The Governors and the New Federalism* (Boulder, Colo.: Westview Press, 1991), p. 86.

20. Thad Beyle and Lynn Muchmore, "Honorable Michael S. Dukakis: Governor of Massachusetts, 1975–1979," in *Reflections on Being Governor,* ed. Jack Brizius (Washington, D.C.: National Governors' Association, 1981), p. 59

21. Ibid.

22. David Osborne, *Laboratories of Democracy* (Boston: Harvard Business School Press, 1990), p. 176.

23. Ibid., p. 75

24. Gaines and Segal, *Dukakis and the Reform Impulse,* p. 126.

25. Beyle and Muchmore, "Honorable Michael S. Dukakis," p. 75.

26. Dolores L. Mitchell, interview by the author, August 26, 1992, Boston.

27. Kenney and Turner, *Dukakis,* p. 102.

28. Beyle and Muchmore, "Honorable Michael S. Dukakis," p. 61.

29. William Geary, interview by the author, August 7, 1992, Boston.

30. Michael Dukakis, interview by the author, September 26. 1995, Boston.

31. Gaines and Segal, *Dukakis and the Reform Impulse,* pp. 215–216.

32. Ibid., p. 216.

33. Ibid., p. 63.

34. Kenney and Turner, *Dukakis,* p. 135.

35. Frederick Salvucci, interview by the author, August 26, 1992, Boston.

36. Martha Wagner Weinberg, "Massachusetts: The Changing of the Guard," in *Gubernatorial Transitions: The 1982 Election,* ed. Thad Beyle (Durham, N.C.: Duke University Press, 1985), p. 193.

37. In Massachusetts this position is formally known as the "chief secretary," but for the purposes of this essay I use the more recognizable term.

38. Michael Dukakis, interview by the author, December 23, 1993, Boston.

39. Weinberg, "Massachusetts," p. 191.

40. For example, between 1975 and 1986, unemployment dropped from 12.3 percent to 3.8 percent, the lowest of any state. Also, whereas in 1975 there had been a budget deficit of over $500 million, by 1985 it had turned into a *surplus* of $400 million. Kenney and Turner, *Dukakis,* p. 195.

41. Michael Dukakis, interview by the author, August 11, 1992, Boston.

42. John Sasso, interview by the author, August 19, 1992, Sudbury, Mass.

43. Alden Raine, interview by the author, September 10, 1992, Boston.

44. Martin A. Levin and Mary Bryna Sanger, *Making Government Work* (San Francisco: Jossey-Bass, 1994), p. 256.

45. Ibid.

46. Martin A. Levin, "Learning How to Manage: Dukakis's Ups and Downs," *Los Angeles Times,* August 21, 1988, p. 6.

47. Kenney and Turner, *Dukakis,* p. 185.

48. Ibid., p. 186.

49. Michael Dukakis, interview by the author, December 23, 1993, Boston.

50. Weinberg, "Massachusetts," p. 208. See also the 1983 inaugural address noted in footnote 4 above.
51. "Inaugural Address," 1983, p. 176.
52. Weinberg, "Massachusetts," pp. 207–207.
53. Levin, "Learning How to Manage," p. 6.
54. Osborne, *Laboratories,* p. 176.
55. Ibid., p. 208.
56. Ibid.
57. Ibid.

CHAPTER 14

Mario Cuomo: A Governor in Search of Policy Decisiveness

ELIZABETH KOLBERT*

It is the last day of the year, and Albany, living up to its cheerless reputation, is gray and frigid. Nevertheless, Governor Mario M. Cuomo has decided to walk to his swearing-in ceremony. He marches down the hill from the State Capitol, a powerful figure in a shapeless fedora, his aides trailing behind him, hugging themselves against the cold.

In deference to the state's bare treasury, Cuomo has forsworn the traditional inauguration party, opting instead for a modest ceremony at the State Court of Appeals building. The whole exercise lasts less than ten minutes. After it is over, Cuomo is about to plunge out into the cold again when a group of reporters blocks his way, and he stops to talk to them under the courthouse dome.

The scene seems, at first, much like an ordinary news conference, with the Governor in the center and a throng of reporters stretching microphones toward his lips. But for Cuomo it is clearly something more. He is standing in the building where he began his career 35 years before as a law clerk, and now he is about to embark on his third term in New York State's highest office. When he is asked to reflect on the challenges facing him as the state goes through a dizzying financial decline, his tone is elegiac.

---

*Originally published as "The State of the Governor," by Elizabeth Kolbert. Copyright © 1991 by The New York Times Company. Reprinted by permission, from the *New York Times Magazine,* February 10, 1991.

"This state has overcome fire and floods and depression and wars, always bringing us to a higher ground," he says. "Sixty years ago this state showed the nation the way out of the depression. So if you remember your history and if you remember the people who came before you, it gets a little easier to look forward to the challenges you have to face."

Cuomo is not a man to draw casually on history, and so this answer, like so many of his remarks, invites speculation. "If you remember the people who came before you. . . ." Are these people like Theodore Roosevelt and Franklin D. Roosevelt, whom historians consider to have been unexceptional governors but who went on to be great Presidents? Or are they people like Alfred E. Smith and Thomas E. Dewey, who imposed their vision on New York State but then lost their bids for higher office?

Since the day of his first inauguration, Cuomo has seemed destined to make his mark according to one of these two models. His tremendous eloquence made him almost immediately a national figure, and within two years of becoming Governor, he was invested with the aura of a potential President. At home in New York, he enjoyed an equally exalted stature—his political sovereignty uncontested, his popularity unmatched. But now, after eight years in office, Cuomo's destiny no longer seems so clear, and his relation to his predecessors has a poignant, almost morbid quality. As he begins his third term, Cuomo, the "Hamlet" of American politics, seems oddly suspended at the edge of history.

Cuomo's uneasy relationship to higher office has been well documented by a national press corps that has tracked his moves with open fascination. When the Governor has traveled around the nation denouncing the Republican administration in Washington, reporters have happily spied signs of a nascent campaign. When he has drawn back, there has been speculation about secreted skeletons and weak knees.

Far less attention has been devoted to the equally curious record of Cuomo's governorship. But it is a record that reveals many of the same themes: an unusual set of opportunities, a mysterious hesitancy to seize them, and a genius for confounding popular expectations.

Some of these opportunities have been created by Cuomo himself; others have been handed to him by good fortune. When Cuomo took office in January 1983, the state was in the final stages of one of its periodic fiscal emergencies. Within a year, however, there were clear signs of economic improvement, and as the 1980's wore on, the recovery turned into a boom. Personal income rose at a startling rate, and state revenues grew apace. In the first five years of the Cuomo administration, the state budget, in constant dollars, increased by 20 percent.

For the Governor, this rare economic windfall was matched by unusual political security. Throughout his tenure, Cuomo has maintained phenomenally high ratings in the polls, and in 1986, he was re-elected by the largest majority in New York State's history. In contrast to Cuomo's robustness, New York's Republican party has for more than a decade been slowly dying of internal injuries. Last year, the party could barely even muster a gubernatorial candidate; at least 19 Republicans turned down the nomination before Pierre A. Rinfret, an economist and political oddball, finally agreed to take Cuomo on. Politically bedridden, the Republicans have allowed

Cuomo to monopolize media attention in the state while raising only a quavering voice of opposition.

Presiding over a time of affluence and lacking a serious rival, Cuomo was well positioned to confront a new generation of needs that accompanied the lavish economic growth of the mid-1980's: AIDS, crack, homelessness. So devastating were these problems that they seemed to demand responses more inventive, and more risky, than traditional government solutions.

Yet Cuomo's response to these problems has been largely incremental, largely business as usual. He has failed to draw on his immense popularity to make New York a leader in new and experimental programs, nor has he undertaken the kind of ambitious capital projects that characterized the administration of Nelson A. Rockefeller in the 1960s. Instead, he has chosen to build cautiously on what was already in place, acting as a conservator of the state's extensive network of social services and its aging infrastructure.

"You have a state that's a perfect laboratory to do something visionary," says Russell Sykes, a senior policy associate with the State Communities Aid Association, a nonprofit advocacy group. "But we have just been taking baby steps."

In the late 1980's and now the early 1990's, New York's economy has been contracting almost as fast as it had earlier expanded, presenting Cuomo with a new opportunity to leave his stamp on the state. Tax collections in New York, as in most Northeastern states, have been dropping precipitously over the last few years, leaving gaping holes between the cost of existing programs and the sum of existing taxes. The impetus for reexamination and reorganization of government services in the state has rarely been greater.

But Cuomo's response to the contraction has been as modulated and circumspect as his response to the years of growth. When money was plentiful, Cuomo distributed it generously and evenhandedly, increasing spending on liberal-minded social programs like welfare, and also on more conservative, law-and-order programs like prison construction. Then he cut income-tax rates and took steps to reduce the state's chronic borrowing. Now with revenues shrinking, Cuomo is meting out the pain just as broadly. He has cut programs for the poor, like Medicaid, and programs for the middle class, like aid to private colleges. He has raised a battery of taxes and then, for good measure, he has raided reserve funds and racked up record deficits.

Perhaps as a result of Cuomo's guarded handling of the state's purse strings, New York has managed to maintain a sense of equanimity in the face of hard times, while many of its neighbors, like New Jersey and Massachusetts, have fallen to bitter squabbling. Cuomo himself has remained remarkably popular despite the pains of retrenchment, and in a period when other governors have been felled, he is still standing. He has retained his power, but some would ask: for what?

"He's holding his political capital tight to him," says Eve Brooks, executive director of Statewide Youth Advocacy, a nonprofit group that keeps a watchful eye on Cuomo. "He's trying to speak to a lot of constituencies and create as few enemies as possible. But the question is: where is he going with all this?"

For his entire tenure as Governor, Cuomo has had to cope with a divided State Legislature: Democrats in the Assembly, Republicans in the Senate. To hear Cuomo tell it, this one fact explains most of the limitations attributed to his record. If he has not been as daring as some would have liked, the Republican Senate is to blame. "'The Senate wouldn't do it,'" says Richard C. Wade, a professor of urban history at the City University of New York and a longtime Cuomo associate. "That's his first response to everything."

That the divided legislature is an impediment to innovation in New York is indisputable. Indeed, many officials in Albany would argue that the sole aim of the Republican Senate is to gum up the gears of state government. But there are many who argue that Cuomo, too, is responsible for the standstill.

Cuomo has always spoken ardently of his desire to win control of the State Senate for the Democrats. But his actions on behalf of Democratic candidates have often seemed to fall short of such passion. In 1986, for example, a year when many Republican seats seemed vulnerable, Cuomo's efforts were so anemic that many in his own party accused him of bad faith. In 1990, the Democrats' last chance to seize the Senate before redistricting, Cuomo played a more active role in the campaign. But when it came to contributing money from his own swollen campaign treasury, he held back, saying the money had not been donated for him to give away.

When it comes to pushing legislation through the Republican Senate, Cuomo's efforts have been similarly tentative. As anyone who has dealt with the State Legislature knows, it is not enough to lay out your case for a bill and then hope for the best. You have to exert constant pressure, to wheedle and threaten and then, finally, make deals. You have to be willing to take risks and alienate some of your supporters to achieve your objectives. This Cuomo has rarely done.

At the start of the year, when he unveils his legislative agenda, Cuomo resubmits the same bills that the Senate rejected the year before: legislation to redistribute school aid, to overhaul the state's election laws, to introduce a system of public campaign financing. Each year, he proclaims that this year will be different. The tide has turned, he proclaims, a new day is dawning, the bills will finally pass. But by the time the Legislature recesses in July, these bills have, once again, been unceremoniously killed off.

The Governor lays out his agenda each year in the State of the State Message, presented to a joint session of the Legislature in early January. The message outlines the Governor's hopes and aspirations for the coming year. In 1982, the last year of Governor Hugh L. Carey's administration, the State of the State Message ran to 24 pages. By 1986, the message had grown to 137 pages, reaching a high of 178 pages last year before dropping back to 121 pages last month.

The expanding State of the State Message is a remarkably apt illustration of Cuomo's style of leadership. Enlarged almost every year, the message has become a statement of inclusivity. Like the Governor's mythic "family of New York," which is supposed to enfold all groups, the elastic State of the State ensures that no one will feel left out. But while the appeal of the message has been broadened, its effectiveness as a statement of the Governor's aims has been dissipated. By the hundredth page, it becomes almost impossible to figure out which of the proposals represent serious policy goals and which are merely wishes that will dissolve on contact with the brutal realities of politics.

Even when pressed on the matter, Cuomo shies away from laying out clear priorities. Shortly after Cuomo delivered one of his State of the State Messages, his staff, responding to reporters' calls on the subject, tried to come up with a list of the Governor's top ten goals for the year. But the task proved too daunting; the Governor's staff could not limit its priorities to just ten. "Under number 1," a former aide to the Governor recalls, "there was 1a, 1b, 1c."

Cuomo entered politics through the side door, first attracting attention as a negotiator in a vicious battle over low-income housing in Forest Hills, Queens. It is a role that he has never abandoned. Assailed by interest groups on all sides, Cuomo often portrays himself as the referee in the great game of government. If one group is unhappy with a call this time, next time it will be the other group. All of the groups have a claim on his attention, and none of them particularly deserves to win.

"One of the failures of our politics is that it has been simplistic," Cuomo said in a recent interview. "So when you have a struggle over the air in the city of New York and it comes down to environment versus economic development, the politicians more often than not will choose one of the sides, and one will be an environmentalist who says, 'The clean air is more important than the jobs,' and the other will be an economic development person who says, 'No, the jobs in the Hudson Valley are more important than the trees,' and both are wrong. Trees are important and the economic development is important."

Cuomo dismisses the idea that his inclusive style of government has liabilities. The press corps's demand for clear priorities is, he charges, simply self-serving. "Reporters have to summarize you at one point," he said. "They have to define you and it's easier if you're in one area and they can call you 'the Education Governor,' or the person who failed to be the Education Governor." As far as Cuomo is concerned, it seems, the only result of having no well-defined priorities is that his public relations are not as good as they might be. "We have a very long list of accomplishments that I think have not been properly noted, because I have never focused on just one issue," he said.

But others see more serious consequences flowing from the absence of priorities. They look at state government, with its tricky politics and its bureaucratic inertia and its many competing interests, and they say coaxing this vast machinery to accomplish anything substantial requires a crystalline goal and a steely single-mindedness.

"The political system doesn't have the capacity to address a lot of important issues simultaneously," says Gerald Benjamin, a professor of political science at the State University of New York at New Paltz, who is active in Republican politics. "What is necessary is to make a dramatic commitment to something and to focus the energy. You have to choose something and be measured by it."

The costs and the benefits of Cuomo's style are clear from his handling of virtually every major issue of the last eight years. Take, for example, the state's fiscal problems, which first emerged in the spring of 1988. Almost immediately, financial analysts urged Cuomo to make systematic, long-term spending cuts to prepare for even harder times to come. But the Governor, hesitant to antagonize the municipal governments, school districts, and other vast constituencies that depend on state dollars, demurred. Instead, he made temporary cuts that left the long-term problems unaddressed. Then he dipped into reserve funds and allowed the state to spend its way into enormous deficits.

It was not until late last year, with a national recession well under way and half the states in the country awash in red ink, that the Governor proposed the kind of budget cuts that others around the state had called for from the start. (Late last month the Governor proposed an additional $4.5 billion in spending cuts.) The price of waiting was high: New York's credit rating dropped to its lowest level ever and became the third-lowest of any state in the nation after Massachusetts and Louisiana. But by waiting, the Governor effectively minimized opposition to the cuts: the problems had become so enormous that the cuts were unavoidable, and everyone, liberal or conservative, Republican or Democrat, acknowledged it.

This tactic—delaying until a consensus finally presents itself—is typical of the Governor's response to controversy. While other governors, like Jim Florio of New Jersey, simply try to overpower their opponents. Cuomo attempts to win them over, no matter what the cost. "What he really likes to do," Wade says, "is defang the opposition."

One of the Governor's favorite strategies for "defanging" his opponents is to appoint a commission to advise him on a controversial issue. At their best, these commissions provide a forum for all sides to vent their anger, and they lay the groundwork for compromise. But too often, critics of the Governor complain, the commissions become a substitute for doing anything at all.

Such was the case with the Governor's commission on the Adirondack park, a collection of private and public lands that together make up the largest wilderness area east of the Mississippi. Under heavy pressure from environmentalists, Cuomo appointed a commission in early 1989 to suggest ways to preserve the park from what he called "an era of unbridled land speculation and unwarranted development." Last May, the commission issued a set of sweeping recommendations, including a yearlong moratorium on new construction in the park and permanent changes in its zoning. Adirondack residents, wary about the impact of the proposals on the local economy, tied up traffic in Albany in protest. Cuomo not only backed away from the recommendations, but even questioned the very premise on which the commission had been founded.

"I didn't assume the park was in trouble," he said. "I said I wanted to know if the park was in trouble." To pacify those who lived in the park, Cuomo turned to a second group, which recommended ways to water down the original commission's plan. It is now two years since the initial commission was appointed, and nothing has been done.

Cuomo is extremely sensitive to charges that he has not imposed a clear vision on the state or lived up to the high standards of achievement set by some of his predecessors. Such criticism, he claims, is an unfortunate consequence of speaking up for what he believes.

Nearly seven years ago, Cuomo delivered the keynote address at the Democratic National Convention in San Francisco. The speech, a ringing condemnation of the Reagan era, not only transformed Cuomo, then a new and relatively untested Governor, into a national figure; it furnished him with what seems to be a perpetual spot on the list of potential Democratic Presidential candidates. Now, Cuomo claims, he regrets ever having made the speech. "Frankly," he says, "I'm sorry I went."

The 1984 keynote address, Cuomo asserts, made him the target of a terrible form of injustice, which he has labeled the "dumb blonde syndrome." Like the proverbial "dumb blonde," the Governor says, he is the victim of an insidious prejudice that works like this: if she's beautiful, she can't type; if he gives great speeches, he must be a lousy Governor. "I think once I made a speech at the keynote that was well received, that became a problem for us," he says. People began to criticize his record, according to Cuomo, saying that it fell short of the rhetoric. "They said, 'See, he gives a speech, what else can he do?'"

Cuomo certainly is right about being treated more critically than your run-of-the-mill Governor. What he seems unwilling to accept is that such criticism follows inevitably from his position as a national leader and potential President. Or it may be that he chooses not to realize it to make a point.

Treating criticism as a fault of the critic is one of Cuomo's favorite tactics. It puts the critic on the defensive ("Gosh, I didn't realize I was prejudiced against great orators"), and it blurs the issue under debate. But the tactic has been only half effective: Cuomo continues to feel harassed by criticism of his record—and to take offense at such criticism. When pressed on the issue, Cuomo can become defensive, measuring himself against some of his more illustrious predecessors—Dewey, for example, or Rockefeller—and suggesting that they have been overrated. (Dewey is credited with building the state's thruway, Rockefeller the state university system.)

"If I had wanted to be the guy with the edifice complex and never mentioned children and never mentioned prisons and never mentioned the environment, I could have talked only about the state university building I've rebuilt and the roads and bridges I've rebuilt," Cuomo said in an interview last year about his record. "Fifty billion dollars worth. You look it up. Where in the Rockefeller years did they do that much in eight years? Dewey didn't do that much."

To further confound his critics, Cuomo has recently taken to chronicling his accomplishments in long, encyclopedic lists. These lists include everything from the significant—"unprecedented prison expansion" (Cuomo has presided over the largest prison construction program in state history)—to the justifiably obscure—"Quebec license reciprocity."

The irony of these limits is that Cuomo rarely takes credit for what is perhaps his greatest accomplishment. When he became Governor, Cuomo inherited a state that was already a hothouse for urban problems: crime, drugs, relentless poverty. During his administration, these problems have grown dramatically. Crack arrived and decimated whole neighborhoods. AIDS exacted a ravaging toll. Reaganomics helped push the state's vast legions of poor further into misfortune.

Much of Cuomo's energies over the last eight years have been devoted to preserving the fabric of New York society in the face of these new threats, a task that has not been easy. AIDS and crack strained the state's safety net; racial tensions grew; the gulf between rich and poor widened. Yet at a time when, in Washington, government was being portrayed as the problem, Cuomo maintained in New York that government was part of the solution.

This message is perhaps Cuomo's greatest legacy to New York State. In a period when the social contract seemed constantly threatened with annulment, Cuomo continued to press for a society in which everyone had a stake and no one was abandoned. He set the tone for the state. When it was easy to sow division, he preached caring and compassion. The achievement is more abstract than most that history records. It is a rhetorical victory, but nonetheless one with real consequences.

Mel Miller, the State Assembly Speaker, is, next to the Governor, the most powerful Democrat in New York. Miller has often battled with Cuomo, but he expresses a grudging respect for him and his ability to sustain a benevolent vision of government in troubled times.

"Cuomo has a traditional Democratic viewpoint that the basic role of government is to help people who need help," Miller says. "His real talent is that he can articulate these issues in a 1990's way. At a time when a lot of people have started to walk from this, he has said that New York is still committed to its progressive tradition, even though times have changed, and this has created a kind of hopefulness."

When Cuomo took office in 1983, he did away with the standard pyramidal model of executive authority and replaced it with a more egalitarian wheel. "I want myself in the center of the wheel," he said, "and a lot of spokes out to the agencies."

The metaphor was a good one for a state government as vast and far-flung as New York's. It stressed cooperation over hierarchy, and it suggested that Cuomo would grant his commissioners the autonomy to exercise their own judgment. But as anyone who has ever had sustained dealings with the Cuomo administration will attest, the reality has never lived up to the metaphor. In the Cuomo administration, "there are no real players," one former administration official says. "There's just him."

Under Cuomo, power has been consolidated to an almost unprecedented extent in the executive offices on the second floor of the State Capitol. No major decision is made by the head of a state agency without Cuomo's clearance, and even many mid-level decisions must await the approval of the Governor or one of his top staff members, a group referred to collectively as "the second floor."

This is a narrow circle, one totally under the Governor's control. Most of its members are able and committed public servants, but their ability to stand up to someone of Cuomo's stature and temperament is limited. Perhaps the highest compliment that can be paid in Albany is to say of a Cuomo staff member: "He argues with the Governor."

One of the few administration officials with enough clout to wrangle with Cuomo—and to speak for him—is Gerald C. Crotty, the Secretary to the Governor, who functions as a chief of staff. Evan A. Davis, until recently Cuomo's counsel, was viewed in Albany as a talented and thoughtful lawyer, but in discussions with the Legislature he was perceived as little more than a mouthpiece for the Governor's position. Many of those who have left the administration over the years look back at the 16-hour days they worked for the Governor and question whether he ever took notice of all the effort they put in.

To call Cuomo a "hands-on" manager is to grossly understate his role in running state government. Cuomo is his own chief negotiator (in a recent fight with the state's public employee unions, he went head to head directly with the union leaders), and he often serves as his own press secretary (he has been known to talk on the telephone with the same reporter two or three times in one day). He calls his aides dozens of times to remind them about one thing or another and asks: "How come I'm the only one who's thinking about these things?"

Cuomo is not fond of internal dissent, and that which exists in his administration is kept under wraps. Criticism emanating from officials outside the administration is harder to silence, but Cuomo is not averse to trying. Recently, for instance, a reporter from *Time* magazine confronted him with a disparaging remark attributed to Assembly Speaker Miller. With the reporter in his office, Cuomo phoned the Speaker and asked him point-blank if he had made the remark, which pointed to a gulf between the Governor's rhetoric and his performance. (Miller reluctantly had to acknowledge that he had.) On days when critical comments appear in the press, legislators, lobbyists and civic leaders have all come to expect threatening phone calls from the second floor.

The contrast between Cuomo's domineering, closed-off style and his open, expansive vision of government is one of the great contradictions of his administration. There is the public Cuomo, pushing a family style of politics that is embracing and compassionate, and then there is Cuomo in private, isolated and unforgiving.

It is the contradictions of his tenure—the record vs. the rhetoric, the politics vs. the personality—that have left Cuomo, after eight years in New York State's most visible office, still with an aura of mystery about him. Attempts to categorize him become entangled in his own internal conflicts, and even those who have watched Cuomo over many years can only shake their heads and conclude that nothing about him is simple or straightforward.

As Governor of New York and the leader of the state's Democratic Party, Cuomo is frequently asked to comment on the political implications of a particular event—an election, a demonstration, an indictment. Just as frequently, he declines. "I'm not good at politics," he says, shaking his head regretfully. "It's not my strength."

This is not the kind of ordinary prevarication that politicians often use to duck tough questions; it is a grandiose lie so patently false that it can hardly even be considered deceitful. Cuomo is a master at such magnificent deceptions. His response to the most direct questions is usually not an answer, it is more a form of entertainment, kind of performance art for the press.

Over the last few months, the speculation about a Cuomo candidacy has been resurrected, providing the Governor once again with a national audience for his circumlocutions. The war in the Persian Gulf has called attention to the Governor's major Presidential weakness—his inexperience in foreign affairs—and remarks Cuomo made in the fall advocating a negotiated settlement to the conflict struck some experts as dangerously naive. But the war has also created new vulnerabilities for President

Bush and made a Cuomo candidacy seem, under certain circumstances, that much more plausible.

Cuomo has been playing the part of the candidate-in-spite-of-himself with characteristic elan. In a recent interview with the author William Kennedy, a friend of his, Cuomo said he couldn't rule out the Presidency even if he wanted to, and he didn't want to: "If I did say convincingly that under no circumstances would I ever run, that would be so unreasonable a position that people would say, 'There must be something in his closet.' Now I wouldn't mind if they said it was a 28-year-old blonde, but they don't say that. They say, 'His uncle is Mafia.'"

Cuomo is acutely sensitive to the peculiar slights suffered by Italian Americans in public life. Indeed, there are few politicians who take their ethical standing more seriously than he does. Cuomo and his wife, Matilda, attend church every Sunday morning, and, according to one of the ushers, the Governor always deposits a $10 bill in the collection basket. The Governor speaks reverentially—and often—about the homespun virtues that his immigrant parents, Andrea and Immaculata, taught him behind the counter of their Queens grocery store.

Nothing, in fact, infuriates Cuomo more than the suggestion that there is a chink in his integrity, or that of his family. Last year, for example, several newspapers reported that the Governor's youngest daughter, Madeline, had been tooling around—and had managed to get into a car accident—with a lapsed driver's license. The Governor's ire was so all-encompassing that even reporters who had not covered the story were told that he would not be answering their phone calls for a few days.

To Cuomo's credit, and immense satisfaction, little damaging evidence about his personal dealing has ever been discovered, despite the best efforts of many in the press. As Cuomo likes to point out, a team of *Newsday* reporters once spent several months trying to uncover corruption in his administration, poring over state contracts and expense records and conducting lengthy interrogations of his aides. The team came up essentially empty-handed. Reporters who investigated rumors about Mafia connections in the Governor's family were similarly disappointed.

These repeated failures have diminished one mystery only to open up another. Cuomo's Presidential hesitancy does not, it seems, have the easy logic of Gothic concealment. Like the disparity between his public vision of government and his private style, Cuomo's relation to the Presidency appears to be wrapped in some strangely personal enigma.

As Cuomo himself notes, enigmas are usually effaced by history, which is remorseless in its demand for decisiveness. Thus history portrays great leaders as unwavering in their pursuits, when, on closer look, one finds that many were consumed by doubt.

Cuomo is eloquent when he describes his heroes, men like Abraham Lincoln and St. Thomas More, who at the crucial moment, he says, were forced by events to transcend their uncertainties: "One of the reasons I enjoy knowing Lincoln and Thomas More is that they were both terribly human, even to the point of suffering fits of ambiguity, ambivalence. Lincoln on the subject of slavery was often perceived as less than totally committed to the idea of the destruction of slavery in this nation.

Indeed, he was perfectly prepared to allow it to continue in parts of the U.S., as we all know.

"The thing about Lincoln and More that makes them appealing to other human beings is that they are like all human beings, capable of not being totally lucid, totally clear, totally in control intellectually of their position on a given issue at all times. Sometimes it evolves, sometimes they slip and slide, sometimes they go sideways."

As 1992 draws close, and as New York enters a time of crisis, it may be that Cuomo will encounter events that will force him to resolve his own ambivalences—and take his place in history. Or it may be that he won't. Events may prove too kind to him, or too cruel.

CHAPTER 15

Christine Todd Whitman: Bringing a "Revolution of Ideas" to the States

*JOHN B. JUDIS**

Last fall [of 1994], New Jersey Governor Christie Whitman was invited to campaign for twenty-two Republican candidates around the country. Three gubernatorial hopefuls, George Pataki in New York, John Rowland in Connecticut and Ellen Sauerbrey in Maryland, called themselves "Whitman Republicans." "Christie," said Haley Barbour, the Republican National Committee chairman, "took the message that Republicans want to make government smaller, not bigger, and that we should promote individual freedom and individual responsibility and not more government power and government responsibility, and she made it the theme of her government." At Barbour's suggestion, Whitman gave the Republican rebuttal to Bill Clinton's [1995] State of the Union speech. Speaking in Trenton before the cheering state assembly, she reiterated her own achievements as a tax-cutter and declared that a "revolution of ideas" had begun in the states and was "sweeping America."

Already, Republican consultants and conservative activists buzz with the idea of Whitman as a vice presidential choice in 1996, to marry the post-Democratic or independent female voter to the Republicans' angry white male. Even one Christian Coalition leader listed her among presidential possibilities, while dismissing Massachusetts Governor William Weld because of his support for gay rights. But many of these boosters seem oblivious to what Whitman really stands for and what, outside of

---

*Originally published as "Hot Toddy," by John B. Judis. Reprinted by permission of *The New Republic,* © 1995, The New Republic, Inc.

her tax cut, she has accomplished as governor. She is not a Northern version of Texas Senator Kay Bailey Hutchison, nor a female incarnation of Michigan Governor John Engler. If she expressed her convictions in a presidential campaign, she might appeal to independents and disgruntled Democrats, but she could also offend many Republican diehards. Whether she succeeds in getting on a GOP ticket in 1996 will be as good a test as any of whether the radical right has taken over the Republican Party.

Whitman's speech last Tuesday was most notable for what she didn't say: she didn't mention Newt Gingrich's Contract with America (she said the revolution began "not in Washington"); she didn't evoke the religious right's "family values" and she didn't try to rebut Clinton's proposal for a higher minimum wage or a more humane version of welfare reform. None of this was coincidental. Whitman is a throwback to an earlier Republicanism. Modern Republican conservatism was born out of opposition to the Eastern establishment politics of New York's Thomas Dewey and Nelson Rockefeller and New Jersey's Clifford Case. What Westerners Barry Goldwater and Ronald Reagan disliked about these Republicans was their emphasis on consensus, their implicit acceptance of the New Deal and their support for civil rights and affirmative action. In background and outlook, Whitman is a direct descendant of these Eastern establishment Republicans. She even calls herself a "Rockefeller Republican."

Today's Republican conservatism also grew out of the merger in the 1970's between an older business conservatism and the social outlook of the new right. Just as opposition to abortion and the support for school prayer were critical to Reagan's coalition in 1980, opposition to Clinton's order on gays in the military helped fuel the Republican sweep last fall. But Whitman is on the opposite shore from the new Republicans on these issues. Gays in the military? "If someone is doing his job, they shouldn't be making an issue of whether he is heterosexual or homosexual," Whitman told me during an interview in the governor's office in Trenton.

Whitman doesn't express her differences with the religious and new right in strident terms, but even when she's being conciliatory, a playful derision comes through. When I asked her if she favored school prayer, she said, "I am for a moment of silence." Then she added, "I wouldn't say prayer, because then you ask what prayer. I don't think there is any problem with a moment of silence. It's when most kids get to think of whether they remembered their shoes for the sixth-period gym class."

Today's Republican conservatism displays a hatred of big government that was forged during opposition to the New Deal and the Great Society. While Whitman declared herself for "smaller government" and "less spending" in her rebuttal to Clinton, she isn't that conservative on the great issues of government. In her first State of the State address on January 10, she merely promised "more effective" government. In her first two years in office, government spending has remained constant. In her first year, the number of state jobs declined only by .3 percent; in her second-year budget, announced last Monday, she has merely created the illusion of drastic job cuts. In general, hers has been a much more centrist administration than that of Engler, Wisconsin Governor Tommy Thompson or other darlings of the Republican right. Whitman sees the irony of her situation. When I told her during our interview that I wanted to understand how she fit in the Republican Party, she threw back her head and laughed. "That's a question a lot of people want to answer," she said.

Christine Todd Whitman is a tall, elegant woman with large, doleful brown eyes, a pencil-thin nose, a long birdlike neck and a small mouth that curls to one side when she laughs. She peppers her conversation with repartee and references to being a mother and having children in school. She insists on being known as "Christie" because her parents called her that. Aides I interviewed repeatedly used the word "nice" to describe her. But she also has an imperious quality that can be glimpsed when she is challenged. Her eyes narrow and her mouth purses, and she pulls herself up and looks hawklike down at you.

Whitman's stately bearing and political views reflect, above all, the influence of her parents. Whitman was a child of the Eastern Republican establishment the same way that Jamie Lee Curtis was a child of Hollywood. Her father, Webster Todd, a multimillionaire contractor who built Rockefeller Center and restored Williamsburg, was a kingmaker in national and state Republican politics—on the moderate side of the party. He was a close friend and supporter of New York Governor Thomas Dewey, who defeated conservative Robert Taft for the presidential nomination in 1948. In 1952 Todd helped convince Dwight Eisenhower to run for the party nomination against Taft and then urged him to put Richard Nixon on the ticket. In 1960 and 1968 he helped Nixon win the nomination.

On two occasions—when the New Jersey party fell on hard times after Goldwater's defeat in 1964, and after it lost the governorship for the second straight time in 1977—Todd took over as party chairman. Both times he stabilized the party's finances and recruited successful new candidates; in the latter instance, one recruit was his neighbor and protégé Tom Kean. Todd was a consummate negotiator, known for keeping his cool under fire and bringing the irreconcilable together. "He had more knives sticking out of his back from his friends than any man I've ever seen," Whitman recalled.

Whitman's mother, Eleanor, known as "the hurricane" for her boundless energy, was equally active in Republican politics. She served as a delegate to Republican National Conventions and was state finance chair for George Bush's 1980 presidential bid. A traditional feminist, she was president of the New Jersey Federation of Republican Women. Whitman believes that if her mother had been born in an era when women were acceptable as candidates, she would have run for office.

Christie, her sister and her two brothers grew up being bounced on the knees of presidents, governors and senators. They became involved in campaigns from the time they could walk. In 1956, when Christie was 10, she sold lemonade at Eisenhower–Nixon rallies in New Jersey. By 1974, when she married John Whitman, a fledgling New York investment banker whose grandfather was governor of New York, it was clear she would someday run for office. "Our marriage vows should have been, 'in sickness and in health and in politics,' " Whitman quipped.

Christie Whitman was raised on Pontefract, a 222-acre farm in the rolling hills of Western New Jersey where other old-money Eastern families—the Keans, the

Frelinghuysens and the Fenwicks—mimicked the English gentry. The Todd children were brought up with a strong ethic of community service and public responsibility. "There was certainly a feeling in our family that we had been very lucky, and you gave back," Whitman explained. She came to envisage politics not as a path of upward advancement but as a means of serving the public.

As the Republican Party moved toward a militant conservatism, Whitman went in the opposite direction. In 1964, when Ronald Reagan was rallying Republicans around Barry Goldwater's presidential candidacy, Whitman and her brother Webster, known as Dan, worked for Nelson Rockefeller's nomination. Although Whitman stayed away from the new left movements of the 1960s, there was one interesting exception: she remembers that sometime in the mid-1960s, as a student at Wheaton College, she took part in a demonstration at nearby Wellesley to protest the arrest of birth-control activist Bill Baird. It was her feminism first asserting itself. In 1968 Whitman backed Rockefeller against Nixon. Then, in 1969, after graduating from Wheaton, she moved to Washington to work for the new Republican administration—first at the Office of Economic Opportunity and then at the Republican National Committee.

At the RNC, while the Republican Party was wooing George Wallace voters and loosening its historic tie to blacks, she and her mother set up a listening post to find out why blacks and young people were not interested in the party. "I was trying to get Republicans to understand," she said. At one point, Whitman recalled, she held a meeting on a winter night with a Chicago gang called the Black Disciples. "They were pretty tough kids, and they started using every word they could think of, but I had grown up around two older brothers and a farmer, so there wasn't much they could describe that I hadn't heard before," Whitman said.

After she left the RNC, she got married and went to live in New York. She began teaching mathematics and English as a second language in Spanish Harlem. When I asked her, "How come?" she shot back with a sly grin. "How come what? Married or teaching?" Then she explained, "We wanted to do something that was needed." In 1982, having moved back to New Jersey, she entered her first race, winning election as a Somerset County representative. In 1987 Kean named her to a low-visibility cabinet post, president of the Board of Public Utilities. She also stayed active in social causes. She was a founder of Republicans for Choice and president of the Community Foundation of New Jersey, which funded homeless shelters, ghetto parks and teaching for the poor. Says an old family friend, "I never saw a stronger sense of noblesse oblige."

As Whitman prepared to enter statewide New Jersey politics in the 1990s, she already had a clear sense of who she was and what she wanted to do in politics. She was a type of Republican common in the Eastern social register but rarely found in the South or West: a combination of upper-class do-gooder, good government proponent, old-line (not radical) feminist and pro-business moderate. What she still lacked was a clear idea of where New Jersey should go. In the 1990s she undertook a crash course in New Jersey politics that culminated in her 1993 election campaign against incumbent Jim Florio.

New Jersey has long been a bellwether state in both its economics and its politics. It was the first state whose suburbs eclipsed its cities as centers of industry and finance. In the Midwest, for instance, manufacturing has abandoned the cities for the suburbs, but the suburbs still remain dependent on Chicago or Cleveland as centers of finance, advertising and law. New Jersey's suburbs, in contrast, look toward Philadelphia and New York, not Newark, Elizabeth, Paterson, Passaic, Camden or Jersey City. These minority-dominated cities have withered as their manufacturing jobs have disappeared. They have become centers of destitution in a state whose suburbs, sustained by pharmaceutical, telecommunications and electronics companies, have prospered. New Jersey has the second highest per capita income in the country, but some of the poorest inner cities. In Trenton, where the state Capitol is housed, you can sit in state offices and hear gunshots from nearby crack houses. Trenton doesn't have a downtown hotel and has only one bookstore. One evening, leaving a state treasury office by the wrong door, I found myself walking among gang members. Yet several miles up the road in Lawrenceville and Princeton, there are elysian conference centers, sleek glass office buildings and palatial homes where the nation's and state's wealthiest people work and play. It is a pattern of poverty amid plenty that may be reproduced across the country in years to come.

The state's odd economic structure is sustained by its tax structure. Like other early Colonial states, which pegged voting to property, New Jersey has always been inordinately dependent on property taxes for local revenue. It had no state tax whatsoever until 1966. As New Jersey's cities began to lose businesses, their property tax revenues began to fall and the schools and other services suffered. In 1974 the New Jersey Supreme Court ruled that the state would have to adopt an income tax in order to help fund the poorer urban school districts. After the court shut down the schools, Democratic Governor Brendan Byrne was able to convince the legislature to pass the state's first income tax, but it was highly unpopular. Voters in the wealthier districts opposed tax increases partly out of self-interest, but, as the urban districts fell apart, middle-class voters argued that the administrations of Paterson or Passaic were so corrupt that they would simply squander whatever money the state sent them. . . .

Opposition to tax increases has produced a political paradox that is a corollary to the state's economic paradox. New Jersey's heavily unionized, cosmopolitan electorate is one of the nation's most liberal on most social and economic issues—from the minimum wage (New Jersey is pegged 25 percent higher than the nation's) to abortion. Normally, a conservative Republican can't get elected to most state offices, as Chuck Haytaian found out in his senatorial bid last fall against the colorless Frank Lautenberg. But there's one issue on which New Jersey's voters have been anything but liberal: the state income tax. Opposing income tax increases and proposing cuts are easy ways for a politician to win office.

Faced with the tax issue, Democratic state officials have often found themselves torn among their own constituencies. Liberal and moderate Republicans, on the other hand, have been able to oppose taxes on Republican fiscal grounds while declaring their commitment on the social front to what Kean called the "politics of inclusion." In 1981 Kean won the governor's race against Florio by promising an income tax cut, which Florio denounced as "irresponsible." Then, after Kean had been forced to raise the income tax, Florio ran successfully in 1989 on a promise not to raise income taxes—even though the state court was expected to rule again that the government must subsidize the poorer education districts. Having won office easily against a pro-life Republican, Florio succumbed to political hubris. Instead of waiting for the court to force his hand, he rammed through a huge increase in both the income and sales tax rates so he could cut a burgeoning deficit and finance school reform. Florio's move spurred a violent statewide revolt, from which Whitman ultimately benefited.

In 1990 Whitman set out on the quixotic task of challenging Senator Bill Bradley. It was her first run for statewide office, and in normal times she would have gotten trounced. But she ran a campaign tying Bradley to Florio, and when Bradley obliged by refusing to criticize Florio's tax hike, she began to climb in the polls. And although three quarters of New Jersey voters didn't know who Whitman was just ten weeks before the election, her debates with Bradley helped. Whitman displayed a remarkable ability to look straight into a television camera and talk to people in their homes. Like Kean, she knew how to speak to people who weren't of her own class, precisely because she knew they weren't. By contrast, Bradley—and even Florio, the son of a dockworker—were stiff and awkward among working-class voters.

By the third debate with Bradley, however, her ignorance of national politics and foreign affairs began to show. At one point, she attempted to turn a question about the Berlin Wall into a question about term limits. "We see the Berlin Wall coming down, but we still have a wall around Congress," Whitman remarked. Although Bradley won by 55,000 votes, Whitman established herself as the GOP favorite to challenge Florio.

Whitman established a PAC to give money to local candidates and began planning her campaign. The big question was how to deal with taxes. Whitman planned, of course, to attack Florio for raising taxes, but she initially refused to call for a tax cut. As the campaign began in 1993, she even denounced the call for a tax cut as "cynical." Her position reflected that of New Jersey's Republican establishment. Republicans such as Kean worried justifiably that a new tax cut could bankrupt a state already facing large deficits and the prospect of another court-imposed school crisis—the result of the legislature rolling back part of Florio's tax increases and payments to poorer districts.

Whitman first put together an odd group of supporters: business leaders who liked her calls for deregulation; the president of New Jersey NOW, who supported her because she opposed Florio's efforts to punish welfare mothers who wouldn't report their children's fathers; and gun owners angered by Florio's ban against assault weapons. But her campaign lacked focus and was damaged by gaffes. By the summer, she was falling behind Florio in polls. At this point, she began to rethink her opposition to a tax cut. She asked *Forbes* magazine heir Steve Forbes, a neighbor in the New Jersey Hills, and Lawrence Kudlow, formerly a Reagan budget official and now an editor at *National Review,* to draw up a tax cut program for her. Their proposals, but not their supply-side arguments, were backed by John Whitman, who believed that cutting taxes would force the state to spend less, and by campaign manager Ed Rollins, who thought a tax cut proposal would direct voters' attention to Florio's tax hikes. At a climactic meeting in September, Whitman agreed to Forbes's and Kudlow's argument for a three-year Kemp-Roth-style 30 percent cut in the income tax. Criticisms that the cuts helped mainly the wealthy were inevitable; Whitman tried to deflect them by exempting New Jerseyans earning less than $7,500 from any tax and by offering a less substantial tax break to people making more than $80,000. At one point, she even proposed granting city dwellers a 50 percent tax cut.

Local newspapers and most economists in the state criticized Whitman's plan. She hadn't explained how the state could possibly pay for it, and the numbers themselves seemed to change every day. Nonetheless, the proposal did exactly what her political aides hoped: it focused attention once more on Florio's tax increases and away from her inexperience. As she hammered the tax issue during the last month of the campaign, she caught and then surpassed Florio, winning by 27,000 votes.

One New Jersey Republican political consultant, asked to grade Whitman's performance during her first year, gives her an "A plus" in public relations, a "B" in policy and a "C" in addressing long-term problems. That strikes me as accurate. Whitman's first year as governor—in contrast to Clinton's first as president—was a textbook example of how to expand a narrow electoral majority into a broad governing one. Even partisan Democrats praise her. Says one former Byrne administration official, "She is warm, accessible, and gives an impression of sincerity." But her fiscal policies did not appreciably benefit the state.

Much of the reason for Whitman's political success is her style. Like her father, she is very cool under pressure and has enormous self-confidence that makes her willing to risk situations that would frighten other politicians. After Rollins claimed he had given black ministers "street money" to suppress the black vote, Whitman immediately issued a sharp denial. When Jesse Jackson and Al Sharpton came to Newark to buttress Democratic demands for a recount, Whitman insisted on meeting with them. After the meeting, both men praised her and exonerated her from any role in the controversy. "She has a balance that few politicians have," says former Kean administration official Hazel Gluck, now a lobbyist in Trenton. "She doesn't get thrown off."

Whitman has also practiced her father's politics of consensus. Her administration is politically and socially diverse. Her welfare commissioner is a holdover from the Florio administration. One of her top budget people is a Democrat. Her press secretary was a political independent who criticized her during the campaign but now swears by her. Her secretary of state is a black woman, and she has appointed the first African American to New Jersey's State Supreme Court. She has handled interest groups deftly. Florio enjoyed labor union support in his campaigns, but as governor, Whitman actually has been more solicitous of labor's opinions than Florio was. She held several meetings with public employee unions to review her forthcoming budget—something Florio never did. She has used commissions to draw potential critics into her administration's broader planning process. Marty Johnson, the president of Isles, a Trenton community organization, was invited to be a member of a subgroup of the governor's Economic Development Task Force that dealt with cities. Johnson now sings Whitman's praises. "I do believe she cares about urban New Jersey," he says. She has even managed to avoid being pinioned in New Jersey's racial politics. After Nation of Islam spokesman Khallid Abdul Muhammad attacked Jews at a state college speech, Whitman arranged a showing and discussion of [the film] *Schindler's List* on campus. During last fall's election, after black ministers protested conservative radio host Bob Grant's racist comments, she refused to make her regular appearance on his show. (After the election, she did appear, but rebuked Grant.)

She has also carefully tacked to the middle in all her policy initiatives. Whitman pleased businesses by appointing a businessman to head the state's Department of Environmental Protection, whose onerous regulations and red tape were often blamed for driving companies to relocate. But she vetoed a legislative measure requiring that state environmental regulations be no stricter than minimum federal regulations.

Whitman kept her promise to cut income taxes her first and second years. She has not, however, used the cuts to hack away at the state government. In her first budget, instead of financing the cuts primarily through genuine spending cuts, she financed the bulk of them through accounting methods reminiscent of Nelson Rockefeller in Albany. To make up most of that year's deficit, she changed the funding of the state's pension obligations, supposedly saving the state $1.3 billion. This year she claims to be reducing the state's work force of 65,000 by 3,300, but the real numbers are considerably lower: according to budget officials, the state will lose 345 jobs through attrition, while another 2,200 jobs will be subject to "competitive contracting"—meaning that, if a private firm demonstrates it can do something better and cheaper, it will get the jobs. In any case, these jobs won't disappear (the state will still be paying for them); and according to a budget official it is "highly unlikely" that many actual state jobs will be lost. That leaves the number of planned layoffs at about 812, roughly the same number that were planned last year. (And last year the number was later reduced to one-quarter of that original goal by the time the budget took effect.) Thus, Whitman's layoffs should run at best 1 percent. Her government might prove more effective, but it will not be smaller.

Whitman has also steered clear of right-wing hot-button issues. During her campaign, she promised Jersey City Mayor Bret Schundler that she would seek a legislative waiver to allow Jersey City to launch a school voucher program that would give parents money to send their children to private and parochial schools. The Heritage Foundation and the Cato Institute, which have sent experts to Jersey City, love Schundler's plan. The teachers' union and many parents with children in public schools, however, oppose it. Whitman failed to seek the waiver during her first year, and then put it off for another year in her State of the State speech. Schundler is furious with her, but few other New Jerseyans care.

In national issues, where she represents New Jersey, Whitman has also sought the center rather than the right. She has opposed Gingrich and the Republicans' welfare plan, which would automatically limit assistance after two years and would prevent legal immigrants from receiving aid. "There should be some recognition that training is necessary and that some people are going to need more than two years," she told me. "I am also concerned that if you haven't been creating jobs, if there aren't opportunities, you can't just say it's two years and out. There has to be some balance there." Like other Republican governors, she has also complained about unfunded mandates from the national government, but she conspicuously did not join California Governor Pete Wilson in refusing to implement the motor-voter bill, which is likely to increase low-income registration. These positions put her at odds with national Republicans, but not with New Jersey's centrist electorate.

While displaying great skill as a politician, Whitman has been less impressive as a policymaker. She has convinced voters of the need for her tax cuts, but not the state's economists—not even some that she herself appointed. For good reason: her numbers still don't add up. During the campaign, Whitman claimed that her tax policies, drawn up by Kudlow, could create 450,000 jobs over four years. But in her first year New Jersey added only 60,000 jobs. The state will be lucky to create half her predicted total in four years.

Whitman claims that her tax policies were responsible for whatever new jobs there have been, but few economists agree. During the first ten months of 1993, when Florio was governor and the state was still coming out of the recession, New Jersey added 45,300 jobs. During the comparable ten-month period last year of Whitman's administration, it added 55,200. The additional jobs, argues Donald Scarry, an economic consultant and a member of Whitman's Governor's Council of Economic Advisers, were due primarily to the national business cycle. "I think the cycle sits there like the Cheshire cat and drives things," Scarry says.

When I asked Whitman about the comparison between 1993 and 1994, she pointed to the psychological boost that business received from the tax cut. "If you look at the state of New Jersey in the past, it was a little bit above the industrial northeast and the surrounding states. After those [Florio] tax increases, we started to fall way behind New York, Pennsylvania and Connecticut. We are now coming back. We are now doing better than New York, Pennsylvania and Connecticut." But New Jersey's recovery began before her tax cuts took effect, or were even announced. From March 1992 to January 1994, when Florio was governor, jobs in New Jersey grew 2.2 percent, while jobs grew by .4 percent in New York and by 1.1 percent in Pennsylvania. The average for Northeast states was 1.4 percent, well behind New Jersey's rate of growth. There is no evidence that Whitman's tax cuts had any effect on the state's comparative rate of growth. They were good politics, but not necessarily good economics.

They might even turn out to be bad economics. The cuts make it much more difficult for the state to bridge the gap between New Jersey's cities and suburbs. In her recent budget, Whitman proposed a five-year annual urban grant of $2 million, to be tripled by banks. Democratic State Assemblyman Wayne Bryant—a moderate black legislator who authored the state's controversial welfare plan—called it "dropping a pin in the ocean." "I don't know how you take cities with crumbling infrastructure, roads, sewers, toxic factories, and do anything about that without dollars," Bryant says. When I asked Whitman about Bryant's comment, her eyes narrowed. "Ask the urban mayors if they are so insulted they don't want part of that," she shot back. But Bryant is right. A paltry $2 million, even compounded over five years, will barely fill a pot hole in Passaic. And Whitman will face still greater fiscal problems from trying to meet the court's demand that by 1997 the government begin spending $400 million more on the state's poorer school districts; this year's budget spends only $100 million. The tax cuts have greatly limited her flexibility in dealing with these problems.

In the end, her tax cut could turn out to be bad politics. As she reduces state payments to cities and towns in this year's budget to pay for the tax cuts, localities will have to make up the difference through higher fees and property taxes. New Jerseyans will soon find themselves with no tax cut whatsoever. Says Scarry, "Anything the state government doesn't do is going to wind up being done by the municipalities. You have to look very carefully when someone says they are going to shrink state government."

With a budget crisis looming, and with property taxes rising, Whitman could be in trouble by 1997 when she would have to run for re-election. Camden Democratic Representative Rob Andrews, who is thinking about running for governor, says, "Her Achilles' heel is that she is not a tax cutter. When her record is examined, most people will find out they are forking over more of their money." But Whitman herself might not be around Trenton when Andrews and the voters make this final examination.

Whitman understands that no one can run for vice president, but she is clearly interested in the position. She has installed her trusted lieutenant Kayla Bergeron, who ran her 1990 senatorial campaign, at the state GOP, where Bergeron handles Whitman's relations with the national party. Says one Washington consultant who has worked for Whitman, "There is no question that she is now trying to position herself."

When I asked Whitman herself if she has ever thought of running for president, I got a denial reminiscent of Clarence Thomas's denial that he had ever thought about *Roe* v. *Wade.* But, while she doesn't like to talk about her presidential or vice presidential ambitions, her family does. Her brother Dan Todd thinks she has the drive to be president as well as vice president. "Does she have the stamina? You bet," Todd says. Her husband worries that the religious right will block her rise in Republican politics. "These people are running around the country like they control the world," he said. "If the moderates don't get organized, then the lunatic fringe right will take over the party." John Whitman complained that, when he accompanies his wife to Washington, Republicans there tell them privately that they like Whitman's "liberal policies." But, he adds, "they won't say it out loud."

When I asked Christie Whitman whether she shared her husband's view that the religious right is a "lunatic fringe," she was much more diplomatic, but her meaning still came through. "There are people in both parties who hold extreme positions at either end of the spectrum," she said. "I don't worry about that. There are a lot of people who would like to see a division within the party, but I think the common philosophies will win out. You just have to be careful. There are a lot of issues that are very personal and that are very divisive, and as a party we don't need to be championing them."

What happens to Whitman in national politics depends, of course, on whom the Republicans nominate for president. On paper, she would make a brilliant match with just about any of the expected candidates—from Bob Dole to Phil Gramm. Insofar as a vice presidential choice can make a difference, Whitman would leaven these men's hard edges among women voters and give them an important boost among political independents in the suburbs—among the people who wouldn't vote for Ollie North or Chuck Haytaian or Michael Huffington. But ordinary voters don't choose vice presidential nominees; presidential nominees pick them under the watchful eye of the party's faithful. Whitman's fate will rest on whether the party's most conservative wing will be willing to have someone on the ticket who holds the same views on gays as William Weld does and the same views on welfare as Ted Kennedy.

Readings for Further Study

ON LEADERSHIP

JAMES DAVID BARBER, *The Presidential Character.* Englewood Cliffs, N.J.: Prentice Hall, 1992.

JAMES MacGREGOR BURNS, *Leadership.* New York: Harper and Row, 1978.

TERRY L. COOPER and N. DALE WRIGHT, *Exemplary Public Administrators: Character and Leadership in Government.* San Francisco: Jossey-Bass, 1992.

JAMESON W. DOIG and ERWIN C. HARGROVE, *Leadership and Innovation: A Biographical Perspective on Entrepreneurs in Government.* Baltimore: Johns Hopkins University Press, 1987.

FRANCES HESSELBEIN, MARSHALL GOLDSMITH, and RICHARD BECKHARD, eds. *The Leader of the Future: New Visions, Strategies, and Practices for the Next Era.* San Francisco: Jossey-Bass, 1996.

BRYAN D. JONES, *Leadership and Politics.* Lawrence, Kans.: University of Kansas Press, 1989.

RICHARD E. NEUSTADT, *Presidential Power and the Modern Presidents: The Politics of Leadership from Roosevelt to Reagan.* New York: Free Press, 1990.

BERT ROCKMAN, *The Leadership Question: The Presidency and the American System.* New York: Praeger Publishers, 1984.

LEONARD R. SAYLES, *Leadership: Managing in Real Organizations,* 2nd ed. New York: McGraw-Hill, 1989.

PHILIP SELZNICK, *Leadership in Administration.* New York: Harper and Row, 1957.

GARY WILLS, *Certain Trumpets: The Nature of Leadership.* New York: Simon and Schuster, 1994.

ON POLICY

GRAHAM ALLISON, *Essence of Decision.* New York: HarperCollins, 1971.

JAMES E. ANDERSON, *Public Policymaking: An Introduction,* 2nd ed. Boston: Houghton Mifflin, 1994.

FRANK R. BAUMGARTNER and BRYAN D. JONES, *Agendas and Instability in American Politics.* Chicago: University of Chicago Press, 1993.

THOMAS R. DYE, *Understanding Public Policy,* 8th ed. Englewood Cliffs, N.J.: Prentice Hall, 1995.

HELEN INGRAM and STEVEN RATHGEB SMITH, *Public Policy for Democracy.* Washington, D.C.: Brookings Institution, 1993.

CHARLES O. JONES, *An Introduction to the Study of Public Policy,* 3rd ed. Monterey, Calif.: Brooks/Cole, 1984.

JOHN W. KINGDON, *Agendas, Alternatives and Public Policies.* 2nd ed. New York: HarperCollins, 1995.

DANIEL D. McCOOL, *Public Policy Theories, Models and Concepts: An Anthology.* Englewood Cliffs, N.J.: Prentice Hall, 1995.

DENNIS J. PALUMBO, *Public Policy in America: Government in Action,* 2nd ed. Fort Worth, Tex.: Harcourt Brace, 1994.

STELLA Z. THEODOULOU and MATTHEW A. CAHN, *Public Policy: The Essential Readings.* Englewood Cliffs, N.J.: Prentice Hall, 1995.

CARL E. VAN HORN, DONALD C. BAUMER, and WILLIAM T. GORMLEY, JR., *Politics and Public Policy,* 2nd ed. Washington, D.C.: CQ Press, 1992.

ON JOHN F. KENNEDY

CARL M. BRAUER, "John F. Kennedy: The Endurance of Inspirational Leadership," in *Leadership in the Modern Presidency,* ed. Fred Greenstein. Cambridge, Mass.: Harvard University Press, 1988.

JAMES MacGREGOR BURNS, *John Kennedy.* New York: Avon Books, 1959.

VICTOR S. NAVASKY, *Kennedy Justice.* New York: Atheneum, 1977.

HERBERT S. PARMET, *JFK: The Presidency of John F. Kennedy.* New York: Dial Press, 1983.

ARTHUR M. SCHLESINGER, JR., *A Thousand Days.* New York: Houghton Mifflin, 1965.

THEODORE C. SORENSEN, *Decision Making in the White House.* New York: Columbia University Press, 1963.

WILLIAM C. SPRAGENS, "John F. Kennedy," in *Popular Images of Presidents,* ed. William C. Spragens. Westport, Conn.: Greenwood Press, 1988.

THEODORE OTTO WINDT, JR., *Presidents and Protesters: Political Rhetoric in the 1960's.* Tuscaloosa: University of Alabama Press, 1990.

ON GERALD FORD

JAMES M. CANNON, *Time and Chance: Gerald Ford's Appointment with History.* New York: HarperCollins, 1994.

JOHN J. CASSERLY, *The Ford White House: The Diary of a Speechwriter.* Boulder: Colorado Associated University Press, 1977.

FRED FERRETTI, *The Year the Big Apple Went Bust.* New York: G.P. Putnam's Sons, 1976.

GERALD R. FORD, *A Time to Heal.* New York: Harper and Row, 1979.

JOHN ROBERT GREENE, *The Presidency of Gerald R. Ford.* Lawrence: University Press of Kansas, 1994.

ROGER B. PORTER, "Gerald R. Ford: A Healing Presidency," in *Leadership in the Modern Presidency,* ed. Fred Greenstein. Cambridge, Mass.: Harvard University Press, 1988.

MARTIN SHEFTER, *Political Crisis/Fiscal Crisis: The Collapse and Revival of New York City and the Liberal Experiment.* New York: W.W. Norton, 1980.

ON BILL CLINTON

CHARLES ALLEN and JONATHAN PORTIS. *The Comeback Kid: The Life and Career of Bill Clinton.* New York: Birch Lane Press, 1992.

JOHN BRUMMETT, *Highwire: From the Backwoods to the Beltway—the Education of Bill Clinton.* New York: Hyperion, 1994.

COLIN CAMPBELL and BERT ROCKMAN, *The Clinton Presidency: First Appraisals.* Chatham, N.J.: Chatham House, 1996.

BILL CLINTON and AL GORE, *Putting People First: How We Can All Change America.* New York: Times Books, 1992.

RICHARD E. COHEN, *Changing Course in Washington: Clinton and the New Congress.* New York: Allyn and Bacon, 1994.

ELIZABETH DREW, *On the Edge: The Clinton Presidency.* New York: Simon and Schuster, 1994.

DAVID MARANISS, *First in His Class: A Biography of Bill Clinton.* New York: Simon and Schuster, 1995.

DAVID STOESZ, *Small Change: Domestic Policy under the Clinton Administration.* White Plains, N.Y.: Longman Publishers, 1996.

BOB WOODWARD, *The Agenda: Inside the Clinton White House.* New York: Simon and Schuster, 1994.

ON AL GORE AND THE VICE PRESIDENCY

RICHARD L. BERKE, "The Good Son," *New York Times Magazine,* February 20, 1994.

AL GORE, *Common Sense Government: Works Better and Costs Less.* New York: Random House, 1995.

AL GORE, *Earth in the Balance: Ecology and the Human Spirit.* New York: Houghton Mifflin, 1992.

AL GORE AND THE NATIONAL PERFORMANCE REVIEW, *The Gore Report on Reinventing Government: Creating a Government that Works Better and Costs Less.* New York.: Times Books, 1993.

HANK HILLIN, *Al Gore: His Life and Career.* New York: Birch Lane Press, 1992.

PAUL LIGHT, *Vice-Presidential Power: Advice and Influence in the White House.* Baltimore: Johns Hopkins Press, 1984.

ELAINE SCIOLINO and TODD S. PURDUM, "Gore Is No Typical Vice President in the Shadows," *New York Times,* February 18, 1995.

JULES WHITCOVER, *Crapshoot: Rolling the Dice on the Vice Presidency.* New York: Crown Publishers, 1992.

ON TIP O'NEILL

PAUL CLANCY and SHIRLEY ELDER, *Tip: A Biography of Thomas P. O'Neill, Speaker of the House.* New York: Macmillan Publishing Co., 1980.

CORNELIUS DALTON, JOHN WIRKKALA, and ANNE THOMAS, *Leading the Way: A History of the Massachusetts General Court, 1629–1980.* Boston: Office of the Massachusetts Secretary of State, 1984.

CHRISTOPHER MATTHEWS, *Hardball: How Politics Is Played by One Who Knows the Game.* New York: Harper and Row, 1988.

TIP O'NEILL, *Man of the House: The Life and Political Memoirs of Speaker Tip O'Neill.* New York: St. Martin's Press, 1987.

TIP O'NEILL, *All Politics Is Local and Other Rules of the Game.* New York: Times Books, 1994.

RONALD M. PETERS, JR., ed. *The Speaker: Leadership in the U.S. House of Representatives.* Washington, D.C.: Congressional Quarterly Press, 1995.

"The Role of the Speaker," in *How Congress Works,* 2nd ed. Congressional Quarterly Staff. Washington, D.C.: CQ Press, 1991.

MARTIN TOLCHIN, "An Old Pol Takes on the New President," *New York Times Magazine,* July 24, 1977.

ON HOWARD H. BAKER, JR.

J. LEE ANNIS, JR. *Howard Baker: Conciliator in a Time of Crisis.* Lanham, MD: University Press of America, 1994.

HOWARD H. BAKER, JR., "Congress According to Baker," *New York Times Magazine,* April 1, 1984.

ROGER H. DAVIDSON, "Senate Leaders: Janitors for an Untidy Chamber?" in *Congress Reconsidered,* 3rd ed., ed. Laurence C. Dodd and Bruce I. Oppenheimer. Washington, D.C.: CQ Press, 1985.

DAVID EISENHOWER, "Howard Baker: Fighting the President's Final Battles," *New York Times Magazine,* September 6, 1987.

SAMUEL KERNELL and SAMUEL POPKIN, eds., *Chief of Staff: Twenty-Five Years of Managing the Presidency.* Berkeley: University of California Press, 1986.

JAMES A. MILLER, *Running in Place: Inside the Senate.* New York: Simon and Schuster, 1986.

ROBERT L. PEABODY, "Senate Party Leadership: From the 1950's to the 1980's," in *Understanding Congressional Leadership,* ed. Frank H. Mackaman. Washington, D.C.: CQ Press, 1981.

MARTIN TOLCHIN, "Howard Baker: Trying to Tame an Unruly Senate," *New York Times Magazine,* March 28, 1982.

ON NEWT GINGRICH

FRED BARNES, "The Executive: The Rise and Rise of Newt Gingrich," *The New Republic,* May 22, 1995.

JASON DEPARLE, "Newt's Fiercest Fight," *New York Times Magazine,* January 28, 1996.

ED GILLESPIE and BOB SCHELLHAS, eds., *Contract with America: The Bold Plan by Rep. Newt Gingrich, Rep. Dick Armey and the House Republicans to Change the Nation.* New York: Times Books, 1994.

NEWT GINGRICH, *To Renew America.* New York: HarperCollins: 1995.

DAVID ROGERS and PHIL KUNTZ, "Jump-Start: How Gingrich Grabbed Power and Attention—And His New Risks," *Wall Street Journal,* January 19, 1995.

KATHARINE Q. SEELYE, "As a Model, Gingrich Takes Presidents, Not Predecessors," *New York Times,* April 11, 1995.

JUDITH WARNER and MAX BERLEY, *Newt Gingrich: Speaker to America.* New York: Signet Books, 1995.

DICK WILLIAMS, *Newt: Leader of the Second American Revolution.* Marietta, Ga.: Longstreet Press, 1995.

ON NANCY HANKS TO JANE ALEXANDER

LIVINGSTON BIDDLE, *Our Government and the Arts: A Perspective from the Inside.* New York: ACA Books, 1988.

RICHARD BOLTON, ed., *Culture Wars: Documents from the Recent Controversies in the Arts.* New York: New Press, 1992.

JOHN FROHNMAYER, *Leaving Town Alive: Confessions of an Arts Warrior.* Boston: Houghton Mifflin, 1993.

PATTI HARTIGAN, "NEA Scripts Self a Smaller Role," *Boston Globe,* January 25, 1996.

ALICE GOLDFARB MARQUIS, *Art Lessons: Learning from the Rise and Fall of Public Arts Funding.* New York: Basic Books, 1995.

KEVIN MULCAHY and MARGARET JANE WYSZOMIRSKI, *America's Commitment to Culture, Government and the Arts.* Boulder, Colo.: Westview Press, 1995.

FRANK RICH, "Who Lost the Arts?" *New York Times,* August 9, 1995.

MICHAEL STRAIGHT, *Nancy Hanks: An Intimate Portrait—The Creation of a National Commitment to the Arts.* Durham, N.C.: Duke University Press, 1988.

ON JACK KEMP

FRED BARNES, "Notes on Jack Kemp: The Obsessions of Jack Kemp," *The New Republic,* May 9, 1994.

MARLIN FITZWATER, *Call the Briefing.* New York: Random House, 1995.

DAVID FRUM, "The Happy Warrior," *National Review,* August 1, 1994.

JACK KEMP, *The American Idea: Ending the Limits of Growth.* Washington, D.C.: American Studies Center, 1984.

JACK KEMP, *An American Renaissance: A Strategy for the 1980's.* New York: Harper and Row, 1979.

RUTH SHALIT, "Disempowered: Empower America Fizzles," *The New Republic,* March 15, 1993.

FREDERIC SMOLER, " 'We Had a Great History, and We Turned Aside': An Interview with Jack Kemp," *American Heritage,* October 1993.

ON COLIN POWELL

HENRY LOUIS GATES, JR., "Powell and the Black Elite," *The New Yorker,* September 25, 1995.

MICHAEL R. GORDON and BERNARD E. TRAINOR, "Beltway Warrior," *New York Times Magazine,* August 27, 1995.

MICHAEL R. GORDON and BERNARD E. TRAINOR, *The Generals' War: The Inside Story of the Conflict in the Gulf.* Boston: Little, Brown, 1994.

HOWARD MEANS, *Colin Powell: Soldier/Statesman—Statesman/Soldier.* New York: Donald I. Fine, 1992.

HOWARD MEANS, "President Powell?" *The Washingtonian,* December 1994.

COLIN POWELL, *My American Journey.* New York: Random House, 1995.

DAVID ROTH, *Sacred Honor: A Biography of Colin Powell.* Grand Rapids, Mich.: Zondervan Publishing, 1993.

BOB WOODWARD, *The Commanders.* New York: Simon and Schuster, 1991.

ON MICHAEL DUKAKIS

ROBERT BEHN, *Leadership Counts: Lessons for Public Managers from the Massachusetts Welfare, Training, and Employment Program.* Cambridge, Mass.: Harvard University Press, 1991.

THAD BEYLE and LYNN MUCHMORE, "Honorable Michael S. Dukakis: Governor of Massachusetts, 1975–1979," in *Reflections on Being Governor,* ed. Jack Brizius. Washington, D.C.: National Governors' Association, 1981.

MICHAEL S. DUKAKIS and ROSABETH MOSS KANTER, *Creating the Future: The Massachusetts Comeback and Its Promise for America.* New York: Summit Books, 1988.

RICHARD GAINES and MICHAEL SEGAL, *Dukakis and the Reform Impulse.* Boston: Quinlan Press, 1987.

CHARLES KENNEY and ROBERT L. TURNER, *Dukakis: An American Odyssey.* Boston: Houghton Mifflin, 1988.

DAVID NYHAN, *The Duke: The Inside Story of a Political Phenomenon.* New York: Warner Books, 1988.

DAVID OSBORNE, "Massachusetts: Redistributing Economic Growth," in *Laboratories of Democracy: A New Breed of Governor Creates Models for National Growth.* Boston: Harvard Business School Press, 1990.

ON MARIO CUOMO

MADELINE WING ADLER and FREDERICK S. LANE, "Governors and Public Policy Leadership," in *Governors and Higher Education,* eds. Samuel Gove and Thad Beyle. Denver: Education Commission of the States, 1988.

KEN AULETTA, "Profile: Governor," Parts I and II, *The New Yorker,* April 9 and 16, 1984.

MARIO CUOMO, *Diaries of Mario M. Cuomo: The Campaign for Governor.* New York: Random House, 1984.

"Cuomo Versus Cuomo: The New York Governor's Race," *The Economist,* September 24, 1994.

MARIO CUOMO, *Reason to Believe.* New York: Simon and Schuster, 1995.

ELIZABETH KOLBERT, "After 12 Years in Spotlight, Cuomo Is Still an Enigma," *New York Times,* December 27, 1994.

JAMES LEDBETTER, "Not-So-Super Mario: Judging the 'Governing Governor,'" *The New Republic,* August 1, 1994.

ROBERT S. McELVAINE, *Mario Cuomo: A Biography.* New York: Scribner's, 1988.

JACOB WEISBERG, "Why We've Fallen Out of Love with Mario," *New York,* August 8, 1994.

ON CHRISTINE TODD WHITMAN

MICHAEL ARON, *Governor's Race: A TV Reporter's Chronicle of the 1993 Florio/Whitman Campaign.* New Brunswick, N.J.: Rutgers University Press, 1994.

ELEANOR CLIFT, "Renegade Republican," *Working Woman,* November 1995.

HOWARD GLECKMAN, "The Ronald Reagan of New Jersey," *Business Week,* October 17, 1994.

SANDY McCLURE, *Christie Whitman for the People: A Political Biography.* Amherst, N.Y.: Prometheus Books, 1996.

JONATHAN WALTERS, "The Whitman Squeeze," *Governing,* November 1995.

JACOB WEISBERG, "The Whitman Hoax," *New York,* March 27, 1995.

"The Whitman Effect," *New York Times,* July 9, 1995.

"Whitman Speech Reflects Upon Revolution," *Congressional Quarterly,* January 28, 1995.

Notes on Contributors

PETER BOYER is a staff writer at *The New Yorker*. His pieces for that magazine include an early report on President Clinton and the Whitewater affair, and a long profile of Hillary Rodham Clinton. A graduate of the University of California at Los Angeles and the University of Southern California School of Journalism, he is the author of *Who Killed CBS?: The Undoing of America's Number One News Network* (1988) and is currently working on another nonfiction book to be published by Random House.

DAVID S. CLOUD is a journalist who covers Congress for *Congressional Quarterly*. A Phi Beta Kappa graduate of the College of William and Mary, he is the magazine's lead reporter responsible for covering the congressional leadership and the Republican takeover of the House and the Senate.

JASON DEPARLE is a staff writer for the *New York Times Magazine*. A summa cum laude graduate of Duke University, he covered antipoverty policy for the newspaper's Washington bureau from 1990 to 1994. Prior to joining the *Times*, Mr. DeParle had been an editor at the *Washington Monthly* since 1987. In addition, from 1986 to 1987 Mr. DeParle was one of fifteen Americans chosen to receive a Henry Luce Foundation scholarship to work in Asia for a year, during which time he lived in, and wrote about, a Manila slum.

JOHN ALOYSIUS FARRELL is the White House correspondent for the *Boston Globe*. A graduate of the University of Virginia with distinction, Mr. Farrell is a winner of the George Polk Award for an investigative series on malfunctioning anesthesia machines.

ROBERT E. GILBERT is a professor of Political Science at Northeastern University. He is the author of *The Mortal Presidency: Illness and Anguish in the White House* and an earlier book on *Television and Presidential Politics.* His articles have appeared in such journals as *Political Psychology, Presidential Studies Quarterly, Congress and the Presidency,* and *Politics and the Life Sciences.* A specialist on the American presidency, Dr. Gilbert was awarded a Kennedy Research Grant from the John F. Kennedy Library Foundation in 1995. Professor Gilbert holds a Ph.D. from the University of Massachusetts, Amherst.

JOHN B. JUDIS is a senior editor at *The New Republic* and has contributed regularly to that magazine since 1982. A graduate of the University of California at Berkeley, he is the author of *William F. Buckley: Patron Saint of the Conservatives* (Simon and Schuster, 1988) and *Grand Illusion: Critics and Champions of the American Century* (Farrar, Straus and Giroux, 1992). Mr. Judis is currently writing a book about the American political establishment from the end of the Vietnam War to the end of the Cold War.

ELIZABETH KOLBERT is a media reporter for the *New York Times.* A member of the *Times*'s staff since 1984, she served as that newspaper's Albany bureau chief from 1989 to 1991 and subsequently covered the presidential campaign of 1992. A graduate of Yale University, she attended Universitat-Hamburg in West Germany as a Fulbright Scholar in 1983 and 1984.

RICHARD A. LOVERD is an assistant professor of Political Science at Northeastern University, concentrating in public policy, public administration, and public sector leadership subjects, and is currently completing a book-length study of the leadership of Michael S. Dukakis. In the past Dr. Loverd has published in such journals as the *Policy Studies Journal, Public Administration Review, Presidential Studies Quarterly,* and *Public Productivity and Management Review,* and he presently serves on the Editorial Board of *Public Voices.* Along with M.P.A. and Ph.D. degrees from Syracuse University, Professor Loverd holds an M.B.A. from Columbia University.

JON MEACHAM is the National Affairs editor at *Newsweek,* supervising coverage of politics and national news events. Before joining *Newsweek* he was an editor for two years at *The Washington Monthly,* and he remains a contributing editor for that magazine. A Phi Beta Kappa graduate of The University of the South, Mr. Meacham began his journalism career with the *Chattanooga Times,* where he was a reporter from 1991 to 1992.

MARGARET JANE WYSZOMIRSKI is a professor of Political Science and director of the Arts Management Program at Case Western Reserve University. In the past Dr. Wyszomirski was the director of the Graduate Program in Public Policy at Georgetown University and director of the Office of Planning, Research and Budget Coordination at the National Endowment for the Arts. She has published articles on arts management, presidential leadership and advisory systems and recently co-authored a book on *America's Commitment to Culture, Government and the Arts* (1995). Professor Wyszomirski holds a Ph.D. from Cornell University.